For Every Indio Who Falls

Rural highlands, El Quiché. Photo by Jean-Marie Simon.

For Every Indio Who Falls

A History of Maya Activism in
Guatemala, 1960–1990

Betsy Konefal

UNIVERSITY OF NEW MEXICO PRESS

Albuquerque

© 2010 by the University of New Mexico Press
All rights reserved. Published 2010
Printed in the United States of America
15 14 13 12 11 10   1 2 3 4 5 6

Library of Congress Cataloging-in-Publication Data

Konefal, Betsy Ogburn, 1967–

For every indio who falls : a history of Maya activism
in Guatemala, 1960–1990 / Betsy Konefal.
p. cm.
Includes bibliographical references and index.
ISBN 978-0-8263-4865-4 (pbk. : alk. paper)
1. Mayas—Guatemala—Politics and government—20th century.
2. Guatemala—History—Civil War, 1960–1996.
3. Mayas—Guatemala—Government relations.
I. Title.

F1435.3.P7K66 2010
972.8105'2—dc22
2009049906

I dedicate this book to the
children of its protagonists.

Contents

Acknowledgments

The story explored in this book has held me in its grip for many years. My profound thanks go to all of those who made this work possible, especially the many Guatemalans who shared their memories of the past, reliving a painfully difficult era, but also showing it to be a time of hope and great courage.

This history was recounted to me by over one hundred interviewees whose patience and willingness to share their experiences were deeply touching and greatly appreciated. A special thanks to Emeterio Toj Medrano for the many hours of conversation, and to Miguel Alvarado, Victoriano Alvarez, Pedro Bal Cumés, Ricardo Cajas Mejía, Pablo Ceto, Gregorio Chay, Amalia Coy Pop, Marco Antonio de Paz, Pedro Esquina, Ricardo Falla, Tomás García, Jorge Luis García de León, Domingo Hernández Ixcoy, Juana, Jerónimo Juárez, Teresa Leiva Yax, Catarina León Medrano, Alberto Mazariegos, Estela Morán, María Elvira Quijivix, Ulises Quijivix Yax, Isaías Raconcoj, Concepción Ramírez Mendoza, Emilia Salanic, Enrique Luis Sam Colop, José Serech, Nicolas Miguel Sisay, Magdalena Tumin Palaj, Fidelina Tux Chub, Juan Vásquez Tuíz, Catalina Ventura, Catarina Xum, the staff at the Voz de Atitlán, and the late Antonio Pop Caal. My thanks to the former *reinas indígenas* who spoke with me about their experiences as activist queens, including one of the young women continuing their struggles into the twenty-first century, the 2000–2001 Rabín Ahau, Mercedes García Marroquín. Maryknoll fathers and brothers were extraordinarily generous with their time, among them Father Dan Jensen, Father Bill Donnelly, Bro. John Blazo, the Rev. Dave La Buda, and Bro. Bob Butsch. Finally, to all of those women and men who wish to be unnamed in this study, my heartfelt thanks for your willingness to speak with me despite the climate of fear that continues to hang over Guatemala.

The Centro de Investigaciones Regionales de Mesoamérica (CIRMA) in Antigua provided an institutional home during this study, and I am especially grateful to the staff of its Archivo Histórico. I'd also like to acknowledge the valuable assistance of the staff of the Biblioteca Nacional's Hemeroteca, as well as the librarians of the Hemeroteca at the Archivo General de Centro América (AGCA) in Guatemala City.

The research for this book was first supported by the University of Pittsburgh and its Center for Latin American Studies (CLAS). I thank Pittsburgh's CLAS for summer field research grants, a Cole and Marty Blasier Research Scholarship, and a Foreign Language and Area Studies Fellowship. I gratefully acknowledge two Andrew Mellon Predoctoral Fellowships from Pittsburgh's Faculty of Arts and Sciences and fieldwork support from a Fulbright-Hays Doctoral Dissertation Research Abroad Fellowship. I would like to thank the US Institute of Peace and its Peace Scholar program for support of writing and the American Association of University Women and their American Fellowship program for support of final book revisions. Thanks, too, to the College of William and Mary and its faculty summer research grants program for research support. All views expressed in this book are mine and do not necessarily reflect the views of these funding institutions.

Thanks to George Reid Andrews, Alejandro de la Fuente, Lara Putnam, and Joshua Lund for their thoughtful and serious engagement with this work from the beginning, and to the readers and editors at University of New Mexico Press, especially Sarah Soliz. For sharing her unforgettable images of Guatemala in the 1980s, a big thank you to a woman who just may be the world's most generous photographer, Jean-Marie Simon. Thanks, too, to others who have read and commented on all or part of the manuscript, among them Abigail Adams, Arturo Arias, Greg Grandin, Walter Little, Ellie Walsh, the anonymous reviewers for *Hispanic American Historical Review*, and at William and Mary, Fred Corney and Andy Fisher. I'd like to acknowledge the important presence of Michael Jiménez in this book as well. Despite the fact that it came together after his death, his wonderfully expansive written comments on early versions remain a source of inspiration. He and all of these individuals made the work exciting, fulfilling, and always challenging. I take full responsibility for the faults that remain.

Outside the academic world my family and I could and did lean on an amazing support system that included Marleni Villela, Elizabeth and the late (great) Ray Konefal, and Jean and Roy Ogburn. Finally, a big *abrazo* to the best research team anyone could hope for, Stephan Konefal and our kids, Ella, Thea, and Jonas, without whom, as they like to say, I would have finished this book years ago! But I wouldn't have wanted it any other way.

x

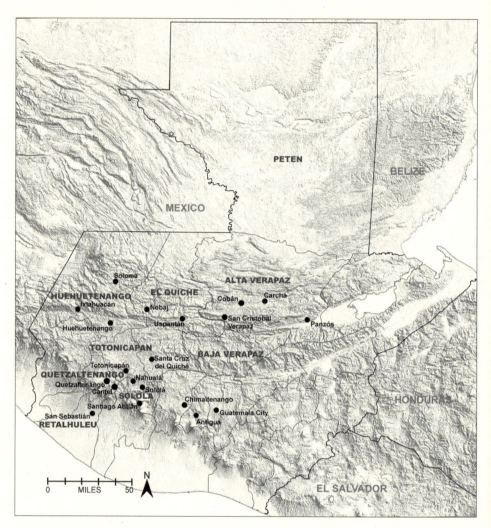

Guatemala. Image courtesy of NASA/CATHALAC/SERVIR, 2005.

Introduction

T wenty-two Mayas appeared in a photograph covering the front page of Guatemala's daily newspaper *El Gráfico* on July 30, 1978. It was a surprising image, considering the time and the place. The young people in the photo came from disparate areas of Guatemala and spoke different languages, which would have been clear to readers because of the community-specific dress worn by the women in the image, and a few of the men.[1] Gathered at the center of the group were indigenous pageant queens, or *reinas indígenas*, young women who represented their specific Maya communities. Yet

Reinas indígenas and supporters protest a massacre of Mayas by the Guatemalan army in Panzós. Source: *El Gráfico*, July 30, 1978.

INFORMACION EN LA PAGINA 4

EN ESTE NUMERO:

INVESTIGAN PLAZAS

despite their different origins, they and the young people around them symbolically posed as one.

Their message was even more striking. The headline at the top of page 1 read "Reinas Indígenas Repudiate This Year's Folklore Festival," an event featuring Maya culture that was sponsored by the Guatemalan government each year. In a strongly worded declaration quoted in the paper, the young people mocked what they portrayed as empty and manipulative state sponsorship of folklore and announced that they were boycotting the festival because of official violence against Maya communities.

In 1978 Guatemala was in the midst of an intensifying civil war. A leftist revolutionary insurgency that began in the 1960s was growing in strength, and the threat was met by violent state counterinsurgency directed not only against the guerrilla armies, but also against reformers and activists of all kinds.[2] Soon extreme levels of state violence would become common even against unarmed civilians suspected of sympathizing with the opposition. But in 1978 that tactic was unexpected. Its first widely known occurence—a massacre of Q'eqchi' Maya campesinos in the community of Panzós, Alta Verapaz—prompted expressions of outrage and protest, including that featured in El Gráfico. On May 29, 1978, army soldiers shot down dozens of campesinos in Panzós who had gathered to discuss land claims with the mayor. It was a pivotal moment in the war: as one of the first in a long series of attacks on Maya communities, it serves as a marker on Guatemala's path toward genocide. Within a few years, the Guatemalan army would routinely identify entire Maya communities in certain areas as likely sources of support for the insurgency and spare virtually no one in their "scorched-earth" destruction of people, shelter, crops, animals, and sacred sites. The army destroyed at least 626 Maya communities in such massacres, and the United Nations–sponsored Truth Commission determined that in some instances state forces committed genocide.[3]

The protestors appeared in El Gráfico just two months after the bloodshed in Panzós. As it turns out, the high profile Folklore Festival was held in the very same area of Guatemala—Alta Verapaz—as the Panzós massacre, and the indigenous pageant queens and their supporters used the festival as an opportunity to confront the violence. Speaking for their dead Q'eqchi' "brothers," the protestors denounced a government that embraced Maya folklore while massacring Maya campesinos. While the blood of "genuine Guatemalan *indios*," as the protestors pointedly termed the Panzós victims, still soaked the ground, they declared that "all the . . . festivals . . . in supposed homage to the indio of

Guatemala are unjustified . . . because in daily reality the right to life is not respected, [nor] the right to our ancestral lands, [nor the right] to our cultural practices without paternalism."[4]

I came across the photograph as I was reading newspapers from the 1970s in Guatemala's National Library, researching the history of organizing and activism by Mayas in the decades leading up to the period Guatemalans call simply *la violencia*, "the violence." It is a bland and safe label—since it elides responsibility—usually referring to the most brutal period of the war, beginning with the Panzós massacre in 1978 and culminating in the army's scorched-earth campaigns of the early 1980s. The *El Gráfico* protest was the first instance I had seen of Mayas appearing in the mainstream press with such an overt condemnation of state repression. The group's racialized imagery and the way they combined Maya symbolism with their pointed and confrontational message to the national government and army were unprecedented.[5] Who were these young people, and how were they connected to each other? Why indigenous pageant queens? What did this protest mean, and how did it fit into the larger picture of organizing by Mayas? I studied each of the faces in the photo with a feeling of dread. Defiantly posing that day, they could not have imagined the horror to come. Had they gotten away with it?

Photo in hand, I traveled through the highlands seeking out the queens and fellow protestors who had gathered before the camera nearly a quarter century before. The newspaper article provided no names, but I began with the communities listed in the photo's caption. With the help of people in each community I identified eighteen of the twenty-two protestors. Most of them—though not all—*had* survived the violence. I talked with sixteen of those photographed, and with dozens of others who had been involved, about their decisions to protest and the historical moment captured in the photo. The story of their protest is recounted in chapter 4.

The story of organizing by Mayas during Guatemala's civil war goes far beyond protesting pageant queens, of course. Though intriguing on its own, the queens' protest simultaneously helped open up a broader story of activism by Mayas in the years before, during, and after la violencia in Guatemala, which is the subject of this book. The protest offered a means to investigate the era's many and evolving forms of organizing and the development of connections between cultural events like indigenous queen pageants and more radical demands for political and economic

3

transformation and an end to violence. The young people involved in the queens' protest were connected to other activists across the highlands and to efforts before and after 1978. They helped expose the networks that activists developed as young people in dozens of communities called for reform, and sometimes revolution. Following their leads, I went knocking on doors in twenty pueblos in the western highlands and the northern highland Verapaces.[6]

By following organizing experiences at multiple levels—local, regional, national, and international—this book explores how (some) Mayas became, in varying degrees, involved in political activism and opposition to a repressive state. It traces how debates around issues of Maya identity and rights evolved among them and how resistance was shaped and reshaped by revolutionary insurgency and genocidal counterinsurgency. It is not a history of all Mayas in this period, or even all who were politically active. This study privileges certain kinds of activism and activists: those who pursued what they saw as economic, cultural, or political justice for a newly envisioned *pueblo indígena*, a pan-community indigenous "people" in Guatemala. It focuses on activists who could and did write; those who could and did speak out in ways that are remembered and can be reconstructed; those who survived the violence that decimated much of the activist community and whole Maya villages, or who have family and friends able to speak for them. It leaves out many, including Mayas opposed to the kinds of activism studied here and those who tried to maintain a distance from state forces *and* its opponents.[7] Additional research into this period is much needed to fill gaps in the historical record.

I also want to acknowledge that as an effort to probe into a difficult, often tragic subject, this project is fraught with methodological challenges and problems. The evidentiary base is sometimes thin; memories are always imperfect; violence and fear remain palpable in the country and limited what interviewees could and did reveal to an inquisitive researcher.[8] The perceived failure of the efforts for change in the 1970s and 1980s, and the shocking magnitude of the violence unleashed to stop them, shape how this history is remembered and recounted by its protagonists. But the method that by necessity I adopted in this study, heavily dependent on interviews, had its silver lining. Accounts of personal experiences revealed a history with nuance and depth, a history as wonderfully complicated as the people who told it.

4

San Pedro Soloma, Huehuetenango

> Well, we were talking and an hour or so passed. Chita brought plantains to the table, milk. . . . I remember that [as] she approached us . . . she said, "Juan, who's coming there?" and she lifted the curtain . . . a yellow pickup with armed men. "Juan, close the door! Hide!"[9]

In 2002 one of the women who appeared in the *El Gráfico* protest photo, a Q'anjob'al Maya named Juana, recounted a scene from a few years later, in 1982. She had witnessed the Guatemalan army abduct her friend and fellow activist Juan Vitalino Calel. She was willing to talk about her experiences, but it was not easy. At the time of Calel's kidnapping and disappearance, state counterinsurgency violence had been at its height, and discussing the period two decades later remained unsettling. At the point when the army entered her narrative, Juana's demeanor changed and her confidence faltered. She glanced at my tape recorder on the coffee table in front of us, posing a question simultaneously answered by the look on her face: "There's not a problem with this?" I quickly turned the recorder off. She continued, her anger rising as she remembered the details of Calel's abduction. After only a few seconds, she looked again at the recorder, and at me. "Turn it back on."[10]

I had made the journey to Soloma, across Guatemala's breathtaking Cuchumatanes mountain range and deep into the Huehuetenango highlands, in hopes of finding and talking with this woman. In 1978, at the age of twenty-two, Juana had been elected to a one-year reign as Soloma's reina indígena. A schoolteacher at the time, she was part of an exciting, radicalizing moment in highland Guatemala, one that reshaped even local queen pageants. Young Mayas like Juana and her friend Juan Vitalino Calel—students, Catholic catechists, young professionals, agrarian activists—were becoming politicized in the 1970s, discussing and asserting demands for cultural, political, and economic reform for what they had come to define as Guatemala's pueblo indígena. Juana's determination to speak out was evident even then. As a reina indígena candidate, she recalls, she was the first to stand in front of her community and deliver a hard-hitting, politicized pageant speech about rights for indígenas. She used the opportunity on stage to argue for pride in Maya cultural identity. She condemned discrimination against

5

Mayas and the concurrent political and economic domination exercised by Ladinos—the term typically used for non-Mayas—in her community. She demanded an end to abusive money-lending practices, she remembers, and the land loss for indígenas that resulted.[11] Her speech was a success, and she was chosen as Soloma's new reina indígena by popular vote.

New ideas about Maya identity and rights shaped politicization in places like Soloma and throughout the highlands in the 1970s, in community after community. Mayas like her at the same time became connected to others beyond their communities, through the Catholic Church and catechist movement, through student organizations and regional secondary schools, and through agrarian organizing. In the mid-1970s, regional discussion groups drew together young Mayas from communities all over the map. Juana's friend Calel, for example, was not a Q'anjob'al like her, but a Pocomchi' Maya from San Cristóbal Verapaz in Guatemala's distant northern highlands, more than a day's bus ride away.

Debates and connections among activist Mayas soon led to pan-community organizing, and that is how I learned about Soloma's indigenous queen. In May 1978, around the same time Juana became queen, Guatemalan army soldiers shot down the Q'eqchi' campesinos in Panzós. Among the many public condemnations of the Panzós massacre was the symbolic and highly charged protest involving the indigenous queens featured in *El Gráfico*.

In the press I learned of Juana as an unnamed pageant queen. She was an interesting figure in other ways, and her experiences parallel those of other activists engaged in efforts for change in the 1970s. Chapters 2 and 3 of this book lay out developments at the local and regional levels in the 1960s and 1970s, which helped shape the thinking of young people like her and opened new opportunities, setting the stage for the kinds of mobilization taking place at the time of the Panzós massacre and into the 1980s. Like growing numbers of Mayas, Juana was able to go to primary school in her community at a Catholic parish school for indigenous students, one of many such institutions founded in the 1950s. She became connected to new ideas about indigenous identity and rights when she was sent in the late 1960s and early 1970s, again with the help of her local priest, to a Catholic secondary school for Maya girls in Antigua, the Instituto Indígena Nuestra Señora del Socorro. Juana

6

graduated from Socorro in 1974 and worked as a schoolteacher in rural Totonicapán and Huehuetenango and passed the ideas she was absorbing and developing to her own students. On weekends, she got together with Mayas from other communities in regional discussion groups.[12] In 1978 she helped politicize cultural events like the indigenous queen pageant in both her local community and at the national level, for the readers of El Gráfico. At the same time, she involved herself in a larger, more radical struggle for revolutionary change: she tells of working in her community for several years in the late 1970s to support the revolutionary Guerrilla Army of the Poor, or EGP.[13]

Juana's relationship with Juan Vitalino Calel illustrates how activism by Mayas like them had developed by the time of his abduction. Though Calel came from a far-off community and belonged to a different language group, Juana explained that the two saw themselves as part of the same struggles. He, too, was involved in local and regional indigenous queen events. He was simultaneously a leader of an agricultural cooperative in his community, San Cristóbal, and involved in agrarian organizing in other parts of Alta Verapaz, including Panzós. After threats from the military due to his work with campesinos, Calel fled his community and took up work in another cooperative, this time in the highland department of Totonicapán. After work and on weekends, he continued to be involved in discussions and workshops with area activists (including reinas indígenas), part of efforts that he and other organizers saw as important to "raising consciousness"—concientización—in Maya communities.

By 1982, Juana herself was no longer participating in those meetings or pan-community discussions, or actively supporting the revolutionary Left. She was married, with a child. Fierce repression by state forces in her community made continued support of the guerrilla insurgency impossible for her, and she'd witnessed a horrific massacre against those the army labeled subversives in the community where she taught, Santa Eulalia, to the north of Soloma. Yet the ties between Juana and Calel remained, and she was visiting him and his wife, Chita, in Totonicapán to inquire about working with his cooperative. From underneath a table in Calel's kitchen, the children gathered around her, Juana watched as soldiers beat him and took him away. He was not seen again. Juan Vitalino Calel is among Guatemala's estimated two hundred thousand dead and disappeared.

7

▓▓▓ Mayas and the Guatemalan Civil War

Scholars writing on the civil war period in Guatemala have disagreed about Maya participation in it, and the historical development of oppositional activism by indígenas in the 1960s, 1970s, and 1980s is poorly understood. With the intense repression of the 1980s and its numbing aftermath, researchers could not easily pose questions about political differentiation among indígenas, or the scope and character of Maya organizing.[14] The specter of genocide, too, seems to have rendered activism by Mayas taboo, as if activism itself were somehow to blame for the horror. After the signing of peace accords in 1996, there remained a deep reluctance on the part of some Maya leaders to speak about or acknowledge an activist past.[15] Only recently has it become possible to begin the process of exploring Maya politicization in some detail—its roots, character, diversity—and assess the effects of state violence on shaping Maya resistance.[16]

We must note that Maya mobilization in its many forms unfolded at the very same time that the two most significant revolutionary groups in Guatemala, the EGP and the Revolutionary Organization of Peoples in Arms, or ORPA, recruited and based their efforts in and around Maya communities. In that context, activists in opposition movements of many kinds—Mayas and Ladinos—engaged in intense and ongoing debates about Maya identity, rights, and revolution. As laid out in this book, some forms of organizing by Mayas in the 1970s were largely articulated around ideas of group identity as Mayas, what activists tended to call *la raza*, or race. Other types of activism sought to unite Mayas and Ladinos in class struggle. Activists who emphasized "Mayaness" came to be known as *culturalistas*, while *clasistas* was the term for Mayas who tended toward class-based organizing in partnership with Ladinos. But those distinctions can be misleading: a lens that tries to determine whether activism by Mayas was motivated by "culturalista" or "clasista" concerns cannot give a clear view of the fluidity of 1970s organizing or the interchanges taking place among activists as these ideas were developing.

When I asked Juana about activist Mayas' motivations, she saw such a differentiation as flawed. As she explained it,

> I don't think any Maya [at the time] would have defined
> his position as either [exclusively] in the class struggle or in
> the cultural struggle. . . . The Mayas on the Left in the class
> struggle believed that it was the path to save us from this

exploitation, this discrimination. Those who spoke of the cultural struggle, we said we have to defend our rights, . . . we all wanted to be heard. . . . The class struggle came from Marxism, from socialism, lines of thinking totally outside our reality as Mayas, but also lines of thinking that sought equality between societies, that was what was understood by many indígenas who supported the class struggle. On the other hand, our identity . . . as *pueblos mayas* [Maya peoples or communities] we had to defend ourselves.[17]

In practice, as Juana suggests, culturalista demands were seldom if ever divorced from issues of economic and political justice, and some—though certainly not all—culturalistas supported revolution. Mayas involved in class-based organizing likewise did not see their efforts as abstracted from their identity as indígenas, and many at the same time took part in cultural "revindication" efforts. Activists did disagree about priorities and strategy, as this study makes clear. Yet the efforts of culturalistas and clasistas unfolded simultaneously and overlapped. Mayas involved in both kinds of organizing interacted with each other and at times formed tentative, temporary alliances in the press, community outreach, protests, and even revolutionary mobilization. Despite tensions between culturalista and clasista agendas, organizing efforts by Mayas in the 1970s and into the 1980s should be examined in relation to each other and to broad and growing movements in opposition to a violent state.

Activism after Genocide

For those familiar with the chilling brutality of Guatemalan counterinsurgency, it will come as no surprise that much of the activism by Mayas developing in the 1970s was deeply altered—in some respects, decimated—by the state-sponsored violence intent upon destroying it. Repression was a catalytic force for social mobilization by Mayas, but as state terror escalated, it had its intended effect: demobilization. This book carries the story of activism and its transformation into a period shaped by unthinkable levels of violence. When terror reached its most extreme levels from 1981 to 1983, the military virtually shut down public organizing; repression forced the opposition movements that remained, paralyzed and polarized, underground. Splinter all-indigenous revolutionary

9

groups broke away from—and sometimes competed with—the Ladino-led guerrilla armies.

When by the mid-1980s the state's most intense repression was deemed no longer necessary, violence eased somewhat, and public activism by Mayas did reemerge. But terror had had profound effects on organized Mayas across the political spectrum. Among activists, the 1990s saw deeper divisions than before between those continuing in opposition struggles focused on economic and political rights and an end to violence, and those who embraced a more focused agenda of cultural rights labeled "indigenous."

The culturally focused "Mayanista" movement, drawing on international indigenous rights language, was especially vocal during the peace process and has been crucially important since the 1990s in bringing debates on indigenous issues to the Guatemalan public arena. Yet the very success of the movement had the effect of circumscribing the definition of indigenous rights and activism in Guatemala.[18] As this book shows, the economic, political, and cultural concerns of activist Mayas were intertwined in symbiotic ways in the 1970s. In the aftermath of insurgency and counterinsurgency, during a "postconflict" era still marked by violence against the reemerging opposition, culturally focused demands became largely abstracted from broader social justice claims.

This history of what came before, what young Mayas in an earlier period were proposing and working for in the name of the pueblo indígena in Guatemala, offers up an important corrective to how indigenous activism is defined. Many Mayas were involved in the struggles that accompanied over three decades of war, especially as that war became directed at the pueblo indígena. Before organizing was transformed by genocide, Mayas in varied ways resisted marginalization and discrimination, state repression and terror. And Soloma's reina indígena was right: as they did so, culture was not necessarily apolitical. Indigenous activism was not always or only about culture.

10

"Two Bloods!"

Defining Race and Nation

*The indígena hides ever more obstinately in his ancestral customs
. . . . By this attitude . . . the indígena becomes a deadweight . . .
for social, economic, and cultural development.*

> —National Indigenista Institute,
> *¿Por qué es indispensable el
> indigenismo?* 1969

*Tecún Umán [conquest-era K'iche' warrior] is a . . . representative of
the land; as clean as our skies, above political conflicts and fratricidal
struggles, sacrificed when the two bloods that run in our veins met,
source of the river of our history.*

> —*Revista Cultural del Ejército*,
> January–June 1979

*What are they without traje [traditional dress]? Nothing but
Indian trash.*

> —Hotel owner, Cobán,
> Alta Verapaz, 2002

*I speak for my race. . . . I speak for the blood that circulates in
my veins, the blood of the kekchíes, the Maya blood! . . . They
[Ladinos] try to incorporate us into their society so we can continue
serving them and they can continue humiliating us, because that
is what the indígena has always been: servant, . . . peon, beast of
burden, . . . until he has become a thing.*

> —Eduardo Pacay Coy,
> in *La Ruta*, September 26, 1971

Race has been a central and problematic theme in Guatemala's vision of itself as a nation. It is a country of profound and remarkably lasting contrasts—linguistic, cultural, and economic—that tend to coalesce around the racialized and opposing social categories of "indígena" and "Ladino," the latter term generally applied to Guatemalans not defined as indigenous. Yet the concept of race can seem problematic when applied to indigenous populations. Scholars usually view distinctions among Guatemalans as "ethnic" rather than "racial," marked by cultural or economic specificities (language, dress, ways of life or work) that an individual or group can maintain, adapt, achieve, or discard. *Race,* on the other hand, smacks of biological determinism. In writing about Maya activism I have wrestled with the question of terminology: does "ethnicity" or "race" better capture the complicated construction of Maya identity? The term "ethnicity" focuses attention on important cultural and economic differences among Maya groups and Guatemalans more generally. But processes of categorizing indigenous groups as one—whether it be Mayas, indígenas, or the more disparaging indios—and ascribing qualities to them have revolved around ideologies of race.

In other words, ethnic differences and the racialization of those differences are important to understanding recent Guatemalan history. Central to the story, too, are the ways in which Guatemalans, Mayas and Ladinos, used the terms. In a society with a large Maya population and a genocidal civil war, when and why did Guatemalans see or assert "race"? For what reasons did people frame identity in ethnic terms? Varied framings have reflected historically produced understandings of difference, often alongside aims specific to the moment.[1]

Activists like Eduardo Pacay in the epigraph wrote of la raza—"the race"—and insisted that Mayas across ethnic boundaries in Guatemala had blood-based links to pre-Columbian Maya ancestors and to each other. This was not only to stress connections between the Maya present and past. It also challenged a *cultural and economic* determinism that defined indígenas as tied to the bean patch and rendered nonindigenous those who were not so tied. In time, the discourse shaped Maya-specific activism as people like Pacay organized opposition to a violent state. Simultaneously, other Mayas and Ladinos on the political Left favored the term *ethnic* in part because it diminished distinctions between them, a construction of difference that was important as they sought to build class-based unity.

Ladino elites' positions reflected other goals. State officials had long claimed for the nation the blood of ancient Mayas such as Tecún Umán, eulogized in the *Revista Cultural del Ejército* (Army Cultural Review). They sponsored homages and commemorations including an annual Day of the Indian, staged the annual Folklore Festival, and even featured an indigenous woman on the national currency. Their views on the present-day Maya were more ambiguous. Ladino elites tended to employ cultural notions to define and disparage contemporary indios, equating identity with traditional practices considered backward and with a low class status, and called for assimilation. Yet underneath official rhetoric were persistent beliefs about the contemporary indigenous "race" as fundamentally flawed, assimilationist views intertwined with a virulent racism that assumed inferiority based in blood.[2] This construction naturalized coercive labor practices that kept modern-day indios at work on Ladino plantations, a fact that Pacay points to: "Because that is what the indígena has always been: servant, . . . peon, beast of burden, . . . until he has become a thing." As Joshua Lund writes of Mexico, the apparent split between revered ancient indígena and disparaged present-day indio is actually no separation at all: it is rather "the constitutive ambivalence of a single, expansionist nationalism. It is a nationalism enabled by a gesture that appropriates while vanquishing, sacralizes while destroying."[3]

Categorizing Guatemala

For over one hundred years, official classification of Guatemalans has taken place and been measured through national censuses. Since 1880, census takers have duly noted whether individuals appeared to be indígenas or not, the latter category usually labeled "Ladinos," or in some cases as the inverse of indígenas: "no-indígenas."[4] In the census data, the two categories coincide with striking material inequalities, within communities and nationally. In the mid-twentieth century—like today—people defined as indigenous were found to be among the poorest of Guatemalans and as a group, lagged behind Ladinos in terms of literacy levels, health, and political participation.[5] The more recent armed conflict itself only widened the distance separating Mayas and Ladinos. Though Mayas make up a little over half of the Guatemalan population, they accounted for over 80 percent of the war's dead and disappeared, an estimated 93 percent of them killed at the hands of the state.[6]

13

The damning figures measuring dead, illiterate, and marginalized Mayas, however, can mask other important social facts. First, Maya communities have long been stratified economically, and indigenous elites' power is derived in part from class-based relationships with the indigenous masses, sometimes in alliance with Ladino elites and officials. A Maya middle sector is important; students, teachers, and social workers, for example, led many of the reform efforts of the 1970s. Second, while a majority of the poor are indigenous, it is also true that a majority of Ladinos are among the poor and are marginalized from economic and political power like their Maya counterparts. The Guatemalan state is understood as "Ladino" because Ladinos dominate positions of power, yet as anthropologist Diane Nelson warns, "Casual reference to a 'ladino state' ignores the enormous costs borne by the majority of ladinos who are not represented there."[7] And third, despite the findings that state counterinsurgency practices amounted to genocide, the war itself cannot be classified as a conflict between Ladinos and Mayas. Before the state adopted its strategy of attacking entire Maya communities, Ladino unionists, students, and leaders of all kinds were the most frequent targets of state assassinations.[8] To complicate matters further still, Mayas filled the lowest ranks of the Guatemalan army, albeit often through forced recruitment, and the state organized a massive civil patrol system in the 1980s—complicit in much of the violence—that required virtually every rural Maya man to patrol his own community for "subversives." Conflicts in Guatemala defy simple explanation. The profound divisions in society that lay at the root of its civil war and motivated activism were based in subordination of Mayas and the poor.

One more layer of complexity should be noted: the linguistic and geographic boundaries that delineate indigenous communities obviously differentiate and separate Mayas in Guatemala from each other. Collective identities as "indígenas" do not necessarily reflect the way individuals have thought (or think) of themselves. Self-identity for most Mayas was and is tied to their local community or language group, and only to a limited extent to a broader indigenous population. As we have seen, activist Mayas stressed links to *hermanos indígenas* (indigenous brothers and sisters) from the western highlands to lowland Panzós. Note that Pacay in the epigraph simultaneously referred to linguistic identity ("*kekchí*") alongside the exclamatory label "Maya!" But communication among monolingual Mayas was limited, and distances separating them from each other were great. The partial breaking down of these barriers—linguistic and geographic—spurred the emergence of the kinds of organizing examined in this book.[9]

The terms *Ladino* and *indígena* thus imply multiple and contested understandings of blood, class, and culture as signaling identity. These labels reflect messy, constructed, and ever-changing social relationships. But despite their mutability, they do have a salience that makes them primary markers

14

of identity in Guatemala. As one recent study argues, while the indigenous-Ladino formulation obscures the diversity found in both of these categories, this bipolarity is a necessary subject of analysis in part because it "occupies a place in the thinking of all Guatemalans."[10]

Where Guatemala has differed (perhaps only in degree) from Mexico and other places in Latin America with large indigenous populations is in the rigid way it has continued to be conceived in binary terms, with two distinct races constituting the nation.[11] Through segregation (discursive and physical), the ongoing use of racialized and overwhelmingly negative images of contemporary Mayas, along with homages to a preconquest Maya past, Guatemala has been imagined and represented not as a merging of indigenous and Ladino cultures or blood, but as a nation of two separate peoples. An effect of a binary understanding and construction of race in Guatemala has been a denial of *mestizo* identities. In the epigraph by the National Indigenista Institute (IIN), it was argued in 1969 that the "deadweight" of indigenous customs must be left behind as indios become Ladinos. In a similar vein, the genetic element of ladinization (becoming Ladino) in Guatemala assumes that Ladino blood "dominates" or overpowers Maya blood. Ladinization, then, is a type of wishful, whitened *mestizaje* (mixing) in which the notion of actual mixing—cultural and genetic—is downplayed. Mestizaje is present in ladinization, but buried within a Ladino exterior understood as not indigenous. It is not uncommon in Guatemala for rude or obtuse behavior to be met with a nasty pronouncement that that Ladino exterior has been ruptured, that someone has let out the indio within: Te salió el indio.[12]

Beliefs about people of the indigenous "race" as culturally and genetically distant from and inferior to Ladinos have reflected, reinforced, and naturalized more material forms of segregation not only in the area of labor, but also education, health, access to land, and effective citizenship. Historian Arturo Taracena argues that such segregation—rhetorical and material—historically has been more powerful than ever-present calls for assimilation, a fact he attributes to the use and function of racialized difference in upholding the economic and political inequalities that have benefited Guatemala's oligarchy.[13] Indigenous resistance to assimilationist pressures, too, has contributed to ongoing segregation between Mayas and Ladinos, as have obstacles of geography and language. Whatever its explanation, a binary understanding of race, a classification of Guatemalans as "indígenas" or "no-indígenas," has penetrated deep into the national psyche. Even at the most obvious and symbolic level of national pageantry, racial boundaries are solidified

15

and naturalized by separate contests for the naming of Guatemala's two national "queens." A Ladina Miss Guatemala has long represented and set the standard for national beauty, before the nation and the world. An indigenous Miss Maya, called the "Rabín Ahau," is the celebrated focal point of the annual Folklore Festival. She personifies the grandeur of the Maya past, an integral part of the nation, but to this day distinct from Ladina—and national—standards of beauty. Anthropologist Carlota McAllister attended the Rabín Ahau pageant in 1988 and described an impassioned President Vinicio Cerezo reminding spectators of the nation's duality: "Guatemalans! We are a people of two bloods!"[14]

Like all racialized groups, the indígena in Guatemala, with his or her ambiguous connotations of blood, class, and culture, has been defined by historical process. The meanings assigned to that identity in Guatemala, the products of racialization, have differed over time and have depended upon who was doing the defining—Ladinos or indígenas, elites or the popular classes, even Maya clasistas or Maya culturalistas. As Richard Adams and Santiago Bastos warn, Guatemala's racial duality does not mean that identity can be rigidly conceived or viewed as a "direct reflection" of what dominant forces may wish it to be. Relations between Ladinos and indígenas "arise . . . within the framework of a strategy of ideological domination but once set in motion, can take their own paths, sometimes at the margins of state control, sometimes"—as we will see in this book—"in opposition to it."[15] But before turning more fully to the contestations over Maya identity, we should consider in more detail the "framework . . . of ideological domination" that elites attempted to construct in Guatemala, the race-related policies and practices of the ruling class.

16 ▨▨▨ "Uncountable Corpses" or Soul of the Nation?

Official calls for the assimilation of Mayas into the nation, as mentioned, contradicted the labor practices of an elite sector that leaned on racial differentiation to ensure a ready and subservient workforce drawn from Maya communities. Prior to reforms in the 1940s, plantation owners could, in fact, secure Maya workers with the full support of the state. The growth of export agriculture, especially coffee, in Guatemala during the Liberal regimes that spanned from 1871 to 1944 relied heavily on Maya labor, the availability of which was guaranteed through various mechanisms of force: debt servitude, labor drafts, and, later, vagrancy laws requiring work of those with little or no land. During that time Guatemala's Constitution no longer differentiated between Mayas and Ladinos, yet ongoing segregation was achieved through legislative policies that enabled labor coercion mainly of indigenous people and through the theories of race that supported them. Scholars of the period point to an ideological discourse inherited from the colonial era and retooled to justify and reinforce such labor practices: indios were capable workers only when forced. They needed therefore to be under the tutelage and firm hand of the state and *finquero* (the landowner).[16] As expressed in an infamous labor regulation from the regime of Justo Rufino Barrios in 1876, "If we abandon the planters to their own resources and do not give them the most effective cooperation from the state, their efforts will be doomed to failure by the negligence of the indigenous class." The decree, which required labor gangs from Maya communities to be sent regularly to area *fincas* (plantations), described the benefits to the pueblos indígenas that would flow from such an arrangement: continual contact with the "Ladino class" was the only way to improve the miserable, abject situation of the indios, the decree argued. Requiring labor on the fincas would convert indios, still untouched by civilization, into something "useful and productive" for the nation. Such policies were backed by the growing coercive capabilities of the state. In the case of Mayas who did not see the benefits of supplying their labor—who "evaded their duty" and "defrauded" the finqueros—the decree instructed authorities of each department to "take special care to punish them to the full extent of the law."[17] Labor was simultaneously made available by Ladino encroachments on the lands of Maya communities, facilitated by new land titling procedures. The nation's progress, in the Liberal view, required pulling the indio away from his small subsistence plot and putting him to work in agricultural production for export.[18]

After an interlude of Conservative party rule, the long Liberal reign of Rufino Barrios (1873–1885) was followed by that of Manuel Estrada Cabrera (1898–1920); Estrada Cabrera's repressive regime was once again at the service of the coffee industry. In 1920 the dictator was removed from office, only to be followed by (somewhat milder) renewed military rule. Yet during the 1920s, ideas of race and nation did undergo a transformation both in intellectual and official circles as *indigenismo* came into being. Described by Martin Stabb in 1959 as a "sympathetic awareness of the Indian," indigenismo brought about a valorization of indigenous culture by Ladino academics, if in

17

the patronizing terms of the times. Developing alongside a new attention to the Maya past were concerns about the problems inherent in integrating the present-day indígena into "Western civilization."

Miguel Asturias, who would go on to win the Nobel Prize for Literature in 1967, was one of the thinkers of the 1920s whose writings from the period have received the most notoriety. (Asturias and his contemporaries at the university worked for the overthrow of Estrada Cabrera, and Asturias made the dictator the protagonist in his chilling novel, *El Señor Presidente*.) The era's debates on Guatemala's "indigenous problem" reflected anxieties on the part of Asturias and other intellectuals about creating a modern nation given the perceived inferior genetic stock of the country and the antimodern nature of labor relations in the countryside. Like theorists elsewhere in the region, Asturias argued in 1923 that the ideal solution to Guatemala's indigenous problem would be a blood transfusion for the nation.[19]

It was not forthcoming, since Guatemala did not attract much-coveted European immigration on a scale large enough to counterbalance the nation's Maya majority. To his credit, in 1923 Asturias also called for structural change in Guatemala to "liberate" the indio. He advocated the study of rural highland communities, which would be undertaken with intensity by North American anthropologists beginning in the next decade and in the 1940s by Ladino *indigenistas* (with both Ladino and Maya assistants) working through Guatemala's National Indigenista Institute. The remote indigenous highlands and indigenous community life in general were utterly foreign to most Ladinos in the 1920s, and to Asturias himself. "Guatemalan territory is of startling beauty," he wrote in his law school thesis. "It is both inspiring and saddening to realize this."[20] For reform-minded Guatemalans, to know the indígena came to be considered a requirement for rescuing him and the nation. Precisely what that rescue entailed would remain ambiguous: aspects of indigenous culture—those related to the pre-Columbian past—were greatly admired by indigenistas. Yet a wide range of contemporary indigenous practices were viewed as problematic. This would be true of the "Generation of 1920" and of those policy makers who followed in their footsteps.

Archaeological discoveries at the time fueled widespread interest in the pre-Columbian Maya, and the celebration of ancient Maya civilization being unearthed in Guatemala's Petén found its way into nationalist discourse in the 1920s. "The Maya empire, nest of our aboriginal progenitors," declared one enthusiast during commemorations of Guatemalan independence in 1923, "is the most elevated example of the culture of the [indigenous] pueblos."[21] The Geography and History Society of Guatemala was founded in 1923, a state-funded institution that set out official discourses on "national historical identity" and worked to foster knowledge about the pre-Columbian Maya past as a pillar of Guatemalan nationalism and tourism. The society created maps and studied social organization and textiles of Guatemalan indigenous communities. In 1926 one spokesperson declared the ancient K'iche' creation text the *Popol Vuh* to be the patrimony of all Guatemalans and published its Spanish translation.[22] A Guatemalan newspaper editorialized that the purpose of making the *Popol Vuh* available in Spanish was to create the "national soul."[23]

Official zeal for studying Mayas was cut short in 1931 by the institution of the long and repressive dictatorship of General Jorge Ubico, who wanted little to do with the spirit of indigenismo. In Guatemala it was a time of increasingly centralized authority and in the midst of worldwide depression, an era in which Ubico sought ever-greater control over rural laborers. Ubico abolished debt peonage but replaced that system with a vagrancy law that affected greater numbers of Mayas, since it required extensive amounts of labor—100 or 150 days per year—of all men holding title to little or no land. He also instituted a tax to go toward construction of roads and infrastructure, typically paid by Mayas through their labor.[24] Ubico refused to allow Guatemala to join the newly founded Interamerican Indigenista Institute because the nation, Ubico argued, had no indigenous problem.[25] But indigenismo was flourishing in Mexico, and enthusiasm for the study of the Maya continued to grow among Guatemalan intellectuals. It would be officially embraced under two successive reformist governments from 1944 to 1954, those of Juan José Arévalo and Jacobo Arbenz, whose administrations are together known as the October Revolution.

The Indígena in the October Revolution

The democratizing pressures of World War II finally brought change to Guatemala: a military coup by junior officers cleared the way for democratic elections in 1944, and Juan José Arévalo, supported by a coalition of teachers, students, and the labor movement, became the nation's president. Guatemala's own National Indigenista Institute, the IIN, was established in 1945.

The indigenous question being debated in the Arévalo administration was shaped in part by an outbreak of violence between Mayas and Ladinos. The October Revolution had been ushered in by a bloody confrontation in the community of Patzicía, Chimaltenango, not far from the capital, beginning just two days after Arévalo took office. On that day, Mayas in the community killed fourteen Ladino supporters of Arévalo. Conflicts seem to have erupted because the party of Arévalo's opponent had made promises of land to local Mayas in exchange for political support. After the killings, Ladinos in Patzicía and from nearby communities took revenge, attacking Maya residents. The number of dead Mayas is unclear, though apparently substantial; the press focused detailed attention on the descriptions of the Mayas' bloody attack on the Ladinos but provided no information on the number of Mayas killed, reporting only that there were "uncountable corpses."[26] The event was portrayed with great alarm in the national press. Dire warnings of impending race wars stirred fears and magnified the urgency of the indigenous problem for the Arévalo regime.

Beyond such tensions, reformers were acutely aware that the staggering problems they inherited from General Ubico had ethnic undertones, since Mayas constituted a great majority of the population in the impoverished rural highlands. Patterns of land tenure were vastly unequal, and large numbers of rural Mayas remained tied to fincas through debt peonage, despite laws making the system illegal. The government emphasized the need for structural reform of Guatemala's economy, especially in the area of land tenure. President Arévalo also made rural bilingual education a priority after an educational census revealed that more than 80 percent of rural Guatemalans of school age had no access to formal education.[27] The governments of the October Revolution argued that access to land and education, as well as health and civics lessons, would make effective citizenship available to Mayas for the first time, and in so doing would create the nation.

Illiterates were granted new voting rights in national elections, and the state set up schools and built roads in some highland communities. The government eased the Ubico-era vagrancy laws, though vagrancy remained a crime.[28] Most significantly, the regime of Jacobo Arbenz (1951–54) not only tolerated agrarian organizing, it encouraged and supported it. The centerpiece of the October Revolution, the June 1952 Law of Agrarian Reform, sought to reform a system that the legislation termed "feudal."[29] It outlawed debt peonage and all forms of servitude, and regulated land rents. Its most ambitious and controversial provisions went much further: they provided for the expropriation of uncultivated plantation lands to be distributed to campesinos through local agrarian committees called CALs. As we will see in the next chapter, these reforms were short lived, but they prompted widespread rural mobilization and shaped the expectations of a generation of campesinos.[30]

Alongside such reforms, the October Revolution focused specific attention on indigenous communities through the National Indigenista Institute. The IIN's first director, Antonio Goubaud Carrera, set out in his inaugural address the vexing questions that confronted reformers. Given the "cultural mosaic" that was Guatemala, how would it become a nation? After decrying Ladinos' lack of a national consciousness, he turned to the challenges posed by indigenous communities: "How many Guatemalans will there be . . . speaking languages different from the national language . . . , dressing in costumes [*trajes de fantasia*] that set them off from the rest of the population, . . . fettered by technologies from thousands of years ago—how many . . . will think that Guatemala is not just that marked by the mountain boundaries of their own social community?"[31]

The questions posed were familiar, but under Goubaud's leadership, a more thoughtful approach to answering them seemed to be in the making, in comparison with indigenismo of the past (and future). Better understanding among Guatemalans needed to flow two ways, Goubaud argued. Only with an awareness among both indígenas and Ladinos of the "two ways of life" existing in Guatemala could a "true Guatemalan nationality" be formed.[32] On the same occasion, the minister of education set out the challenges more starkly. Of all national concerns, he said, the "indigenous problem" was the most acute and "perhaps the source of all the rest we face." Precisely as Asturias had noted twenty years before, he stated that indígenas were foreign to Ladinos: "The first thing demanded by an honest policy is the confession that we know nothing about the Guatemalan indio."[33] To discover the magnitude of the problems the new government faced, the IIN soon commissioned studies in Maya communities across Guatemala.

In 1947 a "sociological guide" was published by the IIN outlining the kinds of information sought in these studies: information regarding ecology, housing, dress, agriculture and other work, sociopolitical and religious structures, health, reproduction, and the supernatural world. Sample questions filled forty-five pages of the IIN *Boletín* and were wide ranging and revealing. Some were straightforward fact-finding: *Is the municipio in a valley, a mountain, near a river? Is the climate cold, temperate, warm? What public services are available? Of what are houses constructed? Roofs? Floors? Are there windows?* Other types of questions seem to have sought information about levels of knowledge and perceptions: *Is it good to have sufficient light inside the house? Is it good for a house to be ventilated?* Still others inquired about habits and preferences and how they functioned as impediments to ladinization: *Do most people in the house sleep on beds, or on the floor? How often do you change your clothes? What do women wear? If the man in the household uses both Ladino clothing and indigenous clothing, what indigenous articles does he use, and why? If he uses Ladino clothing and the woman in the household does not, why? Why don't Indians wear shoes?* Some questions, or at least their phrasing, bordered on the absurd: *Do you wish there wouldn't be: lice? flies? fleas? chiggers? bedbugs? Why? How do you kill lice? If you kill them with your teeth, do you swallow them, and why?*[34]

At the same time, the IIN and the Arévalo administration were greatly interested in indigenous customs of perceived value. Indigenous weaving, especially, was identified as an important part of the national culture and in need of state protection. The 1945 Constitution included an article calling for the protection and conservation of artisan "authenticity."[35] This was to be accomplished both through laws and the creation of museums of indigenous art. In 1947 a detailed, sixteen-part decree aimed to guard the authenticity of indigenous *traje* from "adulteration," ordering the study, cataloging, and even patenting of community-specific weaving designs. It was both the "duty of the state," according to this law, and in the national interest "to protect native industry, a genuine manifestation of the art and tradition of the indigenous element."[36]

During the ten years of the reformist October Revolution, real change did begin to come to the Guatemalan highlands, and most activists of later decades see that period as crucially important. Yet some also look back on the assimilationist mentality of the era's flourishing indigenismo with suspicion. Ambiguities are obvious. How did indigenistas balance the desire to rescue the pueblo indígena through assimilation with the value they placed on certain elements of Maya identity? Recall that the IIN official quoted previously decried the use of *traje* as one of the many challenges facing Guatemala because it set Mayas apart from others and, in effect, apart from the nation. Distinctive indigenous dress was of great significance to the IIN, the focus of much concern and regulation. Yet even Maya customs and products that were deemed valuable, in all their beauty and carefully measured authenticity, seem to have had little place in modern Guatemala and were destined for the museum.[37]

The Indígena in the Post-1954 Nation

The October Revolution, amid accusations of Communist sympathies because of its land reform policies, was overthrown with the assistance of the US CIA in 1954. In the years leading up to the coup, anti-Arbenz counterrevolutionary movements—with the important participation of Guatemala's Catholic Church —viewed the nation's indigenous question quite differently than reformers of the October Revolution.[38] Opponents of Arbenz stressed the need to fortify Guatemalan nationalism with the rhetorical union of (ancient) Maya and Ladino as constituting the nation. But where the Arévalo and Arbenz regimes pursued bilingual education and land reform to achieve assimilation of the present-day Maya, the nationalism of the counterrevolutionary movement demanded that such reforms be reversed. Land expropriations in particular, argued opponents of Arbenz, undermined stability in the countryside and threatened the nation. Their answer was ladinization that involved a combination of citizenship, capitalism, family, Catholicism, and more traditional education (overseen by the church), with the overarching concern being the fight against Communism.

Within weeks of the coup that brought Colonel Carlos Castillo Armas to power, the new Guatemalan government suspended the National Indigenista Institute. It reopened, but with an anemic budget and influence to match. It was overshadowed by a new Guatemalan Institute [Seminario] for Social Integration (SISG) created in 1955, which explicitly focused on state-sponsored economic development to integrate the indígena into the counterrevolutionary nation.[39] The IIN itself was harnessed to the state's anti-Communist programming. In 1955, for example, the IIN translated from Spanish into Mayan languages materials for the Committee of National Defense against Communism, including a piece entitled "A Lesson Dedicated to the Guatemalan Campesinos."[40]

The folkloric component of post-1954 indigenismo involved establishing official and often ostentatious homages to the Maya as a national symbol. In 1955 a "Museum of the Guatemalan Indio" was proposed, "dedicated to exalting the values of the indio guatemalteco, . . . [through] a permanent exhibit of *our* folklore" (emphasis added). The museum was to showcase ceramics, textiles, music, and the "esoteric world" of the Maya and aimed to attract national and international tourism.[41] In 1958 the Ydígoras Fuentes regime designated the official "Day of the Indian," first commemorated on April 19, 1959, a day when present-day indígenas could "focus the spirit of their race and awaken their patriotic sentiment." The indígena deserved such homage, the government declared by decree, because he was the "original architect of the purest Guatemalan nationality."[42]

In 1961 the publication *Guatemala Indígena* was founded at the IIN, with the contradictory goals of integrating indígenas into the nation and showcasing what made them separate. The publication promised to provide information about a Maya "vision of the world" and spread knowledge of "*lo indígena*"—all things indigenous—as the "foundation of our nationality."[43]

23

But an introductory essay set out the "indigenous-national problem" in stark and familiar terms: sociologically, Guatemala was not a unified nation, but "an ethnic mosaic" of indios and Ladinos. As a result, the piece argued, the nation could not reap the benefits of democracy. The solution lay in the integration of the indio, to be achieved through the SISG.[44] In 1969 and 1970, the title page of *Guatemala Indígena* featured the motto "Development of the indígena: The foundation of our nationality." For the next decade, it became "The indígena: The foundation of the national structure." Putting structural questions aside, the journal continued to offer articles limited to folklore and culture: Maya marriage customs, traje, music, pre-Hispanic Mayan manuscripts, and indigenous conceptions of the supernatural.

Preoccupation with folklore once again coexisted with long-held notions about the inferiority of contemporary indios. In 1969 official statements regarding the indigenous problem reflected a finquero paternalism and justified the strong hand of the state in dealing with Mayas. In the IIN's "Why Is Indigenismo Indispensable?" its authors posed a purely rhetorical question: is paternalism at times justifiable? The piece decried that half of the nation's population was ignorant of national laws, illiterate, spoke only Mayan languages, continued to believe in multiple gods and supernatural powers, and was geographically isolated, converting "every hut into a hiding place." (These were some of the same "customs" featured in the IIN's *Guatemala Indígena*.) "Can this population," the IIN asked, "be governed and led in the same way as the other half?"[45] Defending a "special" approach, the IIN claimed that the appropriate means to deal with the indigenous problem would be through an institution "that knows and understands the soul of the indio; that would treat [indígenas] in a special manner, not precisely the democratic way." The IIN claimed that "to know the soul of the indio is not a matter of intuition, nor of improvisation, it is a matter of study and a function of love. This study, understanding and love for the indio constitute the essence of indigenismo."[46]

Homage to Mayas, Massacre of Indios

When activist Mayas segment their history, certain markers are almost always singled out: the conquest, the 1870s Liberal coffee regime, the reformist October Revolution begun in 1944, and the CIA-sponsored coup that overthrew it in 1954. The military (and military-dominated) regimes of the

(Above): Twenty-five-centavo coin, featuring Concepción Ramírez Mendoza. (Right): Concepción Ramírez Mendoza, Santiago Atitlán. Photo by author, used with kind permission of the Reanda Ramírez family.

post-1954 period are not seen as homogeneous, and some stand out as more repressive and others less so. But even the more moderate tend to be viewed as part of a larger, repressive whole. A relatively open environment accompanied the election of Julio Méndez Montenegro (1966–1970), for example, yet one activist described it as a time when you could stick your head up, so it could be cut off later.

Repression against Arbenz supporters following the 1954 coup was swift and extensive. By 1956, the first death squads operated in the country. In the 1960s and 1970s, state forces responded to unarmed reform movements with violent repression. Armed guerrilla groups emerged in the east in the 1960s and in the western highlands in the 1970s. By 1978, counterinsurgency tactics against them included wholesale slaughter of civilians, as was done in Panzós. In the early 1980s, the armed forces carried out the methodological terror of scorched earth.

In that post-1954 era, there seem to be limitless examples to illustrate the state's absurd pairing of homages to Mayaness and disregard for the rights and needs of living Mayas. A case in point involves one of the most familiar Maya images for all Guatemalans, the woman whose profile is featured on the twenty-five-centavo coin. Though she is unnamed on the

25

coin, a press story in 2002 identified her as Concepción Ramírez Mendoza, a Tz'utujil Maya from Santiago Atitlán, Sololá. In 1964 Ramírez Mendoza won a contest held by government officials seeking a new visage for the coin. In Santiago Atitlán women wear a distinctive head wrap, which might explain the state's choice of the community; Ramírez Mendoza's profile replaced that of another Maya from the same town, a woman featured on the coin first minted in 1948.

Santiago Atitlán was a site of nightmarish counterinsurgency violence, and the symbolic Concepción Ramírez Mendoza, like hundreds in the community, experienced the torment firsthand. Her father, an evangelical pastor named Pedro Ramírez, was tortured and killed by the Guatemalan army in January 1981 along with over twenty others in Santiago Atitlán's first massacre, at a coffee finca in nearby Chacayá. She was made a widow nine years later when her husband, Miguel Reanda, was murdered along with three other men by unidentified assailants.[47] No small irony, then, that in 1996 Concepción Ramírez Mendoza was recognized by the Guatemalan state as a "national symbol." At that point the symbolic Ramírez Mendoza was a widow with six children. With her recognition came a small government pension.

One of Ramírez Mendoza's sons, who translated her Tz'utujil into Spanish for me, pointed out that names and information accompany all other figures on Guatemalan currency, but not on the coin featuring his mother. Ramírez Mendoza added that she had been anonymous through the entire process. Her father had arranged her participation in the contest and had received the government's two quetzales, approximately two dollars, when she was chosen. "A curious thing," she said, "is that they never asked me my name."[48]

Empty state homages to the Maya were ubiquitous in the 1950s and 1960s. Growing levels of state-sponsored violence in the late 1970s and 1980s rendered such official gestures outrageous. In 1978 an editorial by Maya activists in their monthly *Ixim: Notas Indígenas* renamed Día de la Raza (what in the United States is known as Columbus Day) as the Día de Desgracia, "Day of Disgrace." The Guatemalan government portrayed October 12 as the birth of Guatemalan nationality, the moment when Guatemala's two races met. *Ixim* editors argued that it was not something to celebrate; instead it signified loss—spiritual, social, political, cultural—and the Maya's prostitution: "For us, this day is a day of sorrow, . . . the day we lost our . . . liberty, to become slaves of the pseudo-Spaniards. On this day they proclaim heroes those who murdered us, those who are the cause of our disgrace, poverty, injustices, urban and rural. . . . We cannot celebrate the Día de la Raza because it . . . meant [our] binding to a . . . system that has only served to prostitute our pueblo."[49] More recently, Maya campesinos have taken to commemorating the Día de la Raza by occupying the nation's highways and plantations to protest state oppression and demand access to land.

Activist Mayas have directed similar criticism toward ever-present state homages to Tecún Umán, a K'iche' leader and warrior at the time of the Spanish conquest. A principal character in state-sponsored folklore, in the late 1950s and 1960s the Guatemalan legislature called for national commemorations, parades featuring Mayas, and monuments to be erected in his honor.[50] In 1960 the state designated Tecún Umán a "national hero" and the rhetorical "first soldier of Guatemala" for his valiant, if misguided, efforts against Spanish conquistador Pedro Alvarado. (Though there is much contestation over the legend, a popularly held version is that Tecún Umán struck Alvarado's horse rather than the man, thinking him a god and the horse an extension of his body. The image of the indio as brave but somewhat mentally deficient cannot be overlooked.) Tecún Umán has been a favored symbol of the Guatemalan army, assigned the rhetorical task of unifying the two "races" that make the nation. He was called upon explicitly to ameliorate rising tensions in the indigenous highlands in the late 1970s. In the *Army Cultural Review* in 1979—exactly one year after the Panzós massacre—readers learned that "Tecún Umán is a . . . representative of the land; as clean as our skies, above political conflicts and fratricidal struggles."[51]

Anthropologist Irma Otzoy has written on the state's use of Tecún Umán and Maya activists' reactions to it. The state chooses a conquest-era Maya as the symbol of Indianness, Otzoy argues, to distance itself from and erase present-day Mayas—especially, I would add, indios like those in Panzós. If Tecún Umán, Otzoy explains, "represents an icon of the Indian space within the nation, . . . [it] is a space in which the Mayas are present in a petrified form, leaving no possibility for their development, inclusion, self-determination or autonomy." Mayaness is "contained" by such a move, argues Otzoy, fixed in the past and divorced from the present.[52]

The state tried to control Maya identity by such maneuvers, but it had a difficult time controlling Mayas. While the *Army Cultural Review* explicitly positioned Tecún Umán as apart from the armed conflict, in 1992 a Maya organization graphically contested that image: Tecún Umán was shown in an anti-Quincentennial poster fighting Alvarado, as legend would have it, but this time the Spaniard took the form of a Guatemalan army soldier equipped with an M16.[53] Diane Nelson describes an even more intense reappropriation of Tecún Umán by Ixil Mayas in the northern Quiché community of Nebaj in 1985. State violence devastated the area in the 1980s, and residents of Nebaj used the image of Tecún Umán to express their grief and fury. He is traditionally a protagonist in annual re-creations of the "Dance of the Conquest" in the community, which again feature the symbolic encounter between the K'iche' warrior and Alvarado. The performance normally ends when Tecún Umán is placed in a coffin and carried through the town. In 1985 he stood in for the staggering numbers of Ixiles dead at the hands of the army. As Nelson writes regarding the events, "At the moment of his death, and throughout the day as the coffin moved through the streets of Nebaj, a torrent of grief accompanied it. People fell upon the coffin shrieking and crying, some cursed the army and called out the names of dead friends and relatives."[54]

With counterinsurgency violence reaching levels that prompted Mayas to compare it to the conquest, whatever disputed claims the state may have had to representing the pueblo maya utterly collapsed.

Mayas Mobilized

President Jacobo Arbenz called the agrarian reform of 1952 Guatemala's first act of justice since the conquest. The ill-fated reform law, which encouraged peasant committees to petition the national government for expropriation of fallow lands, propelled Archbishop Mariano Rossell y Arellano, an ardent anti-Communist, to action. He used the powerful symbols at his disposal to decry Arbenz as a Communist. Most memorably, he enlisted the Black Christ of Esquipulas—a much-revered icon among Mayas and Guatemalans in general—to help rid the fatherland of the October Revolution. When the faithful of Esquipulas nearly rioted at the suggestion that their saint would be removed, Archbishop Rossell commissioned a replica and took that on rounds throughout the country in 1953. This National Pilgrimage of the Christ of Esquipulas was hugely successful and met with expressions of devotion all over Guatemala.

Emeterio Toj Medrano, a K'iche' Maya from an area near Santa Cruz del Quiché, the capital of the department of El Quiché, was thirteen. years old at the time. He was the grandson of campesinos and the son of an itinerant merchant, and, along with many young people in the community, active in the local catechist program, Catholic Action. With the Black Christ, Toj now believes, Archbishop Rossell took advantage of people's attachment to the figure, using these visits to deliver speeches that wildly distorted the Arbenz record. Toj now characterizes the Christ of Esquipulas as the "Captain General" of the so-called Army of Liberation that toppled Arbenz. At the time, though, many Maya Catholics like Toj heeded the archbishop's calls to "rise up as one man against the enemy of God and the Nation."[1] Emeterio Toj supported Arbenz's ouster, what he later viewed as the "overthrow of hope."[2]

Like many Guatemalans, Emeterio Toj now looks back on the October Revolution as a foundational moment for reformism in the country, a period when real change seemed within reach. While he and other Mayas from highland communities went along with the church's anti-Arbenz agenda, many of them saw matters quite differently soon after the 1954 coup. The counterrevolutionary state worked quickly to undo the reforms of the October Revolution and squelch the mobilization that the period had engendered. In that militarized context, Mayas like Toj went from being supporters of the coup to becoming part of community organizing in the 1960s and 1970s criticizing state repression and pressing for change.

This chapter follows local organizing efforts in three places: Toj's Santa Cruz del Quiché, the community of Santiago Atitlán in Sololá, and the department of Huehuetenango. These are just a few of the many examples that could illustrate how local Maya mobilization developed in those years. Each story is in some ways distinct, and community-level efforts reflected local realities and possibilities. Alongside such variations, though, there are strong similarities in the kinds of organizing that unfolded in different communities, and these experiences were for many activists stepping stones toward regional or national-level organizing. We'll use these cases, then, to consider how the stage was set for more collective Maya mobilization.[3]

▓▓▓ Santa Cruz del Quiché

Emeterio Toj Medrano is in some ways typical of activists from El Quiché, in other ways extraordinary. He tells of his grandfather (also named Emeterio) losing his land in the area through debt peonage before the October Revolution. Born in 1940, Toj was raised in an environment of agrarian mobilization and what he calls the "*pensamiento de lucha*," the fighting spirit encouraged by the reformist governments from 1944 to 1954.[4] During the Arévalo and Arbenz years, his grandfather joined the local agrarian committee, or CAL, one of thousands of such groups established under Arbenz and empowered to petition the government for land expropriations. Throughout the country, local leaders channeled labor and land struggles through the October Revolution's new legal mechanisms, supported by the labor federations General Confederation of Workers of Guatemala (CGTG) and the National Peasant Confederation of Guatemala (CNCG). CALs challenged the labor practices of landowners and corrupt officials and, most significantly, petitioned for land redistribution. A study by Jim Handy indicates that in its first three months, the National Agrarian Department received nearly five thousand petitions for land, and an estimated one hundred thousand campesino families were eventually granted parcels.[5] While the agrarian reform law was short lived and soon reversed, the organizing practices and expectations it engendered were not.

Emeterio Toj attended just a year of primary school in 1949, then began to travel on occasion with his father to sell goods in Guatemala City. (He returned to night school as an adult in the 1960s in Santa Cruz and finished his *básico*—ninth year of schooling—in the early 1970s.) His father died when Emeterio was just fourteen, and Emeterio spent most of his childhood and youth living with his grandfather near Santa Cruz. He joined the community's Catholic Action (AC) program in the early 1950s. Mayas of his generation were drawn to AC in large numbers in El Quiché, although many of their parents and grandparents practiced traditional Maya religion known as *costumbre*.[6] Catholic Action, established in the department of Momostenango two decades earlier, grew rapidly in the 1950s, and was harnessed to the archbishop's proactive opposition to Arbenz. Catholic priests viewed AC and similar programs, such as the Maryknolls' Delegates of the Word, as a means both to dampen the appeal of Communism and to counter what many saw as an unacceptably high level of costumbre ritual in the countryside. As Maryknoll father James Curtin wrote in 1963, "The catechist movement has been . . . most important . . . in bringing about better spiritual life in the rural areas. In the cities and the towns, the Cursillos de Cristiandad [Christian workshops or training sessions] seems to be the best instrument for changing the mentality of the future leaders and the present ones among the professional men. It has its effect in giving greater concern for one's neighbour and community, extending the influence of the Church, . . . and lessening the dangers of Communism by creating a social consciousness among Catholics."[7] Priests and their mostly male catechists worked together closely, with the catechists serving as the link between the rural population and the church's goals. AC enabled the church and its anti-Communist teachings to reach into the smallest hamlets, using young catechists who spoke local languages and were part of local communities. Toj recounts that his entire family became AC members, except for his grandparents. Only his grandparents, he says, though they could not read and had no education, had

31

the prescience to reject the church's condemnation of the revolution on which they had pinned their hopes.[8]

The coup in 1954 that overthrew Arbenz was followed by the return of expropriated lands to their former owners, harsh repression against agrarian organizing, and a long succession of regimes headed or dominated by the military. The "fighting spirit," though, remained fresh in the minds of campesinos in places such as El Quiché. Gaining control of restive campesinos was a central aim of the post-1954 governments, but also an elusive one. Agrarian organizing networks from the reform period had extended beyond local communities, linking campesinos to the national labor movement and to the October Revolution itself, and these experiences were not forgotten. As Greg Grandin writes of the period's mobilization, it "tore up and remade social relations and expectations throughout Guatemala."[9] After the overthrow of Arbenz, rural organizing was not ended by the counterrevolution. Instead it emerged in new forms.

Domingo Hernández Ixcoy was another K'iche' catechist, like Toj from an area not far from Santa Cruz. The last son of a campesino family, he was born just before the overthrow of Arbenz and grew up in the early counterrevolutionary period. In his experience, the 1960s were a time when the October Revolution remained strongly in the minds and conversations of his family and community.[10] His parents discussed the reformist governments, he remembers, comparing their own experiences with those of the new revolutionary Cuba, informed via a brother-in-law's shortwave radio. Domingo and the other men of the family would gather together at night to listen to the radio, with news of the outside world translated by his father, a Spanish speaker. There was a great deal of anti-Communist propaganda on the radio, he recalls, from Voice of America and the Guatemalan stations, condemning the former Guatemalan regime and the Cuban government for stripping people of their liberty. "But we in El Quiché, . . . campesinos who traveled to work on the [coastal] fincas," he says, "had a different opinion." His family and campesinos in general had experienced Guatemala's reform period not as a time when freedoms were lacking, Hernández Ixcoy argues, but quite the contrary: as an era when workers could organize and unionize, earn better salaries, and attain lands.[11] These memories, combined with difficult economic circumstances faced by campesinos in the 1960s, fueled social organizing.[12] Much of it, to the dismay of Guatemala's Catholic hierarchy, began in Catholic Action networks.

Catholic Action grew along with an increasing church presence in the Guatemalan countryside. With the coup of 1954, the Guatemalan government lifted restrictions on foreign priests entering the country. In 1960 Pope John XXIII called on the world's Catholics to send priests to Latin America, and the church in Guatemala, with Catholic Action as an integral part, entered a period of rapid expansion. A meager 132 Catholic priests in Guatemala in 1950 rose to 346 by 1959, and then to 608 by 1970, most of them foreign.[13] There were even greater numbers of Catholic sisters and nuns by that time, over eight hundred, again mostly foreigners.[14] US Maryknolls (expelled from Communist China) established parishes throughout Huehuetenango, a few during the October Revolution, but most in the 1950s and 1960s; Spanish Sacred Heart priests arrived in the department of El Quiché in 1955 and were joined by the Jesuits in the 1970s; US, Belgian, and Salesian priests were an important presence in the Q'eqchi' and Pocomchi' communities of Alta Verapaz by the late 1960s, and an Oklahoma mission established itself in the Tz'utujil community of Santiago Atitlán, Sololá, in 1964.

As the reach of the Catholic Church extended more deeply into the highlands, Catholic Action became at once a religious, political, and cultural movement. Maya catechists in Catholic Action began to take part in local politics through the Guatemalan Christian Democrats (DC), a political party founded in 1955, which built its base through Catholic Action. (Emeterio Toj, for one, joined the youth group of the Christian Democrats soon after the party became active in Santa Cruz.) The DC, promoted by Archbishop Rossell and supported with funds from European Christian Democrats, was again viewed as an important "alternative to Communism."[15] Mostly through the Christian Democratic party, Mayas voted, ran for office, and even won election as mayor in some Maya communities. (The DC held control over the mayor's office in Santa Cruz in the 1960s and 1970s.) Through the party, Mayas simultaneously became connected to national politics. In its historical account of the evolving role of the Catholic Church in the department of El Quiché, the Diocese of El Quiché points to the DC as the institution that first channeled local Maya political potential into formal politics connected to the nation. "Between the 1950s and the early 1960s," they wrote,

33

there was very little or no political consciousness among the indigenous population besides the anti-Communism

> inspired by the ideological work of the church or the . . .
> struggles . . . during the decade of the [October] revolution
> (1944–54). But these were not ideas or interests that sprang
> from within the pueblo indígena. They came from outside.
> It is Catholic Action that provided community-level bases
> for this awakening, and DC that channeled this potential
> into party politics, with a national vision that had not
> existed in the communities until that moment.[16]

In the late 1950s and the 1960s, Catholic priests and the Christian Democrats tended to share a paternalistic and conservative view on Guatemala's "indigenous problem," reflecting the positions of Archbishop Rossell (1938–1964) and his successor, Archbishop Mario Casariego. Despite the leadership of Rossell and Casariego, however, newly arrived priests began to adopt an approach to their work that emphasized issues of social justice and focused on a new "theology of liberation." As happened in much of Latin America in the 1960s, the Catholic Church in Guatemala fractured ideologically: the branch aligned with the archbishops held on to positions of power in the capital and continued to staff some rural parishes, but growing numbers of parish clergy applied the new theology in the countryside. Based on the guidance of the Second Vatican Council (held in sessions from 1962 through 1965) and the 1968 Medellín Conference of the Latin American Episcopal Council, priests in rural communities like Santa Cruz began to focus their work not just on the spiritual lives of their parishioners, but also on their social and economic needs. This had far-reaching effects on Maya mobilization. Programs based in liberation theology were not specifically geared toward indigenous people, but in Guatemala they did often focus on Mayas since most Catholic missions concentrated their efforts in the highlands. As one priest explained, the theology's "preferential option for the poor" in many parishes became the preferential option for indígenas. As priests' new mission took shape, they used the catechist model in Maya communities in much the same way that had proved so successful for conservative interests in earlier years.

Adoption of liberation theology did not mean that parish priests necessarily or immediately abandoned their anti-Communist message; many, including the Maryknolls in Huehuetenango and the Sacred Heart priests in El Quiché, continued in the 1960s to condemn Communism as a dangerous force to be defeated. But their approach to that struggle changed, as justice in the countryside—and specifically for Mayas—became identified as the key to diminishing Communism's appeal. Priests intertwined biblical teachings with discussions of everyday needs, or as Maryknoll William Price put it, sought to "save men, not only souls."[17] Over time, too, the ardent anti-Communism among some parish priests waned. Regarding the historical anti-Communism of the church and Catholic Action, the Diocese of El Quiché wrote that a process of "renovation" took place, "of conversion and agony within the . . . movement so that its ideology could be transformed over time and become an instrument of change and liberation."[18] In El Quiché, for example, a priest at the center of the new Catholic theology, Sacred Heart father Luis Gurriarán, has been described as a onetime admirer of Spanish general Francisco Franco. Yet anthropologist Beatriz Manz writes that Gurriarán and several priests in the order were led in "an unexpected direction" by what they encountered in El Quiché. "They focused on the plight of the poor and grew to be a vital part of the community," she observed. "When the church went through its own revolution, they were ready."[19]

No Basta Rezar (It Is Not Enough to Pray)

The ideas of social justice infusing the work of priests in the 1960s and 1970s appealed to second-generation catechists like Emeterio Toj and Domingo Hernández Ixcoy. At the same time, parish priests and catechists used Catholic Action not just to spread the new church doctrine, but as the basis for broader social organizing. Through AC, parish priests supplied young people like Toj and Hernández Ixcoy with resources and networks that helped them develop into community leaders. Both young men became involved in a range of organizing efforts in the 1960s and 1970s, some of them connected to the church, others well beyond church control.

Like many catechists of the period, Emeterio Toj and Domingo Hernández Ixcoy remember a turning point in the church and Catholic Action in the 1960s and the profound effects it had on local organizing. Priests and their catechists began to question the dogma of the church, Toj recalls. He described the impact of priests turning around to face the congregation rather than the altar during Mass, speaking directly to the

35

people through sermons in Spanish instead of Latin.[20] Soon catechists took the priests' new message beyond church walls. Toj explained that "those who accepted and understood that we have to struggle here on this Earth for the body and soul" began to work in community development. With Father Gurriarán, AC catechists set up the first cooperative in the area in 1963, the Savings and Loan Cooperative of Santa Cruz, and Emeterio Toj served as its first secretary. This represented a real change in Santa Cruz, since it freed borrowers from the exorbitant rates charged by traditional (usually Ladino) moneylenders. Gurriarán and AC catechists founded credit and agricultural cooperatives in a half-dozen communities in outlying areas of El Quiché as well. Church run, these were alternatives to state-sanctioned cooperatives that the government oversaw as part of its developmental model, and they were eyed suspiciously by the government and area elites. Despite the fact that Father Gurriarán was known for his anti-Communist views, when he petitioned for official recognition of the cooperatives in 1964 he was attacked in the press for intending to "introduce Arbenz's Communist system and imported models of organization foreign to the indígenas."[21] Soon threats were more direct. To thwart Gurriarán's efforts, the Guatemalan government temporarily expelled him from the country in 1965 and imprisoned cooperativists and catechists working with him.[22] Such repression became the state's response to a wide variety of efforts for reform in and beyond El Quiché. In 1967 the daily *Prensa Libre* calculated some one hundred political assassinations *per month* in Guatemala.[23] In 1971 *El Gráfico* counted 1,248 political killings and disappearances for the year.[24]

Undeterred, priests and catechists in El Quiché protested repression, and the catechist and cooperative movements continued to grow. The diocese claimed in 1968 a total of thirty-six hundred catechists and eighty thousand AC participants. (Each catechist worked with four or five families.) According to these figures, more than 50 percent of young people and adults in the department of El Quiché participated in Catholic Action.[25] In the same year, the diocese was running eighteen cooperatives, the largest of which was the Santa Cruz Savings and Loan where Emeterio Toj was an officer. By 1971 it was the strongest in Guatemala, with 2,246 active members and loans totaling over US$300,000.[26]

A local radio station, Radio Quiché, established by the parish in 1969, became a key part of community organizing, a way to communicate

36

the church's new message to the wider community. Radio Quiché aired programs of liberation theology, literacy training, and civic education, and Emeterio Toj became a broadcaster. At the same time, Toj helped organize culturally focused events in Santa Cruz, reflecting a growing emphasis by priests and young people on the need to value Maya culture and foster pride in "la raza." With area students and catechists, Toj founded the Maya-Quiché Cultural Association to spread ideas about pride in identity. He and other activists fought for control over Santa Cruz's popular contest for reina indígena. Traditionally the pageant had been overseen by Ladinos on the town's festival committee, but Toj and others managed in the mid-1970s to put it in Maya hands.[27]

Catechists like Toj and Hernández Ixcoy started organizing small groups in the late 1960s and early 1970s that aimed to help people in the community get to know the Bible and its connection to the struggles for a more just system. Inspired by these experiences, Hernández Ixcoy describes young Mayas including himself and Toj pushing the local church further in the direction of social engagement. They fought for positions on the local Catholic Action board of directors.[28] Another K'iche' catechist from the area, Gregorio Chay, explained the political challenge they faced: "AC had [in the 1950s] been led by elite groups in Santa Cruz resistant to social change, to a more open Christianity in the social sense." His own family members, Chay said, were among those AC charter members, part of the anti-Communist movement that rose to local prominence after the overthrow of Arbenz and that struggled to hold on to power.[29] These first two generations of AC in Santa Cruz and similar communities came into direct confrontation in the late 1960s and 1970s. Tensions rose between the older developmentalist-oriented AC members and those young people advocating bigger changes, greater social involvement, and more emphasis on concientización, the much-used term for the political process of "consciousness-raising."

In Santa Cruz the young activists prevailed. Emeterio Toj, Domingo Hernández Ixcoy, and later Gregorio Chay won positions on the local board, and their impact was significant. "Masses in El Quiché began to change radically," recalls Hernández Ixcoy, speaking of the 1970s. "Rather than the hymns the priests taught us, . . . we began to sing 'No basta rezar' [It Is Not Enough to Pray], 'Casas de carton' ['Cardboard Houses,' referring to inadequate housing]. . . . The Mass was greatly politicized."[30] The new Catholic Action board members took responsibility for weekly Bible classes and were "in charge of deepening questions

37

of religion among the people," explains Hernández Ixcoy. They infused discussions with issues of economics: "More than talking about God and spiritual questions, . . . we talked about . . . material things—injustice, exploitation, [raised questions such as] who are the owners of the land? What do they do? How do they treat the workers?"[31]

Part of this radicalization of catechists coincided with Jesuit priests from the capital beginning to work in Santa Cruz in 1972, among them Ricardo Falla, Fernando Hoyos, and Enrique Corral. Emeterio Toj by that time had become a well-known broadcaster at Radio Quiché. Toj was approached by Father Hoyos and his team of Ladino university students, many of them active in a Guatemala City–based group called Cráter, which connected socially committed students from the capital to Mayas in the highlands.[32] The Jesuits recognized that Toj, as a catechist and a broadcaster, could link them to the broader pueblo, even distant villages of the department. As Ricardo Falla put it, "Emeterio opened up the *campo* [countryside]."[33]

Together the priests, students from the city, and local Mayas such as Toj and Hernández Ixcoy began more politicized literacy work and concientización in the rural communities surrounding Santa Cruz. They formed small groups to study civics and laws. Toj and Hernández Ixcoy speak of learning and then teaching about the national Constitution in combination with analysis of the Bible. "None of us had read the Constitution [before], we didn't know [it]," remembers Hernández Ixcoy. But quickly "the Bible and the Constitution . . . became our lecture materials. . . . We found that [in the Bible] they denounced injustices . . . , that there had been oppressor classes throughout history, and that pueblos had risen up and challenged oppression."[34]

Marxism shaped their approach, introduced by the Ladino students and priests from the capital. The causes of problems in the pueblo, Toj came to believe, were deeper than could be addressed through existing institutions. Emeterio describes the frustrations that grew from the litany of organizing experiences he had had: he had led culturally focused community organizing; he had worked for years through Catholic Action; he was part of the Christian Democrats; he led cooperatives and literacy training programs. But none of these efforts seemed to bring real change, he said. Regarding the problems of the pueblo, Toj recalled, "We began to realize that there were other much stronger causes, structural causes. So now what? Well, . . . we kept searching."[35] Pablo Ceto, another activist K'iche' from Santa Cruz who

38

was a contemporary of Toj and Hernández Ixcoy, recounts that they formed a more "political" group in the mid-1970s, an organization called Nukuj.[36] The experience quickly led to larger-scale, national-level organizing: within a few years Emeterio Toj, Domingo Hernández Ixcoy, Pablo Ceto, and other area activists, along with people from Chimaltenango, Baja Verapaz, and the southern coast, founded the campesino organization Committee for Peasant Unity, or CUC.

Other Mayas in the community seeking alternatives in the early 1970s took paths that led them out of Santa Cruz to the department's unsettled Ixcán rain forest to the north. Maya mobilization took place against a backdrop of serious economic problems in El Quiché, including grow-ing landlessness and seasonal migration among peasants. Beatriz Manz describes the acute problem of access to land in the municipality of Santa Cruz.[37] Facing poverty and few prospects, in 1970 a group of peas-ants from Santa Cruz and other municipalities of El Quiché, families with experience in the cooperative movement, decided to relocate to the jungle near the border with Mexico, at the time a week's journey from Santa Cruz on foot. Led by the returned priest Luis Gurriarán, the resettlement was one of the first of the church-supported colonization projects that would in the next decade prompt thousands of Mayas to relocate to inhospitable but available land in the northern regions of El Quiché and Huehuetenango and the western part of the Petén.[38]

Despite daunting physical obstacles, settlers from El Quiché founded towns in the Ixcán. They cleared land, planted subsistence and cash crops, and organized agricultural cooperatives with surprising success, which led to more peasants being encouraged to join them. As Manz writes, the success of the Ixcán cooperative movement "bred a new, spirited confidence that in turn fueled social transformations."[39] A young Chilean graduate student at the time, Manz noted the politicization of the settlers when she met them in 1973:

39

> I heard young K'iche' men, the leaders of the settlement proj-ect, singing songs by Victor Jara—the most popular of Chile's singers of the *nueva canción* [new song movement].[40] . . . Up to that point everything that I had read or heard . . . about the K'iche' Mayas had portrayed them as locally centered and apolitical. . . . In contrast . . . , I noticed that the peasants

were interested in me precisely because I was Chilean; it was 1973, and they were surprisingly aware of the social mobilization and conflict taking place in my country.[41]

As it happened, the Ixcán was also the place where in 1972 the first armed revolutionaries from the Guerrilla Army of the Poor, the EGP, entered El Quiché.[42] The community where Manz worked, Santa María Tzejá, was the first settlement that the new guerrilla troops visited, and within several years the EGP had apparently gained the cooperation of a significant portion of the community.[43] Back in Santa Cruz, too, the EGP would have an impact. Soon after Emeterio Toj, Domingo Hernández Ixcoy, and Pablo Ceto helped establish the campesino organization CUC, they would continue seeking "other avenues." Like several of the Jesuits who inspired them—Falla, Hoyos, and Corral—their next step would be to enter the revolutionary EGP.

▨▨▨ Santiago Atitlán, Sololá

Santiago Atitlán, a Tz'utujil Maya community on the shores of Lake Atitlán, is another place where radicalization among young Mayas was under way in the 1960s and 1970s. A progressive Catholicism grew in the village when a US mission from Oklahoma set up residence there in 1964. The mission opened a health clinic and formed a credit union. Within a few years the parish purchased a piece of land and founded an experimental farming cooperative, started a primary school, and set up a community radio station, the Voz de Atitlán (Voice of Atitlán). A thirty-three-year-old priest, Father Stanley Rother, joined the mission in 1968. He tried to create better opportunities for community residents to make a living in Atitlán, rather than migrating to coastal plantations for work. The agricultural cooperative prospered under his oversight, and he also helped set up fishing and weaving cooperatives.[44]

In the 1960s, a few Maya children attended the mission's primary school: Gaspar Culán was one of the first to complete elementary school, followed by several other boys including the brothers Cruz and Miguel Sisay, Felipe Vásquez Tuíz, and Pedro Esquina. While they managed to attend school, they were not well-off economically. Like the young activists in Santa Cruz, they came from families of campesinos and weavers, and several from a young age had migrated to the coast for plantation work. Felipe Vásquez Tuíz was the first person in his family to go to school, and Pedro Esquina was the only one of five children to finish sixth grade, possible with the support of his older brother and the Santiago Atitlán mission priest.[45]

After finishing primary school, Gaspar Culán was invited to study at the Catholic seminary in nearby Sololá. The other students formed a cooperative secondary school in Santiago Atitlán (since none existed) with the help of the primary-school teachers, the church, and their parents. Felipe Vásquez Tuíz was soon chosen to join the Francisco Marroquín linguistics project in the town of Antigua, supported by Benedictine and Maryknoll priests and in the 1970s directed by North American linguists. Father Stanley Rother and another priest in the community arranged for Cruz and Miguel Sisay and Pedro Esquina to study at the Instituto Indígena Santiago, a Catholic school for indigenous boys in the capital.

The Instituto Indígena Santiago was partner to the girls' school in Antigua—the Instituto Indígena Nuestra Señora del Socorro—where Juana, the reina indígena from Soloma, Huehuetenango, was a student. Archbishop Rossell had established Santiago and Socorro in 1945 and 1955, respectively, as part of his anti-Communist crusade.[46] The two institutes aimed to train Mayas as teachers who would return to work in their communities. Like Catholic Action, they were seen as a means of extending the reach of the church into distant pueblos. These were limited opportunities, but parish priests even in small towns managed to secure space for promising local students. A letter from the director of the Instituto Santiago to parish priests in 1974 explained what the school was looking for: young Mayas with the "potential to become influential community leaders." More specifically, they sought students with good health, character, initiative, intelligence, and an "influential Christian family." The required supplies for each student were likely out of reach for most families—bedding, clothing, shoes, and even a second pair for soccer—but those and a ten-dollar per month fee were often covered by scholarships from local parishes.[47]

Despite the anti-Communist beginnings of Santiago and Socorro, the schools experienced some of the same changes affecting local parishes with the growing influence of Vatican II philosophy. In 1965, following the death of Archbishop Rossell, administration of Santiago was turned over to the Catholic La Salle order and Socorro to the Bethlemite Sisters. The schools began to reflect and deepen a new consciousness about pan-community identity in Guatemala, bringing together priests, nuns, and Maya students from all over the linguistic map. Juana from Huehuetenango describes becoming aware at Socorro of the discrimination that Mayas face. "There, . . . we analyzed our situation as indígenas," she said, and "we began to have indigenous teachers, too, who questioned the political situation of our country."[48] The Mayas who gained teaching positions at Socorro and Santiago infused classroom discussions with topics like discrimination and justice. Ideas generated in school, including notions of a broad pueblo indígena and the need for its mobilization, soon made their way back to local communities. They spurred community and regional organizing and shaped indigenous student associations and youth groups in large and small towns alike.[49]

Cruz Sisay, trained at the Instituto Indígena Santiago as a teacher, was the first to return to Santiago Atitlán in 1974. With other young people in the community he formed the Indigenous Students' Association of Santiago Atitlán, ADEISA.[50] His younger brother Miguel describes ADEISA beginning as a group made up of the few students that there were in Santiago Atitlán, along with local Catholic Action catechists and others who worked in the community, perhaps thirty in all. One of their first priorities, Miguel remembers, was to focus on discrimination. Despite the fact that a vast majority of residents of the community were Tz'utujiles, "in those days in Atitlán [it was understood that] the mayor had to be a Ladino, the secretary, the treasurer, . . . no indígena had [this] right. . . . The basketball court was for Ladinos, the *salón de baile* [dance hall] was for Ladinos. . . . [For] the indígena . . . many things . . . were prohibited, many places were off-limits."[51] ADEISA challenged these limits. "These were the kinds of barriers we broke," he said. "[One year] we decided to dance in the salón on the day of the [community] fiesta. We entered with partners and there was nothing anyone could say."[52]

42

A young Pedro Esquina also joined ADEISA, and after his studies at the Instituto Indígena Santiago, he became a campesino organizer. He remembers young people in ADEISA pushing for all kinds of change, sometimes calling on the town's *principales*, or elders, for help.[53] Like Toj in Santa Cruz del Quiché, these activists won control over the community's reina indígena contest, and three of them—Pedro Esquina, Felipe Vásquez Tuíz, and Miguel Sisay—appear in the 1978 *El Gráfico* photo alongside the pageant queens protesting the Panzós massacre. They similarly infused other cultural projects with socioeconomic

Felipe Vásquez Tuíz. Photo courtesy of residents of Atitlán.

and political demands. Felipe Vásquez Tuíz and Miguel Sisay started a musical group, playing the traditional songs of their elders but adding new political lyrics. Vásquez Tuíz, who was trained in linguistics at the Francisco Marroquín project, worked with Cruz Sisay to translate the ancient K'iche' text the *Popol Vuh* from Spanish into Tz'utujil, remembers

Miguel. They were also involved with their community's radio station, the Voz de Atitlán, and created a radio program about the *Popol Vuh*, which they broadcast in Tz'utujil.

These students, aware that they were among the lucky few to receive a good education, tried to help solve the daunting problem of the lack of schooling for most other Mayas in Santiago Atitlán. Pedro Esquina recalls that of the thirty or so children finishing primary school in the community each year, few were Mayas. The group talked to parents and tutored young students, arranging extra lessons during vacations and in preparation for exams. They began nighttime adult literacy training, a hugely popular program. Esquina tells of getting permission from the parish priest to use one classroom in a church building for the literacy project, but soon literacy trainers were occupying five.[54]

Santiago Atitlán is one of thirteen villages that surround Lake Atitlán, and activists worked to reach the wider lake-area population. ADEISA members became involved in cooperatives and campesino organizing in nearby towns and in broader programs of literacy education and consciousness-raising. They gained managerial control over the radio station Voz de Atitlán, forming their own Radio Association and board of directors independent of the parish. In the mid- and late 1970s, they broadcast their literacy programs in Tz'utujil and in Kaqchikel (spoken in most of the other nearby communities) around the lake region.

The Voz de Atitlán was similar to Radio Quiché and other community radio stations in the 1960s and 1970s, most of which were supported by their parishes and coordinated in the Guatemalan Federation of Radio Schools. Aside from stations in Santa Cruz and Atitlán, important Mayan language radio programming was broadcast by the Voz de Nahualá in Sololá, Radio Chortis in Chiquimula, Radio Mam in Cabricán, Radio Tezulutlán in Cobán, and the Voz de Colomba in Quetzaltenango. Programming at all of these stations was geared toward the campesino populations of the highlands and focused on literacy training, agricultural techniques, and the cooperative movement, as well as spiritual lessons inspired by liberation theology. Young Mayas developed and led lessons, and they involved vast numbers of people in study groups throughout the broadcast areas. The Radio Schools Federation estimated in 1975 that in the first ten years of such programming, these radio schools had taught literacy skills to some twenty-five thousand campesinos.[55]

Two Maya students, Marco Antonio de Paz and Vinicio Aguilar, developed a popular liberation theology–based study guide for use in the radio schools, called *Pensemos juntos* (Let's Think Together). Published in 1976 by the Radio Schools Federation, it followed the methods of Brazilian popular educator Paulo Freire. De Paz and Aguilar developed "generating themes," de Paz explained, relating to a variety of issues, including agriculture, military service, social relations, and a category that they called "Ladino-indígena."[56] They designed simple images accompanied by questions to facilitate group discussions. The idea, says de Paz, was based on Freire: after listening to radio lessons, leaders of small groups would present images, and people would "decode" or interpret them through their own experiences. "The objective was not to tell them something, or even teach them, but to facilitate their gaining consciousness of reality, of their problems, and the need to develop solutions."[57]

Miguel Sisay of Santiago Atitlán described how they used this method at the Voz de Atitlán. Some in the Radio Association, he explains, were broadcasters—Gaspar Culán and Felipe Vásquez Tuíz two of the best known. Most of the others worked as literacy facilitators, leading the study and discussion groups. Basing lessons on *Pensemos juntos*, Culán and Vásquez Tuíz broadcast around the lake, where young people and adults got together with facilitators to learn to read, write, and "analyze."[58] They discussed Maya identity on the radio programs, Sisay recalls, and explicitly raised questions about economic exploitation and unjust land ownership that plagued their municipality. The Santiago Atitlán project was very popular, and eventually 150 facilitators— including young women as well as men—worked with some fifteen hundred students in the area.[59] "We used the method of 'generating words' to analyze the reality of Guatemala," Sisay explains, "the reality of each pueblo. It was a very pressing question for us, because we had been outside [the community], we had studied."[60]

Pensemos juntos is worth a close look because it was so widely used by activists around the highlands and, before long, widely condemned by the Guatemalan army. A lesson entitled "Campesino and Labor Contractor," for example, focused on the problem of land shortage, work on distant coastal plantations, and labor contracting. The issues were presented in simple terms: *most indigenous campesinos are poor,* the lesson explained, *and have insufficient land to support their families. They know the land well and have the strength to work, but have nowhere to plant. A Ladino labor contractor always appears in those circumstances, offering money, work, and transportation to coastal fincas.*

This man was not giving money or favors, though, the lesson warned. A key component of *Pensemos juntos* involved teaching people about relevant

45

Lesson entitled "Campesino and Labor Contractor," *Pensemos juntos*. Image courtesy of the Federación Guatemalteca de Escuelas Radiofónicas.

national laws: this lesson included the text of Guatemala's minimum wage law. Participants would then study the image and discuss it, considering questions like these: *Who goes and who does not go to work on the coast? Why are they all crowded in the truck? What is going to happen? How does the labor contractor treat the people? How will they be treated by the owner and overseer on the finca? Why do people have to go? What can we do to avoid having to go? ¿Qué pensamos nosotros? What do we think?*

Another lesson on relations between Ladinos and indígenas explored assumptions about identity. It, too, provided a legal basis for its message, in this case an excerpt from the Guatemalan Constitution declaring that all human beings are free and equal in dignity and rights, and that the state guarantees the rights to life, dignity, and freedom from discrimination. The lesson's image was again accompanied by a list of questions: *Why are the two men dressed differently? What differences are there between the two women? Can the indigenous woman sell well if she doesn't speak good Spanish? What does an indigenous man think when he sees an indigenous*

46

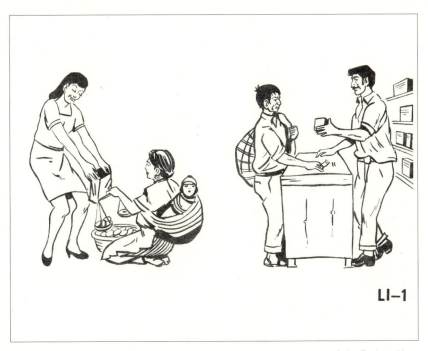

Lesson entitled "Ladino-Indígena," *Pensemos juntos*. Image courtesy of the Federación Guatemalteca de Escuelas Radiofónicas.

woman speaking Spanish? How does a Ladino treat an indigenous customer? How does an indígena treat a Ladino customer? What are the differences between Ladinos and indígenas? Who has made Ladinos and indígenas different? Why do indígenas respect Ladinos so much? Why don't Ladinos respect indígenas? How can the treatment of indígenas and Ladinos become equal? What do we think?[61]

The study guide was cautious in its approach to critiquing the injustices that plagued highland Guatemala, and de Paz described their attempts to "do the most they could do" without appearing subversive. But in the context of 1970s Guatemala, it proved to be an impossible task. Why does the landowner earn more than the campesinos? they asked in one lesson. Why don't you earn more? Why does the army forcibly recruit soldiers, and take only indígenas? Who do the soldiers defend? And perhaps most disturbing from the point of view of the army, what advantages are there to becoming organized?

The army responded to such efforts with severe repression in the 1970s and early 1980s, as we will see. Broadcasters Gaspar Culán and Felipe

47

Vásquez Tuíz began to condemn army violence on the radio, and soon the army targeted the Voz de Atitlán Radio Association specifically.[62] By the early 1980s violence brought these kinds of efforts in the community almost to a standstill. The one important exception was revolutionary organizing. As in Santa Cruz del Quiché, when the army repressed non-violent movements, many of these activists—the Sisay brothers, Felipe Vásquez Tuíz, and others—headed for "the mountains," in their case joining the Revolutionary Organization of Peoples in Arms, the ORPA.

Huehuetenango

Huehuetenango, the highland department that was home to Soloma's reina indígena, was the area of the country chosen by the US Maryknolls for their Guatemalan mission in 1943. It was and remains one of the least accessible of Guatemala's departments, and priests speak of traveling around their parishes on foot and by mule in the 1960s and 1970s.[63] Seventy-three percent of the population of Huehuetenango was classified as indigenous in the 1950 census, and nine different Mayan language groups are concentrated there. The Maryknoll mission chose the region for those very reasons.[64]

The Maryknolls seem to have viewed themselves as intermediaries linking an abstract national developmentalism to the Maya communities that those policies failed to reach. As Maryknoll father William Price wrote in 1974, "The sophisticated Ladino graduates coming from the capital have no language with which to communicate meaningfully with the Indian who lives in a one-room house with his wife and six children, even if the Indian does possess a limited Spanish vocabulary."[65] The Maryknolls were especially critical of the national education system's inability to serve Mayas and the state's refusal to take seriously the need for bilingual education. As Price described educational facilities in the town of Ixtahuacán, "The government maintains a primary school in town, but has no bilingual teachers on its staff. . . . For this reason very few Indians have graduated from the school . . . and very few even care to attend. . . . Life for the Indian in a Ladino secondary school is a nightmare; he is ridiculed, made to feel inferior."[66] To fill the gap, the Maryknolls set up schools for Maya students in places where few had studied previously, with Maryknoll sisters working as teachers. This was

48

the case in Juana's hometown of San Pedro Soloma, where her elementary school was founded by the Maryknolls in 1958. The mission went on to establish thirteen other primary schools in the department, some of them with boarding facilities. They ran several secondary schools as well, and two radio schools.[67] Maryknoll priests offered scholarships to allow accomplished students to study at Catholic seminaries and the regional secondary schools for Mayas, Socorro and Santiago. In 1973, for example, there were at least three young women from Huehuetenango studying at Socorro.

Maryknoll priests, sisters, and brothers also put resources into much-needed social services, founding two hospitals, thirty-one health clinics, and a "barefoot doctors" program of paramedical training. They set up twenty-seven credit unions and eight cooperatives, both artisan and agricultural.[68] Like the Sacred Heart priests would do in the Ixcán region of northern El Quiché, in 1965 and 1966 Maryknoll priests addressed the problem of land shortage in the department by leading agricultural colonization settlements in the unsettled jungle of northern Huehuetenango and the western Petén, clearing land, developing cooperatives, and planting cash crops with the often problematic assistance of the government's developmentalist National Institute of Agrarian Transformation, the INTA.[69]

An explicit goal of the Maryknoll mission was the specialized training of young Maya leaders, and in 1968 they established two centers in the departmental capital: an "Apostolic Center" specifically to train catechists and a "Center of Integral Development" to train community leaders—most of them young adults—in socioeconomic development.[70] Priests in these centers held workshops and programs for young Mayas from the far-flung parishes of the diocese and beyond, catechists and leaders from Mam communities, Q'anjobales, Chuj, and others. Thirty or forty at a time would attend, sometimes more, according to a priest who worked there throughout the 1970s, Father Daniel Jensen.[71] In sessions lasting several weeks, priests combined lessons in civics, democracy, and leadership and discussed issues of discrimination and justice. These in turn were accompanied by what priests termed *trabajo de fortalización*, or strengthening work, an explicitly pan-Maya program of consciousness-raising among more literate Maya students and local leaders, stressing the value of their communities, Maya culture, and history. Father Jensen estimates that fifteen hundred young people, most of them Mayas,

49

attended such courses during the center's ten years of operation.[72]

Father Jensen describes sessions he taught on Maya history. He would start by explaining how students' ancestors may have crossed the Bering Strait, he recalls. He discussed the origins and value of Maya customs and analyzed the common descent of the five or six Mayan languages that might be represented among seminar participants. "That was part of our overall vision," he said, speaking for the Maryknolls, "to give people a greater sense of their own dignity, to recognize the beauty of their own languages." The seminars stressed the need for pride in a pan-Maya identity. "It was at that moment," Jensen said, at the close of history lessons, "that [participants] would be sitting up straighter, and talking to one another." The goal, he explains, was that students together would recognize their worth and dignity, that they would say "'we are beautiful people, we have a culture, traditions that are very important to us, . . . [that] are not backward. . . . They may not [all] prepare us to live in the twentieth century, but then there are areas we can change.'"[73]

Students in the Maryknoll seminars were expected to return to their communities, Jensen explains, "challenged to see what they could do for other people." As Maryknoll sister Bernice Kita observed, catechists from the community where she worked attended the Huehuetenango seminars then gave classes to the community based on what they had learned. Typically seminar attendees were invited back for more intensive training in specialized areas like agronomy, literacy, or medicine. Kita writes that the community supported the catechists by sending along corn, beans, and other produce in the hopes that "the contributions give the men a sense of obligation to give back to the community some of what they learned."[74]

Maryknolls and Vatican II

Given the nature of the challenges they faced in Huehuetenango, it is unsurprising that many priests, sisters, and brothers in the Maryknoll mission adopted the Vatican II approach to their work. Of this transition, William Price wrote that rather than simply converting their subjects, "the poor, the humble and simple people who struggle . . . are converting us."[75] The Maryknolls' Apostolic Center and the Center for Integral Development in particular had a clear Vatican II–inspired mandate. Price explained that these educational programs, similar to those being developed elsewhere in the highlands, were designed to offer "the Indian the . . . information which will allow him to assume the role of his own advancement. The objective is not merely to communicate to them what the missionary has to offer, but also to reveal to them the riches that they themselves already possess. A sincere effort has been made on both the diocesan and parochial levels to help the . . . people see their problems, analyze them, and take steps to solve them."[76]

The Maryknoll interpretation of the social struggle in Huehuetenango was somewhat different from that of priests in places such as El Quiché: both philosophically and practically, most Maryknolls developed an approach to their work explicitly focused on Maya identity. Where the Jesuits supported the growth of alliances between Mayas and Ladinos and some shared a Marxist view of social change, Maryknolls focused more attention on the development of cultural pride and Maya community leadership. At the same time, many thoroughly rejected the idea of assimilation as the answer to problems in the countryside and retained an anti-Communism shaped by the mission's expulsion from China. In 1974 Father William Price wrote that "only when the Indian is allowed to become a part of the Guatemalan national society as an Indian, and not as a potential Ladino, will it be possible for the social revolution to move forward democratically, without interference from Russians, Cubans, or Americans, toward a better life."[77]

Maryknolls were not of one mind on the appropriate approach to their work, of course. Some Maryknoll personnel disagreed strongly with the changing focus of the mission in the 1960s, and sixteen of them chose to leave the region in what one Maryknoll report termed a "Post–Vatican II exodus."[78] Still others held the opposite view, wanting the mission to take a more aggressive stance in the face of state and elite obstruction of reform efforts.

Political tensions over these issues among Maryknoll clergy reached a crisis point only a few years after the Vatican II meetings, exploding into what is known as the Melville affair. In 1967 Maryknoll sister Marian Peter, who organized the Guatemala City–based Cráter (the same group of students who worked with catechists in El Quiché in the 1970s), had befriended a university student involved in the guerrilla Rebel Armed Forces, or FAR. The student introduced Sister Peter to FAR leaders, and Sister Peter in turn arranged a meeting between guerrilla leaders and a

51

number of priests and sisters, among them Maryknoll fathers Thomas and Art Melville, two other Maryknoll sisters, and Sacred Heart father Luis Gurriarán of El Quiché. The group apparently discussed how they might become involved in the movement for revolutionary change;[79] a Maryknoll report accused Sister Peter and the Melvilles of "not [only] supporting but . . . initiating violent revolution [by] forming their own guerrilla movement."[80] Luis Gurriarán, "evidently bothered in conscience by the plan," promptly told the Maryknoll regional superior John Breen about the gathering, and Breen ordered the Maryknoll participants to leave the country in an effort to prevent the entire mission from being expelled.[81]

The Melville incident was politically disastrous for the mission. They were accused of Marxist tendencies both at the official level in Guatemala and by conservative columnists in the US press. But internal reports suggest that Maryknoll personnel in Guatemala had mixed feelings about it. "The issues the Melvilles supported were so close to the interest of the work and effort to help the poor," one report states, "that it was impossible to disregard their conviction."[82] William Price, quoted previously as calling for a social revolution "without interference from Russians, Cubans, or Americans," wrote that "the grinding poverty of rural Guatemala and a series of frustrations" were to blame for the Melvilles' mistake of supporting armed revolution. They "simply capitulated," concluded Price, "to the slowness of the process of change."[83] Price himself in the 1970s would be accused of subversion by the Guatemalan government, though he would argue that he and other missioners were "concerned for the poor not because of Karl Marx, but because of Jesus Christ."[84]

Training and educating rural Mayas no matter what the motivation in the 1970s represented a clear and unwelcome challenge to the status quo. Price, who began working in the Mam community of San Ildefonso Ixtahuacán, Huehuetenango, in the mid-1960s, wrote in 1974 that Mayas in his community were "awakening." "Signs of dynamism are multiplying," he wrote. "A significant development in present-day Ixtahuacán is the entry of the masses into the deep and moving stream of social change. The pressures for change have built up enormously in recent years at Ixtahuacán, as the Indians feel a new strength in numbers. . . . The rural population is beginning to organize and shows capabilities for effective change."[85]

Price was working with Mayas employed in the tungsten and antimony mines, many of whom were catechists, in their struggles with management over unionization and labor rights. He describes police violence meted out against Ixtahuacán miners attempting to organize and the beating and imprisonment of sixteen of them in January 1972. When Price came to their aid, he writes, he was accused of "creating disturbances throughout the area, of being a terrorist or a subversive." The men were freed three weeks later, but only after they agreed to sign a document, as Price describes it, "drawn up by the lawyer of the mine owners [stating] . . . that their arrest was justified because of their attempt to sabotage the mine."[86] Even in the face of such repression, the miners managed to form a union a year later. Immediately after Price wrote about that growing "strength in numbers," the government in April 1974 expelled him from the country for his involvement, barring his reentry until 1978.[87] But the unionists continued. In 1977 a strike by those same Ixtahuacán miners caught the nation's attention as they and supporters, men and women, walked 250 miles from Ixtahuacán to the capital, mobilizing campesinos along the path.[88]

One of the main leaders of the strike, Mario (Guigui) Mejía Córdova, an organizer from Huehuetenango with the National Confederation of Labor (CNT), had been a development and literacy trainer at the Maryknoll Center for Integral Development for several years and, as Price put it, at his "beck and call."[89] Maryknoll sister Bernice Kita described how Mejía, in the course of his work for Maryknoll, would stay in remote villages of the department for a month at a time, organizing and training local catechists and leaders. As someone connected to—and connecting—Huehuetenango's disparate Maya communities, Mejía became an army target. He was one of the hundreds of young people associated with the Maryknoll centers killed by state forces for his organizing work, shot in July 1978, eight months after the miners' strike. Kita attended his funeral, as did thousands of other mourners, and provided a glimpse into the kinds of support offered by Mayas at that moment. Kita was especially struck, she wrote, "by the women wearing orange miners' helmets who lined up to embrace [Mejía's] widow. . . . Now they were conspicuous by their presence at his funeral, as he had been conspicuous by his presence on their march [to the capital]." Four miners, Kita recounts, carried a banner proclaiming that his death was a seed that could now germinate.[90] Mejía was in his late twenties.

Mejía and the miners did have an impact, and one that was felt far beyond Huehuetenango: the Ixtahuacán miners' march is credited with

53

spurring mobilization all along its path. Mayas from El Quiché—among them Emeterio Toj, Domingo Hernández Ixcoy, and Pablo Ceto—watched the efforts of the Mam catechists and unionists closely. As they will recount, the miners' protest helped spark the rise of the national-level campesino movement, CUC.

Envisioning the Pueblo

L ocal organizing like that in Santa Cruz del Quiché, Santiago Atitlán, and Huehuetenango developed throughout Guatemala. At the same time, organizing spilled over municipal and departmental boundaries, and growing numbers of community activists got involved in regional and national efforts. In the 1960s and especially the 1970s, connections among different communities and across language barriers were facilitated in many ways: through priests, cooperatives and other agrarian organizations, schools, and radio programs. Both informally and in more formal meetings, Mayas from different areas began to focus collective attention on shared problems of poverty, discrimination, and political exclusion. Many also developed an interest in pan-Maya cultural revitalization, in discovering and promoting indigenous history and identity.

Over the course of the 1970s, as Mayas engaged in broadening struggles for cultural, economic, and political rights and justice, the two basic tendencies among activists materialized: some activists articulated their efforts primarily around ideas of "la raza" or indigenous identity specifically; others infused their work with ideas of class struggle. Yet Mayas involved in different forms of activism created a web of connections that reached from the western highlands to the Verapaces, relations that activists would deepen and depend on as the full force of counterinsurgency violence hit the highlands.

Race, Class, and Revolution

Mobilization by Mayas in the 1960s and 1970s, and especially its regional and national manifestations, emerged amid intense ideological debates among students, intellectuals, and activists on issues of ethnicity and race, class, and social revolution. Attention to the competing ideas that shaped these debates is important for contextualizing the movements of the 1970s and beyond.

Guatemala's national University of San Carlos, USAC, was the intellectual home to a leftist critique of the nation and its socioeconomic and political structures, a critique most famously articulated by Severo Martínez Peláez in *La patria del criollo*, first published in 1970. Regarding Guatemala's "indigenous problem," Martínez Peláez rejected the idea of racial difference. He argued instead that indigenous ethnic identity was constructed during the colonial period and functioned in modern Guatemala to divide and weaken the struggle between the rich and poor. This perspective was embraced by activists in what came to be known as Guatemala's "popular" movement. They were mostly Ladino unionists, students, and intellectuals, especially at USAC, where Martínez Peláez was a faculty member. But through Ladino students working in the countryside, these ideas came to be shared by activist Mayas like Emeterio Toj and Domingo Hernández Ixcoy. Drawing on Martínez Peláez, leftist revolutionary theorists argued that oppression of Mayas, fundamental to the system they sought to overthrow, would disappear in a social system based on equality. While not denying the endemic discrimination faced by Guatemalan indígenas, the theory insisted that focusing on differences between Mayas and Ladinos was, in fact, counterrevolutionary, since it would undermine a unity of the oppressed that was crucial to a successful revolution.

Sociologists Carlos Guzmán Böckler and Jean-Loup Herbert at the same time articulated a contrasting perspective, arguing that discrimination against Mayas undermined would-be revolutionary unity. They set out the notion of ongoing "internal colonialism" that subjugated the Maya in Guatemala and challenged the inevitability and desirability of ladinization. Also affiliated with USAC in the capital, Guzmán Böckler and Herbert undertook what they called "social investigations" around the city of Quetzaltenango in 1967, in conjunction with local Maya students and intellectuals. Three years later, in 1970 (the same year that *Patria del criollo* appeared), their most well-known work was published, *Guatemala: Una interpretación histórico-social*. The Guzmán Böckler–Herbert treatise argued that racial ideologies based on superiority of the Ladino and inferiority of the indígena underlay Guatemala's problems, which would not be resolved through "integration" or "acculturation" while these rested on assumptions of inequality. Only if a "real and objective dialectic" between Ladinos and indígenas took place, they said—and only if indígenas could recuperate their lands and their history—could *guatemaltecos* together work for a more just "appropriation" of the nation. If colonial domination were destroyed, racialized Ladinos could cease acting as Ladinos, indígenas could be freed of subjugation as indígenas. Most significantly in the intellectual context of the early 1970s, a multiethnic revolutionary movement could then be built to challenge the state: "Only with the disappearance of the colonial relation," they wrote, "will there be revolutionary *compañeros*."[1]

A different set of students and activists embraced the ideas of Guzmán Böckler and Herbert, among them Mayas such as Jerónimo Juárez López from Quetzaltenango, as well as activists in Cobán, Alta Verapaz, and in Chimaltenango, not far from the capital.[2] These were young Mayas of a somewhat different social position than rural catechists and campesino activists: though not well-off, many of them were a step (or more) removed from an agrarian subsistence economy. They lived in or near relatively large communities and studied or worked as teachers, health promoters, in law or social services. Inspired by the arguments of Guzmán Böckler and Herbert and motivated by their own experiences of discrimination, they grounded their activism in identity as indígenas.

Quetzaltenango

When Archbishop Rossell made his rounds of the Guatemalan highlands in 1953 with his sacred "General," the Black Christ of Esquipulas, Jerónimo Juárez López, a K'iche' from Quetzaltenango, was eighteen years old. Like Emeterio Toj from El Quiché, he, too, vividly remembers the archbishop's tour. Juárez was one of five children, four of whom survived childhood, of *comerciantes*, or retailers. His parents sold clothing in local markets, indigenous *traje típica* for Maya women and Western-style clothing for men, and Jerónimo assisted them, working as a tailor. During the Arévalo and Arbenz regimes, he had studied at a local Catholic primary school among priests and nuns who shared a strong anti–October Revolution mentality. Like Emeterio Toj, Juárez recalls this period with bitterness. He, too, supported the overthrow of Arbenz a few years later, "without knowing it was something against us."[3]

In Quetzaltenango, Guatemala's second largest urban area and the country's unofficial K'iche' capital, Mayas like Juárez became involved in a local activist movement that they link to the Sociedad El Adelanto,

57

established over a century ago as Guatemala's first school for Mayas. Jerónimo Juárez explains that for local Mayas, the Sociedad was an important beginning. While its founders had to work within the patriarchal conditions set by the Guatemalan government, he says, sending flowers to Guatemalan presidents on their birthdays or marching in government parades, the Sociedad nonetheless was the first association to demand that the pueblo indígena be respected for what it was and that it be allowed to hold on to and promote K'iche' culture.[4]

As a city with a relatively prosperous Maya middle class, Quetzaltenango—or Xela as it is known in K'iche'—offered greater educational opportunities to area Mayas than were available in most parts of the highlands. Not coincidentally, it was a center of emerging ideas about Maya identity: in the 1960s, discussions about unjust social relations between Ladinos and Mayas began to develop in secondary schools, according to Juárez, and soon within the Xela branch of the national university, USAC.

Jerónimo Juárez recalls the strict governmental regulation and repression that followed the overthrow of Arbenz in 1954. In Xela, the so-called Liberation government prohibited meetings, Juárez remembers. If people wanted simply to socialize, he said, they had to ask for official permission. When would the party be? How many people? Who would be in charge? "Everything was controlled," recalls Juárez. Yet despite government attempts to quell social organizing, Mayas in Xela became an important part of the growing politicization taking hold in highland communities.

Juárez started secondary school in 1950, but when his father died soon afterward he had to withdraw and work to help support his family. Again like Emeterio Toj, he returned to night school in 1961, when he was twenty-six years old and married, taking classes for the next seven years. There, he explains, is where his thinking about identity developed. He confronted blatant discrimination in the classroom, and it became a topic of conversation among Juárez and the few other Mayas at the school. They began to talk about identity, he said, and ideas of race. In the early 1970s, just as the ideas of Guzmán Böckler and Herbert were circulating in Xela, Juárez and several of the others began to take classes at the local branch of USAC, in Juárez's case to become a social worker.

At USAC, Juárez was part of more intense discussions among area Mayas attending the university, though again their numbers were small.

K'iche's from nearby Totonicapán, he remembers, were already engaged in racially focused activism. They had started a local organization in the late 1960s, naming themselves Los Insumisos, "the Rebels," and calling attention to issues of Maya identity. At USAC, they joined with Juárez and other Maya students to form a group called Castajik, K'iche' for "awaken." The group focused on Maya consciousness, Juárez recalls, and the need to "revindicate our pueblo, what is ours [lo nuestro], our beginnings, our values."[5] Another of these students, Isaías Raconcoj, a young man who posed among the protestors in the 1978 El Gráfico photo, notes that their thinking in Castajik developed alongside intensifying debates about identity and revolution taking place in the university.[6]

Mayas who were students in the 1970s remember the local Xela branch of USAC and the main campus in the capital as places where differences between Mayas and Ladinos were magnified. With Mayas a small minority among a mostly Ladino student body, Juárez remembers, discrimination was experienced as a "great choque," a direct confrontation between indígenas and Ladinos. Marxist discourse was strongly dominant, and charged discussions took place among university students and faculty both from the local university and the capital, including sociologist Guzmán Böckler. Most Ladinos, Juárez recalls, firmly supported the Left's position as argued by Martínez Peláez. In response, Mayas like those in Castajik began to stake out a position on the specificity of racial discrimination in Guatemalan society. "We wanted to develop our own ideological positions," Raconcoj remembers, "develop an ideology, valorize ourselves, . . . build on historic social bases to revindicate the pueblo indígena."[7] Their emerging critique was voiced in a publication they simply titled Castajik, the first Maya publication to claim any sort of regional presence, if only for a short time, and something of a precursor to the more widely known periodical Ixim: Notas Indígenas. Raconcoj, like Juárez, was trained at USAC as a social worker. In the course of his work, he traveled the departments of El Quiché and Alta Verapaz, using his access to the countryside to distribute Castajik to local community leaders.

Several of these Quetzaltenango-area Mayas, including Jerónimo Juárez and a teacher and unionist named Ricardo Cajas Mejía (yet another figure in the queens' protest photo), at the same time became active in local politics. They formed a predominantly Maya civic committee in 1972 called Xel-jú as a means to voice local demands and gain political power in municipal government. Xel-jú members charge

59

that fraud in the elections two years later kept their mayoral candidate from gaining office, but several members of group—including Jerónimo Juárez—won seats on Quetzaltenango's community council in 1974.[8]

Their activities in the next several years help illustrate how different forms of activism by Mayas came to overlap in practice. Xel-jú itself maintained a Maya-specific focus, but several Xel-jú members individually became tied to "popular" opposition movements in partnership with Ladinos. As state repression mounted in 1978 these distinctions blurred even more: the civic committee, for example, campaigned in Xela under the slogan "Only the pueblo saves the pueblo."[9] In the context of growing revolutionary opposition in the region, the motto could be interpreted as setting out a Maya-specific identity (because the Xela "pueblo" was understood as indigenous), but also linking their struggle to leftist oppositional politics, a pueblo broadly understood as multiethnic.[10]

Cobán, Alta Verapaz

Other figures developing a racially defined social and political critique came from Cobán, a Q'eqchi' community and the departmental seat of Alta Verapaz. Antonio Pop Caal, a Q'eqchi' seminarian and law student, was especially influential, so important to activists' thinking that Maya intellectual Luis Sam Colop has described him as the patriarch of today's Maya movement.[11] Born in 1941 in a rural community near Cobán, Pop Caal as a child was another of the promising young Mayas identified by parish priests as a gifted student. He was sent to primary school in Guatemala City, then to a Catholic seminary in Quetzaltenango. When he graduated in the early 1960s, the church sent him to study theology and philosophy in Spain.

Pop Caal returned to Guatemala in 1969, but after his studies he rejected Catholicism and the church. He began to study law at USAC in Guatemala City in 1972. In the capital, Pop Caal took an active part in debates about indigenous identity and led a small group of activist Mayas—from the Cobán area, San Cristóbal Verapaz, Chimaltenango, and Huehuetenango—calling itself Cabracán. The group's name had a dual and symbolic meaning: Cabracán is the "god with two legs" and lord of earthquakes from the *Popol Vuh*. Antonio Pop Caal explained that the choice reflected the idea of Mayas standing on their own two feet and also referred to the earthquake that devastated the highlands in 1976.[12] Cabracán's founders were mostly young men, but there was one woman among them who was permitted by her parents to join the group on the condition that her brother join as well. Members of Cabracán studied in the capital and several of them lived together, though they did not publicly identify as belonging to the group because they thought of it as clandestine.[13] Activists outside of Cabracán almost always describe the group as "radical," in part because Pop Caal and other Cabracán members famously rejected Western goods and habits.[14]

Antonio Pop Caal made a name for himself by authoring—and publishing in a Ladino weekly—a scathing critique of ladinization and spelling out basic rights of indígenas. His "Replica del indio a una disertación ladina" (Reply of an Indio to a Ladino Discourse) appeared in the December 12, 1972, issue of the Guatemalan journal *La Semana* and caused a stir among fellow Maya activists and intellectuals, and Ladinos as well.[15] Ladinos were always writing about indígenas, Pop Caal explained in an interview, but indígenas were never allowed to respond, at least not in print; his was the first major rejoinder he and other activists recall appearing in the mainstream press.[16]

In the article Pop Caal took issue with Ladinos claiming to be authorities on all things indigenous. He cataloged a range of problems confronting the indígena, some of them echoes of Guzmán Böckler and Herbert, and virtually all of them still part of pan-Maya politics three decades later: ongoing colonialism, internally and externally; agricultural exploitation and land loss; political domination; and denial of the right to use of native languages. He discussed the "anxiety" of Ladinos over their own ambiguous identity. To well-worn suggestions (long expressed in *La Semana*) that all indígenas needed to become Ladinos, Pop Caal had this to say: "Anyone who analyzes this cultural entity of the Ladino with sincerity and scientific exactitude . . . must conclude that this idea has nothing to offer the indio."[17] This is the same article in which Pop Caal urged activists to adopt the label *indio*, as many would do. *Indio* by that time had evolved into a term with derogatory connotations, especially when used by Ladinos. But in part due to the urging of Pop Caal, it took on a politicized, radical meaning for Maya activists. "We know that [indio] is a word . . . which reflects a 'fetish' of slanderous character by those who use it," he wrote. "But we have accepted it, and it brings us honor rather than denigration. . . . [W]e have accepted it, and such an identification signifies nothing less than a challenge to Ladinos."[18]

61

Miguel Alvarado, a K'iche' from Cantel, Quetzaltenango, remembers that activists asserted, "With the name [indio] with which they've destroyed us, with the same name we'll revindicate ourselves."[19] The multiethnic Left, too, adopted it. Ricardo Cajas described a banner hung by the campesino organization CUC at the symbolically charged Iximché ruins following the deaths of over two dozen CUC members at the hands of the state in 1980: "For every indio who falls," the banner read, "thousands of us are rising up."[20] Mayas' reclaiming of the term *indio* was both an assertion of a pan-community indigenous identity and an explicit rejection of the meanings attached to that identity by Ladinos.

The Catholic Church and Pan-Maya Organizing

Just as the post–Vatican II Catholic Church was an important catalyst for local Maya mobilization in Guatemala, parish priests and national-level efforts by the church encouraged and supported pan-Maya organizing. There was a clear desire on the part of large sectors of the Guatemalan Catholic Church to "know" the pueblo indígena in order to better serve and support it. There were also explicit church efforts to link Mayas from different regions to each other, to foster a more collective identity, and as Maryknoll William Price put it, to promote that "new strength in numbers." For some priests who fostered ideas of pan-Maya identity, it was a matter of instilling cultural pride; others, like Price, had more explicitly political motives. Price believed, as he wrote in 1974, that "Christianity must become more of a catalytic force in the development of a new type of opposition to the Ladino power structure," an opposition that arguably depended on pan-Maya unity.[21]

62

The Jesuit Rafael Landívar University in Guatemala City was an early proponent of these efforts, holding training programs on "Social Promotion" for Maya community leaders beginning in the 1960s. Within a few years of the 1968 Medellín conference, the Catholic Church in Guatemala also convened regional and nationwide meetings for priests and lay pastors focused on indigenous issues. To institutionalize their efforts, they established an overarching Pastoral Commission on the Indígena, which brought together church workers to discuss local experiences and issues of Maya culture and history, and to analyze the needs of Maya communities and parishes. Priests in these meetings also sought input from Mayas. Jesuit Ricardo Falla describes the gatherings as an opportunity for local priests and the capital-based church leadership to meet with each other and with representatives of the pueblos indígenas, to engage young Maya leaders in discussions about the work of the church.[22] The meetings could include up to one hundred people, he explained, from all parts of the country.

By the early 1970s, a few Mayas had been ordained as Catholic priests and sisters, among them Father Tomás García, Father Arnulfo Delgado, and Sister Juana Vásquez. These three, active among organized Mayas in the years to follow, took part in the Pastoral Commission meetings, or *encuentros*.[23] Mayas active in Catholic Action as well as local community activists like Jerónimo Juárez participated. Juárez remembers the meetings with Ricardo Falla fondly. It was a time of reflection, he said, about the needs of Maya communities. At that time "we never talked of the 'Left' or the 'Right,' but about social movements, 'the situation,' what to do."[24] As Falla put it, "Historically, the church and its priests taught." But the meetings of the early 1970s were an attempt to take a new approach: "'We aren't going to teach,' we said, 'we are going to learn.'"[25]

Maryknoll Dan Jensen recounts that what priests "learned" from Maya participants often came as a surprise. The Mayas whom many thought of as passive and childlike, he said, were in fact able and willing to contradict the church and stand up for themselves. Jensen recalls a meeting in the early 1970s at the Catholic seminary in Sololá when the presiding bishop at the time, Father Juan Gerardi, referred to Guatemala's Maya population as "*nuestros inditos*," "our little Indians." One of the Maya participants jumped up, Jensen recalls, and said, "We're not yours, and we're not little children." As Jensen explains, "I think that was a moment of conversion for the bishop. No one would ever speak to a bishop that way. And this guy had no qualms about it."[26]

Bishop Gerardi soon organized another such encuentro in the diocese of the Verapaces, in early 1973. Academics—an anthropologist, a sociologist, and a theologian—from the National Center for Assistance to Indigenous Missions (CENAMI) in Mexico were guest speakers at the conference in Cobán, as they would be at several other seminars on the Maya for religious workers in Guatemala. The meeting focused on the need to develop a new, more inclusive approach to the church's work in Maya communities, though the language of one commentator

63

seemed quite similar to IIN indigenismo of the same era. Father Luis de León, a Salesian priest working in Carchá, Alta Verapaz, described the meeting's purpose: "The Catholic Church recognizes," he wrote, "that its traditional methods of Christianizing the indígenas were not good in all respects; [recognizes] that a change of mentality is needed . . . ; that to work successfully among the indígenas requires knowing them, appreciating them, loving them." As de León continued, "The missionary has to have great sensitivity to and understanding of the environment in which he works, know the history, culture, language, the customs of the pueblos." Priests must not, he warned, "come with the airs of a conquistador, a reformer, a know-it-all."[27]

Some Mayas did not think priests at these meetings succeeded in leaving their traditional views and methods behind. Moreover, some complained that Catholic Action itself was assimilationist. The newly ordained Father Tomás García, a K'iche' from Totonicapán (home, you may recall, to the racially focused Maya group, the Rebels), made such charges about the first Pastoral Meeting for Indigenous People of Quetzaltenango in October 1973. The structure of the meeting did, in fact, reflect priests' intent—as Falla pointed out—to learn rather than teach. Father García recounted that as observers, the priests were not to speak but to listen to the Maya catechists who were invited to take part. But this hardly meant, he complained, that priests were getting an "indigenous" point of view. Sharply criticizing the church's patriarchal positioning on Mayas, he argued that indigenous catechists at the meeting simply supported the ideas of the nonindigenous priests. The conference did not address "real indigenous issues," "*lo que es propio del indígena*," Father García wrote. "Many indígenas spoke," he charged, but not as indígenas. "Their language [as catechists] was already corrupted/contaminated [*viciado*] by the process of acculturation."[28]

64

Despite such tensions, priests involved with the Pastoral Commission on the Indígena, including Father Tomás, kept the dialogue going. An agenda of a monthlong seminar convened the following year by the Pastoral Commission reveals some of the concerns and interests of priests and participants and suggests a truly national scope for their meetings. It was held at the Instituto Indígena Santiago in the capital, with academic assistance again from the Mexican CENAMI. According to a participant list, eighty-one religious workers from departmental capitals and small towns throughout the country attended the seminar, including the recently ordained Mayas mentioned previously.[29]

Nearly as wide ranging were the topics covered in the seminar: themes of politics, economics and society, culture and anthropology, religion and justice. Meeting five days a week, attendees discussed "the indígena in Guatemala's socio-political, economic, and religious reality" and current indigenous policies in Guatemala.[30] There was a panel by Mayas on the indigenous *problemática*, and the conference addressed the pressing issues of the links between evangelization and culture and evangelization and justice. Attendees received lectures on theories of cultural relativism and structuralism and discussed new interpretations of the Bible and liberation theology. They were offered a lecture by Father Tomás García on the theological meaning of the sacred K'iche' text, the *Popol Vuh*. There were even transcriptions of several speeches by candidates for local indigenous community queen included in conference materials, apparently used as a window into contemporary demands of the pueblo maya.[31] Clearly "knowing" the indígena was on the church's agenda.

Seminarios Indígenas and the Coordinadora Indígena Nacional

In the early 1970s, at the same time that the Pastoral Commission on the Indígena was examining Maya issues and Antonio Pop Caal set out his "Reply," Mayas attending university in the capital, once again working with Catholic priests, established the Association of Indigenous University Students. The association began by organizing workshops, speakers, and discussions about Maya culture and identity. The discussions, first held in the National Conservatory, featured speakers such as Father Estéban Haeserijn, a Belgian priest and anthropologist working in Alta Verapaz who compiled a dictionary of the Q'eqchi' language. Ricardo Cajas from Quetzaltenango took part in the workshops and recalls that in the dictionary's preface, Haeserijn echoed Pop Caal and Guzmán Böckler by articulating the idea of Ladinos as colonizers in Guatemalan society and indígenas as the colonized. In the conservatory Haeserijn spoke to his audience, Cajas remembers, about ongoing race-based colonialism and its tendency to pass for class relations.[32]

65

Soon these discussions took place in yearly Seminarios Indígenas, "Indigenous Seminars" or "Workshops." These were novel and important because young activists from all over Guatemala attended, including Mayas from the departments of El Quiché, Huehuetenango, Sololá,

Chimaltenango, Quetzaltenango, Totonicapán, San Marcos, and Alta Verapaz. The first national meeting was held in Quetzaltenango's Casa de la Cultura in 1972, ironically, says Ricardo Cajas, with seminar folders printed by INGUAT, the Guatemalan tourist bureau. (Maya activists would rail against INGUAT for viewing the pueblo indígena as a commodity for tourists.)[33] In subsequent years they were held in Tecpán in the department of Chimaltenango, in Santa Cruz and Chichicastenango in the department of El Quiché, and again in Xela.[34]

The Seminarios were organized predominantly by Mayas associated with racially focused efforts, who also founded the Coordinadora Indígena Nacional (National Indigenous Coordination), an umbrella group that aimed to formalize links and maintain communication among activist Mayas all over Guatemala. Participants remember the forceful presence in the Coordinadora of Ricardo Cajas, from Xela; Antonio Pop Caal, from Cobán; and Kaqchikel Maya activist Demetrio Cojtí Cuxil, from Tecpán, Chimaltenango, who (re)emerged as a leader of the pan-Maya culturalist movement of the 1990s. Among its founders there were also Mayas from El Quiché, the town of Chimaltenango, and the capital. Coordinadora leaders were mostly intellectuals—teachers, social workers, health promoters—people who, as one campesino activist put it, had little or no experience "living under the oppression of a *finca patrón*," or plantation owner.[35] Yet the umbrella group claimed members from all of Guatemala's Mayan language groups, and it did include a broad cross section of activist Mayas. Participants describe the Seminarios, which took place over several days each year during December holidays, as retreats involving as many as 150 people. There were religious workers, participants explain, anthropologists and academics from Guatemala City, but also community leaders and organizers of all kinds—catechists, literacy workers, cooperativists, and campesino leaders.

Emeterio Toj from Santa Cruz del Quiché was one such leader who attended the meetings. In those first years, he remembers, "we got together . . . [simply] in search of an identity that could represent or be the voice of the pueblo indígena."[36] Ricardo Cajas of Xela recalls discussing very basic issues in the first meetings: what should indígenas call themselves, for example, indígenas, *naturales*, Mayas?[37] In the early 1970s, *Maya* was mostly an academic, anthropological term, but some young activists adopted it for its rhetorical value.[38] Reflecting the influence of intellectuals like Antonio Pop Caal, Seminario participants discussed whether and how to use the term *indio*, Cajas remembers. Precisely because it symbolized oppression, leaders argued, they should use it for its power of "revindication."[39]

With activist Mayas bringing diverse organizing experiences and expectations to the Seminarios Indígenas, participants debated a range of topics: Maya identity, culture and history, economic exploitation, poverty, class struggle, and violence. A written declaration from the 1974 Seminario (one of the few Seminario documents that have been uncovered) expressed concerns about indigenous betterment (*superación*), justice, and defense of Maya interests and identity. It called for Mayas to develop and articulate their own thinking and their own objectives. And it called for the unity of all Guatemalan indígenas, so that they could "reappropriate" their history and culture and "penetrate" the Ladino power structure.[40]

I asked people who attended these meetings if and when activists began to differentiate a "clasista" (class-focused) and a "culturalista" (Maya specific) perspective. Participants remembered such differences emerging at an early moment, but some recall them as evidence of diversity rather than division. (Tensions may have felt more significant at the time and seem modest today only in comparison to the divisions that followed.) Emeterio Toj, for instance, portrays the Coordinadora Indígena as a single body with multiple ways of "seeing reality . . . and proposing solutions." "There were debates," Toj explained, "but with a . . . richness, we were alike/twins [*cuates*], we were friends joined together in the Seminarios and the Coordinadora."[41] Ricardo Cajas of Xela similarly describes the Coordinadora's character, linking disparate interests and areas and facilitating discussions of culture and politics: "The agenda was mixed. The indígena at times made class demands, at times ethnic, it was a combination of the two. [Participants] talked of the need to revitalize indigenous languages but also spoke of *latifundismo* and *minifundismo*, like crossing currents."[42] Others remember a greater gulf between culturalistas and clasistas from the very beginning. Domingo Hernández Ixcoy from Santa Cruz del Quiché asserts that members of each group paid lip service to the interests and demands of the other but continued to stress their own positions and interpretations, failing to address issues of Maya specificity and class in any integrated way.[43]

67

▓▓▓ CUC and a Multiethnic Pueblo

As activists began to define their positions on identity and rights, a natural disaster fundamentally changed Maya organizing. A massive earthquake hit the Guatemalan highlands on February 4, 1976. Dozens of interviewees point to the experience as an awakening, a moment when they became aware of the ethnic profile of poverty in Guatemala and the national scope of problems for Mayas. The experience solidified notions among activist Mayas of belonging to a broad pueblo indígena. The earthquake killed twenty-six thousand people and left a million homeless, and the vast majority of both groups were Mayas. It was called the "earthquake of the poor" and the "earthquake of the indio" and generated widespread discussion of the connections between ethnicity, poverty, and injustice on Mayan language radio stations and in churches, study groups, and organizations. It prompted the Catholic Church to speak out officially in the name of justice and rights and publicly to champion the rights of the pueblo indígena.[44] As one activist describes it, the earthquake consolidated an indigenous movement: "We didn't know at the time that the earthquake, a national tragedy, could bring the unification of so many indígenas."[45]

The enormity of the destruction motivated young Mayas to assist in recovery efforts outside of their communities, especially in the earthquake-ravaged departments of Chimaltenango, El Quiché, and Baja Verapaz. Pablo Ceto of El Quiché describes traveling with other students to help earthquake victims, a process that opened up the country to young activists, he says, and allowed Mayas from many areas to meet each other. "When the earthquake of 1976 hit," Ceto explains, "all of us were involved. . . . We . . . helped in Tecpán, Joyabaj, Chimaltenango, helped people organize brigades to repair houses, held meetings with the people, got to know other areas." They worked nearly the entire year of 1976, Ceto recalls, intensively for three months, and continuing throughout the year on weekends.[46]

Immediately following the earthquake, Emeterio Toj left his broadcasting position at Radio Quiché and went to Joyabaj, also in the department of El Quiché. He began working with the Institute of Socioeconomic Development for Central America, IDESAC, the development wing of the Christian Democratic party, on recovery in the departments of Chimaltenango and Baja Verapaz. Like Pablo Ceto, Toj describes the experience as leading to a heightened awareness of the problems confronting

68

Mayas in Guatemala and, at the same time, facilitating connections among activists from the affected areas and those coming to their aid. Why were indígenas the ones most affected? they asked. Why were Mayas' dwellings the ones to fall down? As Toj tells it, the work allowed him "to widen my field of knowledge/action [*cancha*], to know more of the country's reality, because the earthquake showed Guatemala for what it is."[47] Toj traveled to Rabinal, to Rio Negro, to Chimaltenango, to San Martín Jilotepeque, meeting Maya leaders and campesinos in communities struggling to rebuild.

Connections like these spurred the creation of the Maya-led organization that would change the face of the Guatemalan popular movement: the Committee for Peasant Unity, CUC. From the wreckage of the earthquake, activists like to recount, CUC was born. It was also a product of years of organizing within the cooperative movement and Catholic Action. Along with founders Emeterio Toj, Domingo Hernández Ixcoy, Pablo Ceto, and other former catechists and organizers from El Quiché were Mayas from Chimaltenango and from Rabinal, Baja Verapaz. CUC eventually linked campesinos from Guatemala's highlands to its coastal plantations, pooling local agrarian organizing experiences, some inherited from the Arbenz period, others developed through the Catholic Church and its cooperative movement and grounded in the liberation theology discourse of the late 1960s and early 1970s.

When CUC was in the process of formation, its organizers helped support the 1977 strike by Mam miners from Ixtahuacán, Huehuetenango. Like the tragedy of the earthquake, the miners' struggle was a catalyst in CUC's development. Pushing for better wages and working conditions, the Ixtahuacán miners on November 11 began the 250-mile march from their community to Guatemala City. Starting with a group of seventy, the miners wound through the indigenous highlands on a nine-day journey down the Pan-American Highway, growing in strength along the way. Soon-to-be CUC activists coordinated food and support along their path and accompanied the workers toward the capital. The protestors soon numbered in the thousands, then tens of thousands. The Guatemalan government, in an effort to stop the march before it reached Guatemala City, forced mine owners to acquiesce to workers' demands, but the marchers kept going, taking up banners to support striking sugar workers near the capital, in Pantaleón. An estimated one hundred thousand protesters finally entered Guatemala City on November 20, 1977.

69

Maryknoll father William Price, the priest who had worked with the miners in Ixtahuacán before he was forced to leave the country, was clearly moved by their efforts and felt a personal connection to the march, though he hadn't yet returned to Guatemala: "When they arrived in the capital," he wrote, "they began to sing 'The Song of Ixtahuacán' (that I had taught them in the '60s) to the tune of 'Anchors Away' (from my Navy days). Through this simple but beautiful song, I was part of their march. . . . Never before had workers and peasants, Indians and Ladinos, the Indians of different ethnic groups showed such solidarity with each other."[48]

Activist Mayas remember the event similarly, especially its power in linking Maya and Ladino campesinos along its path—from Huehuetenango, Quetzaltenango, El Quiché, Totonicapán, Sololá, and Chimaltenango. Domingo Hernández Ixcoy describes the event as the first time Maya campesinos held up banners and proclaimed demands "that came from their hearts, [that] were their own." Some had worked politically through the Christian Democrats, he said, but the miners' march was different, more personal, a struggle by indígenas. "The solidarity with the miners of Ixtahuacán . . . was born in the hearts of our communities," he explains. "We recognized [the miners] as our brothers—brothers as indígenas, and brothers in the same poverty as us."[49] After activists triumphantly entered Guatemala City with the miners, he said, they returned to their communities to discuss the experience.[50] Five months later, in April 1978, CUC was officially founded.

The new organization did much more than connect distant local organizing efforts: due to its leaders' connections to university activists, the Ladino-led popular movement, and the Jesuits, CUC would link campesinos from various parts of Guatemala to national-level opposition politics. And while founded and led by Mayas, CUC was explicitly multiethnic: its campesino members included Ladinos and Mayas. It connected Maya campesinos and the *cuadrilleros indígenas*—Maya work gangs that traveled to the coast to work in the cotton and sugar fields—with the more permanent Ladino coastal workers in Escuintla and other plantation areas. It was important and unique because it was the first national-level campesino organization in Guatemala and the first major political movement to link Mayas and Ladinos.

CUC was also shaped by a clandestine alliance with the revolutionary EGP, active in El Quiché at the time of CUC's formation. As a mass peasant organization, CUC provided the EGP with access to the Maya

70

EGP guerrillas at a party in a highland community. Photo by Jean-Marie Simon.

countryside. The formal relationship between CUC and the EGP remains somewhat murky, but Pablo Ceto—a member of both—maintains that he and many others established their first contacts with the EGP shortly after the 1976 earthquake.[51] By the time CUC became public, Emeterio Toj explained, the EGP was involved in the organization and significantly shaped its political positions. (Toj, too, was a member of both organizations.) In its first public statements, the influence of a Marxist position on ethic differentiation is clear: CUC refrained from any reference to indigenous identity, simply using the word *campesino* to describe those who filled its ranks and whose cause it championed. Gregorio Chay described a CUC workshop where Jesuit priest Fernando Hoyos, who was later killed in his role as an EGP combatant, presented CUC members with an analysis of identity that stressed the class-based explanation of ethnicity—in direct opposition to the seminars being offered to Maya students by educators like Father Haeserijn mentioned previously.[52]

While closely tied to national politics and the revolutionary Left, though, CUC gained its tremendous strength because it focused on the most pressing concerns of local campesinos, like the high cost of living in the 1970s and rising prices of equipment and fertilizer. It pushed for

71

just wages on plantations and for better prices for crops.[53] At the time of CUC's founding, issues of ethnicity were barely mentioned, though this would change somewhat in time. As Gregorio Chay (once again, a member of CUC and the EGP) argued, CUC felt that the primary needs of campesinos were not Maya revindication, language, or traje, but better wages, working conditions, land; "lo étnico," he said, was a subject more for intellectuals than the rank and file of CUC.[54] Emeterio Toj, looking back on this history, offered a similar explanation. "We fought hard in the beginning of the 1970s for cultural issues, but nonetheless, we weren't able effectively to unite [culture] with political questions." Culture, he argues, would not have resonated with CUC's constituency. "If CUC had said, 'muchá, you need to wear traje,' we would not have had echo. The questions felt by the people [were economic]. . . . You could exist without traje, but not without food—that was our thinking, and I think it is still valid."[55]

A "Culturalista" Response

CUC's rhetoric evolved and in time came to incorporate Maya specificity and symbolism, but the initial position on ethnicity reflected in CUC statements was alarming to activist Mayas drawn to the ideas of Carlos Guzmán Böckler. They insisted that Mayas' identity as indígenas could not take second place to their class identity. Participants in the Seminarios Indígenas remember real divisions among activists emerging for the first time in a meeting held in Santa Cruz del Quiché at the very time and place the idea of CUC was taking shape.[56] Differences in emphasis among activists and their struggles were becoming polemical disagreements about how to achieve change. The ideology and rhetoric of class struggle prominently shaped the Santa Cruz meeting's agenda, participants remember. Emeterio Toj recalls "tremendously strong" discussions among Seminario Indígena attendees, in which "clasistas" like himself argued that activism focused on Maya revindication would not resolve major problems. "The issue is land!" Toj told fellow activists.[57] He describes a delegation of indigenous clasistas coming to the Santa Cruz meeting from Chiapas, Mexico. Despite the fact that Toj is quoted praising the "richness" of debates between clasistas and culturalistas, he remembers being thrilled that the Mexicans attended, giving the Quiché-area activists intellectual allies in the meeting.

72

Participants remember that other activist Mayas attending the Seminario, including Antonio Pop Caal and Demetrio Cojtí Cuxil, insisted on the importance of Maya-specific claims and protested the class struggle–focused agenda. Some (certainly not all) of the activists in the culturalista camp agreed with clasistas that revolutionary change was necessary in Guatemala, but they were distrustful that the "indigenous problem" would be resolved by a Ladino revolutionary government as the Left promised. They began more forcefully to speak of a double oppression, and argued that class exploitation could not be privileged above the discrimination suffered by Mayas.[58] At that moment there was greater clarity in the arguments, Ricardo Cajas recalls, greater differentiation between a struggle based on identity as indígenas and one based on class position. "We resisted joining a revolutionary struggle," says Cajas of the Santa Cruz meeting, "without first addressing . . . [the issue of] interethnic relations in our country. I think that is where the group divided in two."[59]

After a vote won by the culturalista camp, the agenda was revised to include a greater focus on the struggle of indígenas as indígenas, as activists put it. We insisted, Cajas recalls, that indígenas had to have their own well-defined culture and their own movement. "We were radical," he says, "it's a radical issue. . . . That's where we began to develop the idea of *nacionalidades indígenas*," "indigenous nations."[60] Emeterio Toj, Cajas remembers, countered with the argument that only as a single nation could they defeat the state and create a new nation.

▓▓▓ Clasistas, Culturalistas, and the Catholic Church

73

Two separate church-funded institutions functioned as resources for the clasista and culturalista tendencies among activist Mayas, both located in impoverished areas of Guatemala City and founded in 1973. The first was a center in Zone 5, the Center for Investigation and Social Action, CIAS, run by the Jesuits. The other was a house in Zone 8 run by the Maryknolls. The Jesuit project housed a community of eight priests who considered themselves "vanguard" or "radical," as Ricardo Falla put it, "Jesuits who were no longer tied to the university, but to the countryside." Among them were "organizers" and "investigators," Falla explained, and they focused on work among campesinos in the highland communities of Comalapa, San Martín Jilotepeque, San

Antonio Jilotenango, and Santa Cruz del Quiché. They became intimately involved with the formation and development of CUC.[61]

Around the same time, the church's Pastoral Commission on the Indígena envisioned another gathering place in the city, a center for Maya organizing and discourse. The "Centro Indígena" in Zone 8 of the capital was opened in 1973, financially supported and run predominantly by the Maryknolls.[62] Father Jim Curtin was at its head from 1973 until early 1979, followed for a short period by Father Dan Jensen. The center, a complex with ten or twelve rooms, served many purposes: it was a resource for growing numbers of young Mayas, men and women, who were going to the city in search of jobs, a place for domestic workers, students, and activists to gather, meet, learn, and organize. Curtin and his fellow teachers gave workshops on how to speak Spanish, which was the language of work and the city, and the means for Mayas from different areas to communicate with each other. They taught basic arithmetic for young men and women working as gardeners and maids. The center organized student work brigades, teams that helped in earthquake reconstruction in nearby communities. It offered a meeting place for a wide variety of organizers; CUC met there on occasion. There were also Sunday afternoon dances, which activists remember fondly, where young women and men came to socialize. Members of Antonio Pop Caal's organization Cabracán were some of the most active at the Centro Indígena, several of them living in student quarters there and in another nearby house as they attended university. One young woman in Cabracán described the meetings taking place at the Centro Indígena, with Mayas in the city gathering every Sunday. "It was happy, lively when we met there," she remembers. "I wanted to be part of all of it. I used traje again, wanted to help my compañeros." She was always humiliated when she wore traje in the city, she said, but she did it anyway, to work to change discrimination.[63]

Ixim: Notas Indígenas

By 1977, the broad meetings held by the church to discuss Maya issues had broken down, perhaps, as Ricardo Falla suggests, as a result of the Jesuits pushing the church to be more radical in its approach to justice for the pueblo maya, and also due to dramatically escalating violence.[64] While the Jesuits worked closely with a radicalizing campesino movement, the Maryknolls remained somewhat cautious and tended toward an indigenista rather than a Marxist approach in their efforts (with the Melvilles being notable exceptions). The Maryknolls' Centro Indígena was geared toward Maya-specific organizing, and an important component of it was a new periodical supported by the Maryknolls, *Ixim: Notas Indígenas.*

Ixim offered an indigenous critique of both the state and the Left. It was produced by a team of Maya students and activists, among them Jerónimo Juárez and Ricardo Cajas from Quetzaltenango, with four or five in charge of production at one time: one to raise money for printing, several more to work as reporters, others to serve as editors and take care of meetings and correspondence. The publication used the connections of the Coordinadora Indígena Nacional to solicit articles and circulate the issues, with local community activists handling distribution. *Ixim* was officially registered with the state, a move its founders say was intended to signal an independence from the popular Left. *Ixim* quickly blurred any such distinctions that officials might have perceived, however, by forcefully condemning government policies and practices related to Mayas and at times calling for revolution.

The pages of *Ixim* reveal how activists' thinking and strategies evolved in its short period of existence, October 1977 through October 1979. It purportedly aimed for a Maya audience that included intellectuals and campesinos or, perhaps more realistically, literate agrarian leaders. With rather lengthy articles and small print, it was a far cry from the simple publications CUC produced for the campesino masses, yet its first editorial introduced *Ixim* as a means to link the city with the countryside, and its front cover depicted a Maya campesino. The periodical also sought explicitly to connect Mayas of different linguistic groups in Guatemala to each other, its editors wrote, and had adopted the name *Ixim* because it had the same pronunciation and meaning— \ē-shēm \, "maize"—across Mayan languages. The editors expressed the hope that *Ixim* would nourish readers and inspire action by facilitating the sharing of experiences in the countryside and in the city. It sought, "in a small way, to fulfill the request of our ancestors written in the *Popol Vuh* . . . : May all rise up, may all be called, may not one group nor two among us be left behind the others."[65]

75

The subject matter of the first issue of *Ixim* dealt both with cultural matters and with issues driving the campesino movement. One article asked, "What is culture? What is folklore?" while another discussed in basic terms the idea of cooperativism. Yet another piece, reflecting an early CUC concern, described campesino organizing to secure reform in the forest laws to ensure access to wood.[66]

An article that had a rather large impact detailed a protest by "organized indigenous groups from different communities . . . , both student groups and campesino organizations," to demand indigenous students' right to wear traje in public institutions and schools and to speak Mayan languages. In a letter addressed to the Guatemalan minister of education, it noted the contradictions inherent in state-sponsored exhibitions like the National Folklore Festival that celebrated traje and "cultural values," while rules existed prohibiting the wearing of indigenous dress in public schools. "What is going on, Señor Ministro? What does this mean? Would this be the way to promote our cultural values?" Calling on the basic tenets of democracy, the Universal Declaration of Human Rights, and quoting the Guatemalan Constitution's equal protection and nondiscrimination provisions, the protestors called on the minister of education to respect the dignity and liberty guaranteed to all human beings, by ensuring Mayas' right to dress and language use: "We demand: free access, with trajes típicos, for all persons who desire it, to any educational establishment in the country and that at no time will use of maternal languages be prohibited. Rather, we ask that these cultural values be respected." The minister's response was published alongside it, guaranteeing students' right to wear traje and calling on all schools to respect it.[67]

The publication was widely read. At its height only five hundred copies of each *Ixim* issue were produced, but it was enthusiastically received by activist Mayas, passed around and reproduced, sometimes surreptitiously. Gregorio Chay, soon a CUC and EGP member, but in 1977 a student in Santa Cruz, recalls making hundreds of copies of the *Ixim* traje article when it appeared, secretly using his school's mimeograph machine. He and other students plastered the school with them, he says, put them in the bathrooms and halls, slipped them under the doors of all the teachers and school officials. "It was my first clandestine action!" he said. School officials were furious: the school's director threatened that if students did not appear in an upcoming community parade in proper uniform, they would be held back a grade and would risk not graduating. The protest primarily involved female Maya students, Chay explains, because in Santa Cruz they were the ones who wore traje, but their male counterparts pledged solidarity, agreeing to boycott the event if the women were not allowed to wear indigenous dress.[68] On the day of the festivities "the *compañeras* arrived in traje," Chay recalls. "We stood firm, . . . joined the parade, and no one threw us out. We all passed on to the next grade. It was the greatest victory!"[69] His response to the issue shows that at least for some Mayas—even future CUC and EGP members—traje (at least for women) was a topic with "echo."

Subsequent articles in *Ixim* focused on links among Mayas, within Guatemala and even abroad. One piece detailed Maya last names in the Guatemalan highlands, for example, and the similarities found in different areas and language groups, an obvious effort to suggest a pan-Maya affiliation across geographic and linguistic space: the name Xom was common among K'iche's in Chichicastenango, for example, Oxom among Q'eqchi's in Cobán, and Xoyom among Kaqchikeles in Chimaltenango.[70] Another article reported on a September 1977 meeting in Geneva of indígenas of the Americas, convened by the UN Human Rights Commission. Indígenas across the continent "are waking," reported one contributor, "and seeking [their own] solutions to their problems. Many of their problems are the same as ours here in Guatemala, and we have to recognize . . . as brothers and be in solidarity with indígenas of América."[71] This became a central theme in the periodical and in other writings of Mayas tied to this movement: the need for indígenas to define their own solutions to the problems of the pueblo maya.

Editors, including Jerónimo Juárez and Ricardo Cajas, continued to combine themes such as the need to reconstruct Maya history in Guatemala with contemporary issues relating to the campesino, but the way they wrote about the latter reveals the gulf that existed between the kinds of activists involved in *Ixim* and those in CUC. The first issue's very simple treatment of cooperativism, through an imagined discussion among campesinos, for example, was picked up in the second issue and, for illustration, turned to a discussion of the Ixtahuacán miners' march that was under way at the time of publication. That is "cooperation," said a character named Cristóbal, "what many men and women, mostly indígenas, are doing to offer food and . . . more . . . to the brother miners who, coming from San Ildefonso Ixtahuacán . . . are on their way to the capital to demand justice . . . , carrying out a protest march to demand better salaries." The writer, in this case "Kakul'ja" (contributors often adopted Maya pseudonyms for publication), wanted to inform his readers about the march, but his impressions of it differed in important ways from those of campesino activists like Domingo Hernández Ixcoy, quoted previously. "What is really astonishing," Kakul'ja wrote, "is that the march is on foot."[72] While Hernández Ixcoy had seen the miners as brother indígenas and brothers in poverty (and thus on foot), Kakul'ja's imagined campesino stressed the miners' Maya identity, but was "astonished" that they would walk the 250 miles to the capital.

Despite the relatively privileged class position of some *Ixim* writers, the journal became increasingly bold and began to include pieces that advocated revolution, armed if necessary. (They perhaps misleadingly attributed some articles to indígenas elsewhere in Latin America.) In April 1978 they asked readers to consider the arguments of a Colombian, for example, who (they claimed) expressed the following thoughts in a periodical called *Exposición*: "I am uncomfortable with the world as it is. They call me revolutionary. . . . They say that I am a friend of violence. But my violence does not go against men but against whatever system of oppression offends men. . . . Should I be resigned? Should I wait for justice to fall from the skies? . . . Is it possible today to love mankind without feeling the impulse toward a revolution?" *Ixim* editors asked their readers to ponder the position. "We have to ask ourselves," they wrote, "what are we doing? Are we helping those who help the pueblo? . . . [Or] are we standing by, thinking only of ourselves as individuals?"[73]

If public calls for revolution were not enough to alarm their Maryknolls sponsors at the Centro Indígena, *Ixim*'s writers soon profoundly insulted them when they took an aggressive position on what they called the "colonialist" Catholic Church in Guatemala. Cover art on one issue depicted a Maya bent over by the weight of a cross he was carrying; on the cross sat a priest, his hand held out for money.[74] "We aren't referring to you [the Maryknolls]," Ricardo Cajas remembers telling the priests at the Centro Indígena, but they were deeply offended nonetheless. "They wanted us to be grateful, but not critical," said Cajas.[75] Father Dan Jensen recalls the church's perspective, with people beginning to say, "We've nurtured an asp in our bosom!" "There is a saying in Spanish," Jensen told me, "nurture crows, and they'll take your eyes out. And they were always quoting that, because these people were not being the docile little Indians that people thought they were."[76] Production of the publication abruptly moved from the Centro Indígena in the capital to Quetzaltenango, where it was overseen by Xel-jú activists Juárez, Cajas, and others at a distance from its Maryknoll sponsors, although the Maryknolls continued to support the periodical financially.

By issue number eight, May 1978, produced in Quetzaltenango, the initially cautious and simple tone of *Ixim* was abandoned completely. The authors were now clearly writing for an educated Maya activist readership, and one highly critical of the government. They condemned army practices of forced recruitment and demanded to know why recruits were predominantly Mayas. They accused the military of turning "honorable [Mayas] into criminals." The front cover depicted Maya soldiers in the army, with a caption asking them, "Brother, who are you going to defend, your pueblo or the world of the whites?" Accompanying this racial critique of army forced recruitment was a vitriolic condemnation of the state-sponsored National Folklore Festival, which is examined in the next chapter.

In the following issue, *Ixim* writers condemned government abuses in the colonization zones of El Quiché, northern Huehuetenango, and the Petén. By then campesino settlers in these areas were suffering intense repression at the hands of state forces. *Ixim* editors renamed the area "*la fosa común*"—the common grave—"of the indio maya." Along with state violence, *Ixim* writers repudiated the fraudulent usurpation of colonized lands by high-ranking military officials when the area was found to contain oil and other valuable minerals. "There has been a change," they wrote. "Historically the army served to defend the interests of the rich; now they are the rich."[77]

Ixim did more than criticize government abuses, though: analysis of the Ladino-led Left was nearly as biting. Throughout its issues, virtually from the first to the last, *Ixim* activists challenged the Left's position that ethnicity was a "false" identity that stood in the way of change. By mid-1978, the argument was explicit and forceful. One of the most radical of the writers, another K'iche' from Xela, wrote that beyond physical violence, Ladinos "can kill with ideas, like class struggle," a concept he labeled "*culturicidio*," "culturecide."[78] Another contributor rejected the idea of homogeneous Guatemalans. "We can't pretend we are all *sanjuaneros*," wrote L. Yaxcal Coyoy regarding community politics in San Juan Sacatepéquez. "It is only an intellectual exercise and there will always be *sanjuaneros indios* and *sanjuaneros ladinos*." The "refuge in false solutions" represented by ignoring "racial" identity, he charged, took place at the national level, too: "The concept 'guatemalteco' pretends to supersede the concepts of 'indio' and 'Ladino.' The territorial reality is put forward as a substitute for the racial reality. And this is an error because a nation cannot be constructed negating the identity of

79

the human elements that constitute it. . . . [T]o reconcile indios and Ladinos is not to negate the existence of indios and Ladinos."[79]

▒▒▒ Party Politics and the FIN

In the early 1970s, participation by Mayas in formal electoral politics had expanded at the local level, primarily through the Christian Democratic (DC) party. DC candidates won mayors' races in a number of towns, and two Mayas were even elected to the national congress in 1974, Fernando Tetzahüic Tojón as a representative of Sololá and Pedro Cumez from Comalapa. Yet few young Maya activists saw elections as the answer. Fraud was especially widespread in 1974, and many activists—like Emeterio Toj who quit the DC that year—emerged from the experience deeply critical of formal politics. Many in Quetzaltenango believed that Xel-jú member Augusto Sac Raconcoj (a K'iche' assassinated in 1981) won a majority of votes in the 1974 mayor's race, but was prevented from taking office through fraud. On a national scale, the DC candidate for president, the future evangelical dictator Efraín Ríos Montt, won the popular vote, but the army nonetheless installed Minister of Defense General Kjell Laugerud García as president.

Despite this unpromising context, an indigenous political party was conceived in 1976, the ill-fated "National Integration Front," or FIN. The party had its roots in a political group affiliated with Congressman Tetzahüic called Patinamit, which had sponsored his successful run for office two years before. Led by Tetzahüic and other professionals from Chimaltenango, FIN cast itself as a political party of *verdaderos y auténticos guatemaltecos*—true and authentic (Mayan) Guatemalans— and claimed a vast constituency: the country's four million indígenas, the majority of Guatemala's "disinherited" and "exploited," along with the nation's campesinos and "workers in general."[80] FIN started with the name "National Indigenous Front," but its founders substituted the word *integration* for *indigenous* when they met intense public pressure and accusations of racism. No matter, the press continued to refer to it as "the indigenous party," often with alarm and warnings of racial conflict.

When it came to policy positions, FIN set out a moderate platform, "neither Right nor Left," and focused most of its efforts on gaining seats in Congress. Almost immediately, local power struggles with Maya candidates of the Christian Democratic party belied FIN's claims about representation, and the party itself divided over allegations of fraud and disagreements over which presidential contender to support in the elections of 1978.[81] Amid dissention, FIN leaders made the fatal mistake of siding with candidate General Roméo Lucas García, a leader who would soon oversee the beginnings of scorched-earth in highland Guatemala. In a speech celebrating their alliance, Lucas García, a landowner from Alta Verapaz known for his indigenista rhetoric, assured FIN members assembled at the symbolic ruins of Iximché, former capital of the Kaqchikel kingdom, that he shared their concerns and understood their problems. He had felt what indios suffer in his own flesh, he claimed. He had walked without shoes among indígenas as a child, had known hunger and thirst, had carried wood with a tumpline across his forehead. "I have deep knowledge of the situation," Lucas García told a crowd of FIN supporters. For that reason he was certain, he said, that the actions of his government would immediately be felt among the indigenous population.[82] Opponents of the alliance commented at the time on the irony of the choice of Iximché as the site for the announcement: it was the same place, they asserted, where Kaqchikeles had historically betrayed the K'iche's by allying with the Spanish invaders; again, they charged, indígenas were betraying "their own culture."[83]

The alliance was similarly condemned by younger Maya activists. Those I spoke with, considerably more radical than their counterparts in FIN, did not admit connections to the party, though a few had links to its precursor Patinamit. I am missing key *Ixim* issues from the months surrounding the 1978 elections (December 1977 through March 1978), but in those that I have, a clear anger is apparent regarding party politics. Writers refrained from explicit mention of FIN, but they condemned mainstream politicians and "false leaders." After the 1978 elections one writer commented that as usual most Mayas had remained outside the political system and were expected to follow politicians like sheep. He wrote that "brother indios" should open their eyes well and remember that their problems were never solved through electoral politics. All the parties were the same, he asserted: the Right, the Center, and the "so-called Left," all were opportunists.[84] The editors of *Ixim* reprinted a lengthy and unflattering analysis of FIN by Jesuit Ricardo Falla, adding that the experience with the failed party "should be known and studied to draw the greatest possible number of lessons from it."[85] The disdain expressed in the periodical for the FIN-supported General Lucas García was unequivocal. He was not only singled out as a military official

81

enriching himself illegally by usurping lands in the northern colonization zones; during his tenure as president, his name in *Ixim* would generally be accompanied by the word *assassin*.

It is important to mention, though, that FIN leaders, too, suffered violence at the hands of the state, despite their mainstream positioning and strategic alliances. Charlie Hale has found that of twenty-two people originally listed in the press as FIN leaders, by 1982 at least twelve of them were dead and three were in exile. He quotes FIN leader Marcial Maxía as saying that General Lucas García allowed FIN to submit an application for party recognition so that its members could be easily identified and murdered.[86]

Activist Mayas would go on debating about the rights and needs of the pueblo and the profound failures of Guatemala's political system, as the stakes rose with mounting state repression. In an increasingly tense context, relations among Mayas in opposition movements were ambiguous and in constant flux. Disagreements among clasistas and culturalistas were sometimes heated; at other times activists drew closer together as state-sponsored violence against the pueblo indígena had the effect of solidifying Maya opposition. An important turning point, both in patterns of state violence and Maya opposition to it, was the Panzós massacre of 1978.

Reinas Indígenas and the Authentic Maya

4

On May 29, 1978, hundreds of Q'eqchi' campesinos in the community of Panzós, Alta Verapaz, entered the town square to present a document to the mayor regarding land claims. In one of the first large-scale counterinsurgency assaults against Mayas, army soldiers fired into the crowd of men, women, and children, killing at least thirty-five and wounding dozens more. The violence did not end in the plaza. Campesinos fleeing into the hills and river were pursued by army helicopters, gunned down as they tried to escape the mayhem. It was a massacre on a scale not yet seen in Guatemala's civil war, though such mass killings would become almost routine practice within a few years.[1] In 1978—unlike the early 1980s—the killings were met with massive public protests, among them the symbolic denunciation of army violence by indigenous pageant queens in El Gráfico.

Even considering the public outrage that followed the massacre, the audacity of the queens' protest in the press was extraordinary. The ominous headline of an unrelated article (at least technically) hung above the young Mayas featured on El Gráfico's page 1: "A 'Death Squad' Is Operating in the Country; Interior Minister Claims It Is Not Connected to Security Forces." (The minister's claim would prove to be false.) Amid mounting violence against oppositional organizing, how and why had these activists decided to make such a public repudiation of the army massacre? And again, why queens and pageants to protest state killings?[2]

83

---

* Originally published in a slightly different form as "Subverting Authenticity: Reinas Indígenas and the Guatemalan State, 1978," *Hispanic American Historical Review* 89, no. 1 (2009): 41–72. Reprinted by permission of the author and the publisher.

84

Front page of *El Gráfico*, July 30, 1978.

░░░ Pairing Massacre and Folklore

Years of repression and violence had preceded the killings in Panzós, but that massacre was perceived as different: the mass killings of Q'eqchi' campesinos—it was believed at the time that there were over one hundred victims—ratcheted up tensions in Guatemala and gave state violence a racialized cast. Within three years of the Panzós killings, counterinsurgency practices that equated "Maya" and "subversive" in entire areas of the highlands—much of El Quiché, northern Huehuetenango, parts of the Verapaces, and elsewhere—would reach a level that the UN Truth Commission determined to be genocide.

Yet at the same time and in the same department of Alta Verapaz, the Guatemalan government maintained its indigenista tradition of folk-loric homage to the nation's Maya "soul," most visibly in the National Folklore Festival held each July in the departmental seat of Cobán. The festival aimed to showcase the nation's Maya heritage, one folklorist explained, and to "keep watch over [velar] its authenticity."[3] As symbols of authentic Maya identity (as judged by non-Maya folklorists), Maya women—and especially reinas indígenas—played a central role in state indigenismo and in the annual festival. Since 1971, festival organizers had summoned local indigenous queens from across Guatemala to compete in the Folklore Festival's centerpiece, a national competition for the title of Rabín Ahau.[4] Through dress, language, and dance, contestants were called on to embody Mayaness for the nation. Government officials including the president typically attended the pageant. The Rabín Ahau was held up as the national representative of the indigenous race, embraced by the president himself.[5]

In Guatemala, indigenismo had long involved a supposed valorization of the country's pre-Columbian heritage, primarily through folklore and homages to long-dead Mayas. As we saw in chapter 1, the same sentiments did not seem to extend to living Mayas themselves. Guatemalan officials were not alone in this—such incongruities underlay indigenismo everywhere—but in the late 1970s, discrepancies in attitudes toward past and present Mayas in Guatemala were extreme. Similar to other instances when repressive governments have professed to celebrate elements of the nation while in fact assaulting them, the very contradictions inherent in state actions created a means of resistance. As Jennifer Schirmer writes of "motherist" movements in Latin America, the states' "contradictory doctrine of at once valorizing and destroying the family . . . made [mothers'] resistance possible."[6] In Guatemala after the 1978 massacre of Q'eqchi's, the state's own celebration of Guatemala's Maya folklore provided protestors with compelling language and imagery with which to denounce the crass inconsistencies in government actions. It was no accident that the protestors, too, positioned the gendered symbol of indigenous identity—Maya women in community-specific dress—as the focal point of their protest. The

85

group set out their demands in the name of the Maya communities the women as queens represented. Drawing on but contesting the state's ideas of Maya authenticity, they argued that the dead in Panzós were "genuine" Mayas and their "brothers." They displayed Maya identity through dress, yet protested against the state as they did so: several of the reinas wore Maya clothing symbolic of mourning; one young man in traditional dress—Felipe Vásquez Tuíz from Santiago Atitlán—raised his clenched fist in the air.

In the eyes of the military, the dead in Panzós had nothing to do with "genuine" Maya heritage. Politicized campesinos in Panzós were not Mayas to be celebrated; officials charged instead that they were enga-ñados (duped), the tools of leftist insurgents. The protest offers a snap-shot, then, of contestation between a repressive state and Maya activists over issues of identity and justice, both cultural and political. By staging their protest within the government-sanctioned space of Maya women's pageantry, could these young people get away with confronting an abu-sive state? Could "authentic" Mayas, ironically, manage to subvert the state's definition of lo auténtico?

The protestors were a diverse lot, not only geographically, but also politically.[7] In 1978 they were involved in many of the efforts develop-ing in the highlands: these women and men were teachers and students, Catholic Action catechists, literacy workers and radio broadcasters, campesino leaders, and young people who would become revolutionary combatants and supporters. Juana from Soloma, Huehuetenango, is there, along with activists and soon-to-be guerrilleros from Santiago Atitlán, Felipe Vásquez Tuíz, Pedro Esquina, and Miguel Sisay. Two young women from Santiago Atitlán are among the group as well, though they seem to have been less engaged in community organizing. El Quiché is repre-sented by the reina from Chichicastenango. Organizers from Xela occupy the back row, among them Ricardo Cajas and Isaías Raconcoj. Their reina is there, too, and the photo itself was taken in front of her house. La Esperanza and Cantel, communities on the outskirts of Xela, are rep-resented, as is Nahualá, in Sololá. A land rights activist, the queen from San Sebastián, Retalhuleu, occupies the photo's very center.

The group's union of economic and political demands with cultural rights claims clearly stands out and belies a tidy differentiation between them. In reina indígena pageants, embraced by culturalistas and cla-sistas alike, the queen contestants' very words wedded concerns about cultural identity, land, rights, and justice. The protest is important not because it succeeded in its aims (it did not), but because it helps illustrate a moment when pan-Maya organizing in Guatemala was relatively new and qualitatively different from what reemerged in the aftermath of genocide. As seen in the last chapter, activists of different types disagreed about strategy and priorities in the 1970s; some felt strongly that Mayas could not achieve justice within Marxist movements that subordinated Maya-specific concerns to class struggle. Yet such differences did not preclude discussions among activist Mayas of different persuasions or informal alliances in what many saw as collective defense of the pueblo indígena. In July 1978, differences of opinion about identity did not preclude queens and campesino leaders, culturalistas and revolutionaries, from standing before the same camera, together opposing a manipulative and violent state.

▓▓▓ The Community Reina Indígena Pageant: Identity and Politics on Display

The intensification of highland activism taking place in the 1970s was reflected in local reina indígena pageants. Virtually all of the activists discussed so far—those in Santa Cruz del Quiché, Santiago Atitlán, Huehuetenango, Xela, Totonicapán, Cobán, San Cristóbal Verapaz—became involved in their local indigenous queen pageants. Over the course of the decade, such pageants became part of broader processes of highland politicization, one means by which activists (mostly young men, but through young women) could spread new ideas of Maya identity and rights. Maya women had long served as visual markers of indigenous identity in Guatemala, weaving and wearing *huipiles* (blouses), skirts, and elaborate hair wraps whose designs and colors signify culture, place, and, in the eyes of the world, nation. Within Guatemala, each weaving pattern is recognized as specific to a given locale, and a woman wearing traje is identifiable not only as indigenous but as a member of a certain community. Since men in many Maya areas no longer wear traditional dress, men and indigenous communities as a whole depend on Maya women to produce and display the symbols that mark them all as indigenous.[8] The indigenous queen's symbolic role was even more explicit: as a chosen representative of her community, she embodied local identity. What that meant—what she stood for—was undergoing important change in the 1970s.

87

There are two distinct kinds of reina indígena contests in Guatemala: local pageants, some of which began in the 1930s, and the national indigenous queen pageant, established in 1971. Despite similarities between local and national contest formats, community reina indígena pageants were independent affairs, usually held during annual festivals in honor of a local patron saint. Before the establishment of reina indígena contests, even towns with majority Maya populations typically had Ladina beauty queens presiding over local fairs. To counter exclusion from such festivals, in the 1930s Mayas fought for the establishment of their own queen pageants in towns such as Cobán and Quetzaltenango, though Ladino mayors and judges typically officiated, and indigenous "reinas" in the first decades of the contests adopted European-style crowns and other adornments similar to Ladina queens.[9] Mayas did not, to my knowledge, push for inclusion in Ladina contests, but instead advocated parallel, racially separate indigenous pageants, which exist to this day. These gave an indigenous representative a spot beside the Ladina queen or behind her, in a community parade. Soon common even in small highland municipalities, the pageants staged a community's indigenous identity as separate and distinct from Ladino identity.[10]

Community reina indígena pageants varied somewhat from place to place, but most shared a basic structure. Unmarried Maya women could

1936–1937   1942–1943

take part, sponsored by a community group or institution. Contests were held in a town's central plaza or theater, which was set up with a stage, microphone, and marimba and decorated with symbolic renderings of the Maya past. The contests drew large crowds and garnered press coverage. People speak nostalgically of plazas overflowing with spectators and recall the festive feel of the nights.[11]

The pageants would begin with each contestant making her way through the crowd amid clouds of incense. Wearing ceremonial dress, each young woman would move forward slowly to the sound of marimba, carrying a basket loaded with goods symbolic of her pueblo and the fecundity of the land, or with her head bent and arms clasped behind her, dancing a traditional dance called the *son*. The final component of the pageant, and the one that changed most significantly in the 1970s, involved a speech by each candidate given both in her maternal language and in Spanish. It was a unique and likely often daunting opportunity for women to speak before an entire community. Spectators cheered on their favorites and hissed at the less articulate or those unable to speak Spanish well. Successful *discursos* (speeches) have been described as highly poetic, full of symbolism, and delivered with passion.

At issue even in local reina indígena pageants was whether a contestant represented the community and la raza—the "race" as locally

89

(From left on facing page) Reinas indígenas of Quetzaltenango. Source: *1934–1984: Historial del certamen de la belleza indígena de Quetzaltenango.*

1953–1954

Reina indígena of Quetzaltenango, 1970–1971, Thelma Beatriz Quixtán Argueta. Source: *1934–1984: Historial del certamen de la belleza indígena de Quetzaltenango.*

understood—with authenticity. In the politicized 1970s this could be a contentious subject. Activist Mayas, culturalistas and clasistas alike, made local reina indígena pageants a focal point of their cultural revitalization efforts, a means to introduce new ideas and foster pride in la raza. Activists demanded and won changes in the events. Struggling with Ladino officials, they first pressed for equality with Ladina queens in terms of prize money and titles.[12] Soon they focused on questions of symbolism and the meaning of "authenticity." What would be represented in the contests? Would Mayas or Ladino "experts" plan and judge the events? In community after community in the 1970s, activists gained control of the pageants and designed contests that they considered to be more culturally appropriate.

At the same time, themes of rights and justice made their way into some queens' speeches, alongside frequent references to a broad pan-Maya identity. As Greg Grandin notes, the tomb of Thelma Beatriz Quixtán Argueta, the 1970 reina indígena of Quetzaltenango who died shortly after being named queen, is inscribed with the epitaph, "We have been beaten and humiliated, but the race was never defeated."[13] Perhaps not coincidentally, Quixtán, the thirty-sixth indigenous queen of Quetzaltenango, was shown in a commemorative

90

Reina indígena of Quetzaltenango, 1978–1979. Source: *La Nación/ Quetzaltenango*, August 14, 1978. Photo courtesy of Salvador Bonini.

history of the contests not in a formal portrait, but speaking into a radio station's microphone, addressing the pageant's audience in the theater and beyond its walls.[14]

In a similar image of the Quetzaltenango reina elected in 1978, the photographer and his newspaper readers again seem to have been interested in the queen as speech maker. The newspaper image also captures changing ideas about authenticity: in 1978 the queen cast aside the elaborate crown, collar, and flowing cape that had adorned indigenous queens of earlier decades. A year later the indigenous representative was no longer called "reina" but was renamed U-mial Tinimit, "Daughter of the Pueblo" in K'iche'.[15]

▓▓▓ "May All Rise Up!": Envisioning the Pueblo Indígena

In a surprising number of communities, activists went beyond symbolic changes and managed to appropriate reina indígena contests for political ends, as stages for the expression of oppositional discourses. Leftist community groups growing at the time sponsored queen candidates and shaped pageant speeches. Not all contestants' speeches in the 1970s, or even a majority, could be construed as voicing resistance. But opposition groups could and did put forward contestants who protested discrimination, poverty and exploitation, and, increasingly, state violence. A new type of discourse took its place alongside traditional speeches. The words of activist-sponsored contestants were poetic, as tradition dictated, but politically charged as well.

One young K'iche' woman, a student at the Instituto Indígena Nuestra Señora del Socorro and reina indígena of Quetzaltenango in 1973, provides an example. In her farewell speech in 1974, the reina indígena intertwined references to Maya blood lineage with explicit calls for economic justice. In a reference to class conflict in and beyond Maya communities, she called for an end to economic exploitation of campesino "brothers," whether by "foreigners" (meaning non-Mayas) or fellow members of la raza:

> I, a genuine representative of the Mayas, feel proud to be a descendant of the greatest civilization of the Americas, . . . the race that will never die, a race that . . . clamors for justice, an oppressed and bitter race. . . . My race, become once again free and powerful . . . ! [Ancestors] illuminate our path and our understanding, [so we may fight for] the well-being of our campesino brothers who are vilely exploited, not only by foreigners but also by our own race.[16]

The Quetzaltenango reina indígena elected in 1978 similarly spoke of unity and solidarity with the exploited. She pledged to women— rural and urban—and to campesinos in general that she shared their struggles. She called on the pueblo as a whole to follow in the footsteps of the ancestors, to walk forward together in solidarity.[17] Yet another K'iche' reina from San Sebastián, Retalhuleu, later at the center of the 1978 protest photo, demanded in a 1977 speech that Mayas recognize their own worth.[18] She called for pan-Maya unity in Guatemala and for Mayas to rise up together in common political cause: "Our pueblo suffers so much exploitation, . . . so much violence," she told a reporter. "My pueblo will only move forward by unifying, because in unity is strength." Like many other reinas of the 1970s would do, the San Sebastián queen drew on the sacred K'iche' origin narrative, the *Popol Vuh*: "I exhort . . . the pueblo indígena . . . of Guatemala," she said, "to take up the counsel of our ancestors, 'may not one, nor two be left behind, may all rise up together.'"[19]

The idea of pan-indigenous unity in Guatemala developed as activists from different areas were in fact getting together. By 1974, the newly formed Coordinadora Indígena Nacional brought together activists for meetings and workshops. The 1976 earthquake had connected activist Mayas to each other, as young people from distant communities worked together in relief efforts. In 1977, *Ixim: Notas Indígenas* became a conduit of pan-community activism and communication. That same year, the strike by miners from Ixtahuacán, mostly Mayas, drew the attention of organizers all along Guatemala's Pan-American Highway, and within months, CUC linked local agrarian activists, Mayas and Ladinos, to each other and to national opposition movements.

In these same years, reinas indígenas became involved in pan-community organizing. Beyond sponsoring their own candidates, Maya organizers invited reinas and their supporters from other municipalities to their local pageants. Sometimes visiting reinas spoke on stage about experiences in their pueblos. The young Maya women at the Instituto Indígena Nuestra Señora del Socorro formed a marimba group and played at pageants in many communities. Queens and their sponsoring groups met in regional meetings planned by Maya students and funded by the Catholic Church, and organizers offered workshops for the women and supporters, inviting teachers and other professionals to take part. Adrián Inés Chávez, a Maya linguist and translator of the *Popol Vuh*, was an influential figure in these efforts. He traveled to communities far and wide to introduce young people to the text, which helps explain its appearance in many speeches. The 1978 reina from Soloma, Huehuetenango, remembered Chávez playing a vital role for her and her friends, sharing a version of Guatemalan history that included the experiences of Mayas, absent from school textbooks.[20]

As connections among pan-community activists grew, reina indígena pageants became a convenient place for people from different areas to get together. This became even more important as increasing state repression accompanied the growth of highland mobilization. By the late 1970s, few places remained for students or campesino organizers to meet, and fairs and pageants, held throughout the year on community patron saints' days, could provide cover. At the same time, pageants were cultural and gendered events (and therefore deemed nonpolitical), so they represented a relatively safe means by which activists could speak out. As Ricardo Cajas of Xela explained, "The reina indígena [pageants] were a space we appropriated for political action. We were using the girls [*señoritas*], we have to admit that. But there were no alternatives left."[21] When the military labeled most other forms of activism "subversive," indigenous queen contestants like those in the 1978 protest became activists' symbolic spokeswomen.

Consequently, queens like those quoted previously delivered speeches that advocated mobilization. A few urged their listeners not only to rise up, but also to join a class struggle that united them in common effort with poor Ladinos. A contestant in the 1978 Quetzaltenango pageant, sponsored by the activist group Acción Juveníl (Youth Action), embraced class struggle and condemned a racial politics that divided Maya and Ladino campesinos.[22] With a leftist insurgency growing in strength, her speech was practically a call to arms.

94

Certainly not all pageant spectators would have agreed with the sentiment she and others like her voiced. Regarding the contestant from Acción Juveníl (who did not win the contest), one Maya observer commented that she seemed "to forget that she was participating in an indigenous event," speaking with "resentment" against her "brother indios."[23] Similarly, members of other communities, Mayas among them, sometimes reacted negatively when queen contestants advanced an unwelcome political opinion or overstepped the bounds of appropriate speech. Critics charged that by such displays they rendered themselves not representative, but inauthentic. These moments of local contestation over authenticity offer an important message: radicalized speeches represented only one facet of a complex story, as intensifying violence deepened divisions within Maya communities.[24]

Activists or *Patojas*?

Politicized pageants raise an obvious question: were the young women who gave voice to oppositional politics being used by activists, as Ricardo Cajas suggests? (In interviews, he referred to reinas not only as señoritas, but also patojas, "little girls.") Queens could be as young as fifteen, but most were a few years older, sometimes even twenty or twenty-one. Many outspoken queens had experience in community groups and in contemporary newspaper interviews seemed quite savvy. Yet women's roles as activists were and are less obvious than men's. As Grandin observes of activism by Q'eqchi' women in Alta Verapaz, "Women's actions tended to be more covert, as planters, military commissioners, and the like were less likely to recognize them as agitators than they were men."[25] One woman active in the 1970s noted an invisibility that made her organizing possible: "'As an indigenous woman, I lived a clandestine life.'"[26]

Gender ideologies that allowed women's activism to go unseen acted in concert both with local cultural practices and indigenista zeal for folklore to further render queens apolitical. Of course, the protestors (like the "clandestine" Q'eqchi' woman) leaned on those very understandings to create a space for political activism. The protest participants I spoke with, women and men, were aware that queens' symbolism gave them all room to speak out. Interviews suggest, moreover, that the women knowingly and willingly lent their "authenticity" to the group.[27] Consider the composition of their photo, taken by an organizer from Xela. Nearly all of the reinas, framed by their male supporters, wore solemn and composed expressions. The men's mannerisms were strikingly different: Ricardo Cajas and another organizer smiled as they exchanged glances in the back row, and Felipe Vásquez Tuíz grinned with his fist clenched. The single woman without a serious expression (in the center) had long been challenging gendered norms as a land activist in her community, San Sebastián. Yet the more composed women, their expressions dutiful markers of indigeneity, seem to authenticate both her and the male activists.

Given these gendered stereotypes, politicized speeches by queens sometimes aroused suspicion and accusations that their words were not their own. It is true that the women typically prepared speeches in consultation with their sponsors, and their speeches generally reflected sponsors' aims. There is also remarkable similarity in the speech themes voiced by reinas, which suggests that pan-community and church-based organizing efforts had significant effects. Yet it is not safe to assume that the messages delivered by reinas were simply memorized, or that the women did not take ownership of them. A majority of the reinas I spoke with insisted that they were the ones to give voice to the words on paper. Juana from Soloma, and other women, claimed to have written their speeches themselves.

What the women as reinas actually did was not wholly determined by their assigned roles, their sponsors, or any given script. Those I interviewed accepted rather than challenged their position as symbolic queens, but several of them used that position in surprising ways. While some of the women limited their participation (or it was limited for them by family or local authorities) to speaking with relative caution on the pageant stage, others went beyond what might have been scripted to graphically protest racism and terror. One reina in the 1978 protest, for example, stood before a plaza filled with spectators shortly after the Panzós massacre. With an intensity that was remembered by another participant twenty-five years later, she paid tribute to the dead by internalizing and giving voice to their suffering: "Hermanos de Panzós," she said, "¡su sangre la tenemos en la garganta!" (Brothers of Panzós, your blood is in our throats!)[28] Young women like her pushed the boundaries of what the reina indígena stood for and conveyed to the community and the state.

▓▓▓ Authentic Mayas at the National Level

Ironically, as local contests became more politicized, folklorists and successive Guatemalan military governments adopted the local pageant format as their own, staging a reina indígena pageant at the national level for the first time in 1971.[29] The National Folklore Festival of which it became a part had been created two years earlier by Cobán resident Marco Aurelio Alonzo, a Ladino teacher and folklore promoter. Alonzo organized the festival to celebrate Guatemala's Maya heritage, he explains, and save it from "inevitable" decline and corruption.[30] Soon other folklorists took control of the festival, including the wife of soon-to-be-president General Kjell Laugerud García. Along with the change in organizers came the new highlight of the festival, the contest for Rabín Ahau.

The National Folklore Festival, while a Cobán-area inspiration, fit perfectly into the government's symbolic efforts to forge a nation of the fragments within Guatemala's borders—a modern nation of guatemaltecos, but one with a glorious Maya heritage. The selection of a national indigenous queen was a natural addition to official homages to the Maya, an opportunity to personify, for Guatemalans and tourists, the "indigenous spirit" of Guatemala.[31] State officials became enthusiastic patrons of the Rabín Ahau contest. Local-level reinas indígenas were called to the national competition from towns all over the highlands, sometimes forced to attend by local Ladino mayors. The army press office printed pageant brochures. Presidents gave speeches and posed for the cameras with queens. In 1972 the Rabín Ahau was crowned by the wife of President Carlos Arana Osorio, who was also in the pageant audience.[32] In 1976 President Kjell Laugerud García danced with one of the candidates on stage, and the press noted the visual impact of the young woman's traje side-by-side with the general's army uniform. His wife appeared at the pageant dressed in traje típico from a community in Alta Verapaz.[33] The juxtaposing of Maya queens and generals by that time had become terribly ironic, given the nature of state violence. "No to death," said one young reina in her pageant speech. Future president General Romeo Lucas Garcia was in the audience that year and, according to the press, had "made the event, with all of its splendor . . . possible" through his financial support.[34] Lucas García continued to attend and support the festival while president (1978–1982) and appeared in a photo in the 1981 festival program, a time of fierce brutality in the highlands, smiling and "contentedly" embracing a Rabín Ahau contestant.[35]

Like the local reina indígena pageants, the Rabín Ahau contest since its beginning has been racially segregated from the national, exclusively Ladina, Miss Guatemala pageant.[36] Like her local counterparts, the national Rabín Ahau was understood as a symbol not of beauty but Mayaness. A Folklore Festival organizer, the Belgian priest Father Esteban Haeserijn, explained that the Rabín Ahau was not just another beauty pageant, "not the same as the election of a Ladina queen, chosen for her physical beauty." "The Rabín Ahau," he insisted, "is chosen for the way

"Beauty" versus "Authenticity": Ladina queens (upper photos) and their indigenous counterparts (lower photos). Source: Programa General de Feria 2002, Cobán, Alta Verapaz, courtesy of Imprenta y Tipografía El Norte.

she expresses her *identity*, manifested by . . . her maternal language; . . . the purity of her traje . . . ; and her . . . dance (son)."[37] She was an idealized symbol of Maya essence, a symbol, as Carlota McAllister has argued, understood as separate from and subordinate to national Ladina beauty.[38] A striking contrast remains between images of Ladina and Maya queens even in recent years, as represented on the back cover of the 2002 Rabín Ahau pageant program. Maya authenticity as embodied by Princesa Tezulutlán on the lower right, always a favorite of Folklore Festival spectators, continues to require an open blouse.[39]

For the Guatemalan military regime in 1978, symbolic Maya women were viewed both as essential and safe, an apolitical way to celebrate Guatemala's Maya soul and attract tourists. As noted, however, the same officials applauding candidates for Rabín Ahau applied a very different label to Mayas in general. The familiar and ugly underside of indigenismo had long held the contemporary indio (read as male) to be a deadweight on society. With the rise of the guerrilla insurgency in the highlands, state and military officials went a step further and defined entire Maya communities as potentially subversive and a danger to the nation. The state's hypocritical positioning on the Maya—embracing and appropriating a female essence, while defining the broader population first as a problem and then as subversive—stood out in especially sharp relief in 1978.

Denouncing Paternalism and Massacre

While many activist Mayas were involved in local reina indígena pageants, bitterness toward the state-sponsored Rabín Ahau event was intense. Even before the events in Panzós, activist Mayas used the festival as an opportunity to protest what they perceived as the emptiness of state indigenismo. Countering official or family pressures on reinas to participate, activists tried to prevent their local queens from going to the festival pageant.[40] They recounted rumors about mistreatment of reinas in Cobán, of inadequate food and housing, and of disrespect and disregard for the women wearing the celebrated traje. They condemned the event as manipulation of the Maya by the government for its own gain.[41]

In May 1978, shortly before the Panzós massacre, a group of activist Mayas published an article in *Ixim*, taking aim at the National Folklore Festival.[42] The authors' critique in "Requiem for Homages to the Maya

Race" was fierce. Blasting the Folklore Festival as a modern vestige of colonialism and exploitation, the authors charged that under the pretext of maintaining cultural authenticity, the state sought to obstruct social change, to halt the development of the Maya community at a stage of history convenient for Ladino domination. The festival, the authors asserted, since it required Mayas to compete with each other to be the most culturally authentic, turned indices of exploitation—bare feet, heavy loads, the alcohol abused by the campesino worker—into cultural elements to take pride in. "Poverty is art," they wrote, "a constitutive part of the authentic indigenous culture." The Ladino contemplates the beauty of indigenous poverty, they asserted, becoming a "connoisseur" of the misery of the indio. With biting irony that highlighted the gulf that separated Maya and Ladina queens, they wrote, "¡Viva la belleza de la pobreza!" (Long live the beauty of poverty!)[43]

The authors observed the contradictions in celebrating as folklore what was repressed in real life. While folkloristas praised and judged Rabín Ahau contestants for their maternal language fluency, Mayas were prevented from using indigenous languages in schools, in the workplace, even in church. While the most authentic clothes were prized in the contest, Maya women routinely faced rules prohibiting them from wearing traje in state and private institutions and the workplace. And who were Ladinos, the authors demanded, to judge and value indigenous culture? They suggested in a footnote that perhaps Mayas should begin to hold events to elect a "pretty Ladina" or offer homages to the Ladino race. Or why not establish a "Ladino Institute" to "teach [Ladinos] not to live at the expense of indígenas?" a reference to the Instituto Indígena Nacional, dedicated to observation and documentation of indigenous life.[44]

The article is extraordinary for the boldness of its tone and for the ideas it expressed, several of which remain key components in the discourse of the pan-Maya movement today: the persistence of colonialism, assertion of rights to the use of Mayan languages and dress, the allegations of the absence of any true Ladino identity and culture, and most forcefully, the conception of a modern Maya race in Guatemala, which rejected an identity circumscribed by the past. In the passage that gives the piece its name, the authors wrote, "May HOMAGES TO THE MAYA RACE rest in peace, now that the Mayas of today need no type of homage . . . [and] have no confidence . . . in false actions in favor of the indígena [which] . . . never . . . give real benefit to the pueblo indígena."[45]

Already in May 1978, the authors of "Requiem" and likeminded activists strongly opposed the National Folklore Festival. The subsequent massacre in Panzós made their critique seem shockingly prophetic: a government that purportedly embraced Guatemala's Maya past murdered Mayas in the present.

Activist Mayas involved in a variety of efforts—organizing campesinos, working with reinas, writing for the publication *Ixim*, participating in discussions of indigenous identity and rights—were at the center of public protests against the killings in Panzós.[46] Those who had worked with queens in the past devised a plan to stage a boycott of the upcoming National Folklore Festival. They convinced a significant number of reina contestants to speak out against the massacre and denounce the festival. Women took to stages in their own communities to demand justice and joined together for the symbolic national-level denunciation featured in *El Gráfico*. The events were organized primarily by young men, and the reinas once again lent their services as spokeswomen. Yet the reinas' words and stories suggest that they, too, became invested in the struggle against repression.

Condemning Massacre on the Local Stage

In Carchá, Alta Verapaz, the contest for local reina indígena took place just days after the Panzós massacre, and one local Q'eqchi' woman named Fidelina Tux Chub used her presence in the pageant to condemn the killings. The reina candidate, sponsored by a local development committee, approached the stage walking slowly through the crowd, refusing to dance the son as required, as a sign of mourning and protest.[47] With this gesture, Tux Chub asserted her own understanding of the pageant's traditional dance: rather than a symbol of authenticity, it was a display inappropriate at a time of tragedy. She continued her protest in her speech, drawing parallels between the lives of those in Panzós and in her community. Her speech was preserved in a church publication, which now hangs on the wall of her living room:

101

> *Señoras y Señores*, brothers, . . . I am here with sadness. . . . I
> did not enter dancing because our pueblo is living a tragedy.
> Why am I sad? You know why, because of what our brothers
> of Panzós just experienced; you know that they were killed,
> and we don't know why. It could be because they are
> indígenas, or it could be because they are poor. . . .

I could not dance . . . knowing that my brothers and
sisters are crying for their loved ones. . . . I feel . . . what
[they] are experiencing. They have not a piece of earth to
live on and for this they were demanding their rights to
what truly belongs to them, their lands, and for this they
have been killed. You have heard the news on all the
radios, . . . read it in all the papers, we all know it. . . .
Tomorrow it could be us, *verdad?*[48]

Intertwining questions of race and class in her speech, she asked why the
campesinos were killed: was it because they were indigenous or because they
were poor? She answered the question herself: it was both. They were killed
because they were Mayas pressing claims for land.

After requesting a minute of silence to honor the dead, Tux Chub
invoked a now-famous refrain from the *Popol Vuh*, calling for all to rise up
and walk forward together, leaving no one behind.[49] Though her performance
was apparently well received by the audience, which gave her "abundant
applause," she was promptly disqualified by the Ladino jury of the contest
for her refusal to dance.[50] She believed her message about Panzós was also
unwelcome, though the jury refrained from comment. They simply pointed
to a requirement that she failed to fulfill, rather than dispute the content of
her speech. Whatever its reasoning, the jury ensured that Fidelina Tux Chub
would not be queen, she would not represent the community locally or in the
Rabín Ahau pageant.

The press supported Tux Chub's interpretation of events, publishing an
article with the headline, "Reina Candidate Disqualified for Requesting a
Minute of Silence for the Victims of Panzós."[51] The young woman went into
hiding for a few days, she told me, but then returned home, saying, "if they
come, they come." Her fears were not unfounded because the army targeted
people for less. But no one came.

In another town in Alta Verapaz, the Pocomchi' community of San
Cristóbal, a reina indígena candidate named Amalia Coy Pop was sponsored by cooperative leaders, men who sought to transform the local fair and
reina contest into "indigenous" events.[52] (Among Coy Pop's sponsors was
campesino organizer Juan Vitalino Calel, whose abduction was later witnessed by the Soloma reina, Juana.) Young people from many communities
attended the pageant that year, as did Adrián Inés Chávez, the K'iche' linguist and teacher. People remember the evening vividly—the decorations,
the traditional feast, marimbas, and women and men from all over the highlands dressed in vibrant traje.

Again, the timing of the community's festival and pageant was significant: just six weeks had passed since the massacre in Panzós. Coy Pop and her sponsors saw the pageant as an opportunity to call attention to the violence. She described the other candidates' speeches as "pretty" and "poetic." "Then I came, brave me! And my message was very different." She spoke about identity and discrimination, economic exploitation, and repression. She mentioned the Panzós killings explicitly: "Our brothers [in Panzós] are suffering too for speaking out," she remembers saying to the crowd. "We cannot be afraid . . . , and no one can silence us, no one can take away who we are."[53]

San Cristóbal was experiencing important political changes in 1978. Coy Pop's sponsors, Juan Vitalino Calel and other local leaders, had formed a strong agricultural cooperative, politicizing area campesinos. A Maya man, a relative of Coy Pop's, had recently won election as the community's mayor. In this context, the outspoken reina candidate was named queen. The festival committee presented Coy Pop with ceremonial traje and took photos. There was marimba music and visiting with guests. After midnight she went home.

San Cristóbal's activist Mayas had indeed made gains, but the events that followed show how tenuous they were. That very night, residents of the community (remembered as mostly Ladinos, but some Mayas as well) gathered in the town square to protest her election. They charged that the young woman was a *guerrillera*, a member of the insurgency, and this time the speech itself was condemned. The protestors demanded that the title be taken from Coy Pop and that she not represent the community. Military officials arrived from nearby Cobán to investigate the "content and meaning" of her speech.

The committee in charge of the festival quickly moved to appease the protestors and military officials, stripping Coy Pop of her crown. They named the previous year's queen as representative for a second time, despite the young woman's unwillingness since she was planning to marry.[54] In a long line of reinas' photos in the Casa Cultural in San Cristóbal, Amalia Coy Pop is absent. Under her predecessor's picture are two printed cards: "1977" and "1978."

Despite threats, the young woman was unharmed. She returned to the secondary school she was attending in Sololá on a government scholarship. There she was urged by her teacher Otilia Lux (more recently Guatemalan minister of culture and part of the UN-sponsored Truth Commission) to go to the press with her story. She did, and El Gráfico printed an article about the events in San Cristóbal, reporting that Ladinos in the community had pressed for the removal of her crown.[55] It is unclear whether Coy Pop had not mentioned Maya opposition to her election or whether the paper gave the story a "Ladinos versus Mayas" slant. In any event, this version of events was immediately contested in another national daily by an association of women from Alta Verapaz, many of them Ladinas living in the capital. They asserted that Mayas and Ladinos together had opposed the queen and that the local festival committee had rescinded her election "for the dignity of the [indigenous] race."[56] Their explicit reference to the recent massacre in Panzós reveals the tremendous racial and political tensions that underlay events in San Cristóbal: "Considering the events of Panzós," they asserted, "it was incorrect to blame Ladinos, or the army, or the government [for what happened in San Cristóbal]. . . . Only disastrous events occur when there are resentful persons counseling the indígena to act outside the law. . . . Not wanting to convert our pueblo into a bloodbath [campo de sangre], we consider it prudent . . . to assign responsibility to those who try to destroy the peace and order in San Cristóbal."[57]

Insisting that outside instigators must be behind any Maya action "outside the law" (without, in fact, specifying any illegal act), the Alta Verapaz women accused these same unnamed people of wrongly converting "a cultural and social act [the indigenous queen contest] into a political meeting," in a community known for its "cordial and fraternal" relations between Mayas and Ladinos. In a scarcely veiled threat against the young woman and her school, they added, "Hopefully . . . [Coy Pop] will realize that the studies . . . she is pursuing in the school of Santa Lucía Utatlán in Sololá as a student with a government fellowship, [are] not a weapon to bring indígenas against Ladinos, . . . unless that is the orientation she is receiving there, which would be distressing for the progress of education in Guatemala and for the prestige of said institution."[58]

Repression and bloodshed in San Cristóbal became severe in the next few years. Coy Pop's two sponsors were among the victims of state violence, likely targeted for their work organizing campesinos. Juan Vitalino Calel moved his family away from San Cristóbal after receiving threats but was dragged from his new home—with Juana as witness—and disappeared by the army in 1982. The army disappeared a second sponsor, Ricardo Policarpio Caal, in the early 1980s. Amalia Coy Pop feared returning to San Cristóbal and lived in another area of the country until 1998.

National Protest

Condemnation of the 1978 Panzós massacre came in many other forms. Several Maya organizations explicitly criticized state-sponsored folklore in light of the killings; among them were groups in the Verapaces region (home both to Panzós and the Folklore Festival) and in Comalapa, Chimaltenango. Representatives from communities in the Verapaces notified *Inforpress* that they would not send their local reinas indígenas to participate in the Cobán festival because "they did not want [them] to serve as entertainment for those who killed" campesinos in Panzós.[59] In a Maya publication, *Cha'b'l Tinamit*, an article signed simply "Kekchíes" held that if the Folklore Festival took place, the Rabín Ahau should bind her skirt with a black belt of mourning for the death of her brothers, "her crown and staff should be soiled with Kekchí blood, her eyes should shed . . . tears like the waters of the Polochic, darkened with blood."[60] The Polochic River runs through Panzós and after the massacre bore bodies of the dead.

Activists in Comalapa requested the festival's suspension in a message to the new president, General Romeo Lucas García, stating, "The Association of Indigenous Students and Professionals of Comalapa . . . respectfully requests that in the interests of national dignity, the Folklore Festival of Cobán be suspended due to the bloody tragedy of Panzós which our country is mourning."[61] This time the letter to Lucas García was not anonymous but was signed by the group's president, Antonio Mux Cumez. The army abducted him a few years later, and he, too, is counted among Guatemala's disappeared.[62]

Activists organizing the festival boycott meanwhile met with the Quetzaltenango reina indígena, a young K'iche' woman named Teresa, to ask for her help. It was important that the Quetzaltenango indigenous queen participate in the protest, since she was something of a celebrity at the Folklore Festival due to the importance of Quetzaltenango as Guatemala's second largest city. She readily accepted. As she told the press, "Due to . . . the massacre in Panzós, I have become part of the general protest [against] . . . this bloody act. . . . I will not participate in the festival in Cobán. . . . [It] would not be acceptable, while our brothers in Panzós suffer the irreparable loss of their loved ones, . . . that we their blood brothers would be traitors participating in a fiesta like that."[63] Another valued participant was the previous year's Rabín Ahau, a K'iche' woman from San Francisco El Alto, Totonicapán. To the delight

105

of organizers, she agreed to participate in the boycott, to join protesters rather than travel to Cobán to coronate her successor. She took an active role in the group, attending local pageants to protest the Panzós killings. The group considered the Rabín Ahau crown, then in her possession, to be the key to the protest. They contemplated using it in a counterfestival of their own in Quetzaltenango (no such event took place), or presenting it with their declaration to the press in Guatemala City; it would *not*, they insisted, be used to crown another Rabín Ahau.

Reinas and supporters met in San Cristóbal, Totonicapán, for a boycott planning event that participants remember involving over one hundred people, as usual held under the auspices of the community's fair and reina indígena pageant. Many reunited in Quetzaltenango a week later. The twenty-two most "valiant" of the group, as one organizer put it, assembled for the photo that would appear on the front page of *El Gráfico*.

The group, however, faced a disappointment. The 1977 Rabín Ahau in the final moment was unwilling or unable to boycott the Folklore Festival. Rumors circulated that she had been threatened or paid off by army officials with links to the festival. According to one organizer, such pressure was applied indirectly through two young women—both wealthy indígenas, in fact—whose families were close to the government and army. I talked with both of these women, and one remembered that she had visited and talked with the Rabín Ahau about the importance of her participation in the festival.[64] (This development, like the combined Ladino and Maya opposition to the dethroned Amalia Coy Pop, once again underscores growing divisions within Maya communities as violence rose.) Ultimately the protestors decided to go through with the boycott even without the Rabín Ahau and her crown. Some twenty or thirty of them—memories vary on this point—boarded a night bus and made their way to the capital, about six hours away, to deliver their statement to the press. Juana from Soloma was on board and remembers arriving in Guatemala City, being received in a small room in *El Gráfico*, and presenting reporters with the photo and the declaration of protest.

As the queens and their supporters expressed in the declaration, the state's celebration of Maya "authenticity" a mere two months after the killings of indigenous campesinos in Panzós reeked of hypocrisy. "The reinas indígenas believe," the press article stated, "that considering the events of Panzós, in which genuine Guatemalan indios [*verdaderos indios guatemaltecos*] lost their lives, this Festival should be suspended." The queens declared

> that the recent massacre of our brother indios of Panzós
> . . . [represents] the continuation of centuries of negation,
> exploitation and extermination initiated by the . . .
> Spanish invaders.
>
> That the Folklore Festival of Cobán is an example of
> [an] . . . oppressor indigenismo that . . . makes the reinas
> indígenas into simple objects for tourists to look at, without
> respect to our authentic human or historic values.
>
> That while the wound of Panzós still bleeds, the failure of
> the organizing committee of this "show" [written in English]
> . . . to suspend it . . . demonstrates . . . the degree of disrespect
> [they have] for the lives of us, los indios. [65]

Government officials' comments following the Panzós killings make it clear that they viewed massacred campesinos quite differently. Like the women of Alta Verapaz decrying the politicization of the San Cristóbal pageant, the mayor of Panzós stated that the campesinos in his community were incited by "agitators" who deceived them with strange ideas about land rights. The outgoing president, General Laugerud García, expressed a simi-lar sentiment: "I know the campesino as peaceful, honest and hardworking, but he has been incited, . . . indoctrinated."[66] In statements to the press, officials chose not to describe the victims in ethnic terms at all.

The protestors directly contradicted these positions. By using the very image embraced by the state, the revered indigenous queens, the protestors refuted characterizations of massacred Mayas as engañados, duped, by insisting that they and the dead in Panzós were one and the same, los verdaderos, los indios. The protesting queens, they claimed, and not the officially sanctioned Rabín Ahau, represented true Guatemalan Mayas—Mayas who lived and breathed, bled and died.

107

▓▓▓ Lessons from 1978

Ricardo Cajas of Xela noted that the violence and repression following the Panzós massacre included the disappearance and killing of scores of people linked to reina indígena pageants, but the queens themselves were spared. "It was for the best," Cajas concluded, "that we did not manage to 'kidnap' the crown." Given the military involvement in the Cobán festival, he suggested, especially with its patron General Lucas García assuming the presidency in July 1978, the response against the reinas could have been deadly.[67]

The reinas did, in fact, remain safe in 1978. To return to a question posed earlier, could purportedly "authentic" Mayas be subversive? The boycott suggests that notions of a gendered authenticity prevented reinas—and the men around them, at least temporarily—from being seen by the state as subversive. Yet that same quality gave them the space and voice to challenge the very definition of "genuine" Mayas and to do and say things that others could not.[68]

That was not the case for the Maya campesino victims of the Panzós massacre, women among them. It was not the case for the thousands of Maya men, women, and children killed in scorched-earth campaigns during the next few years. In those campaigns, military thinking about Mayaness and gender was very different. As investigators have documented, the army massacred Maya women along with whole communities to prevent the "seed" of insurgency from reproducing. Pregnant women could receive especially brutal treatment. But in the infamous words of General Efraín Ríos Montt, that was not "scorched-earth," it was "scorched Communists."[69] Not, we might add, authentic Mayas.

As a tool to confront a genocidal military regime, ideas like authenticity proved to be painfully limited. The National Folklore Festival of 1978 was not cancelled. The festival organizers were able to assert, in the same newspaper that had published the protestors' statement, that the festival was not linked to politics.[70] The 1977 Rabín Ahau, despite her short-lived role as a protestor, passed the crown to her successor. She claimed that most reinas from the western highlands boycotted the event, but the government recruited other women to take their places, and there were a total of forty-nine contestants. In *La Nación*, a government spokesman stated that "despite the negative criticisms and the pressure exerted on indigenous delegations not to participate, the festival surpassed that of the year before, both in number of participants as well as the presentation of the folkloric acts. It was an eminently folkloric program . . . without any political taint." President Lucas García met personally with the reinas, a fact publicized in the press. "Those indigenous delegations that were present," the article continued, "were received in a special audience by the President of the Republic. The

Army directing local festival in Nebaj, El Quiché. Photo by Jean-Marie Simon.

interview lasted more than three hours, and the president had the opportunity to learn [directly from] . . . the representatives of the indigenous race their problems and their concerns."[71]

Reina indígena pageants would no longer provide activists with cover as Guatemala became an outright terror state from 1981 to 1983. As part of counterinsurgency strategies to control the rural Maya population, Ladino officials and military commissioners in conflictive highland zones took over direction of local reina indígena pageants in the 1980s.[72] In a 1983 publication by a group calling itself Movimiento Indio, a drawing depicted a Guatemalan army officer, a rural massacre, and indigenous queen contestants side-by-side. The officer held a grenade in one hand and with the other, crowned a reina indígena.[73]

109

Despite getting away with the protest in 1978, the young people who assembled for the photo did not emerge unscathed from the violence. Several of them followed the campesino organization CUC underground; several joined or aided the guerrilla insurgency or splinter all-indigenous revolutionary groups; a few went into exile, where one still remains; another continues to live clandestinely in Guatemala, despite a tenuous peace; yet another wanted no part in discussing this painful history. As I searched the faces and clothing in the photo, I had been particularly concerned about the

Violence and pageantry. Source: "Guatemala," Movimiento Indio, January 1983.

young man grinning in the back row with his fist in the air. Felipe Vásquez Tuíz, the musician and linguist, community activist, literacy worker, and eventually a member of the guerrilla group ORPA, was disappeared by the Guatemalan army in 1982 after being taken forcibly from his community, Santiago Atitlán. His body has not been recovered.[74]

In 2002 María Elena Winter Flor, an intriguing figure in the history of Alta Verapaz indigenismo and the Folklore Festival, echoed the 1978 festival organizers' assertion that the event was not political. The protesters had been misguided, she told me, because the Panzós massacre and the state's Folklore Festival had nothing to do with each other.[75] The young Mayas protesting in 1978, on the contrary, had felt themselves and the pueblo indígena violated by both.

Radicalizing Violence

Guatemala . . . land of eternal spring, land of eternal Panzós.
—*Ixim: Notas Indígenas*, June/July 1978

The army killings in Panzós in May 1978 were followed less than two years later by another galvanizing episode of violence against mostly Maya protestors: the massacre at the Spanish embassy in Guatemala City. When campesino protestors occupied the embassy to call attention to brutal violence in northern El Quiché, state forces set fire to the building and then stood by while over two dozen CUC activists burned alive. Violence of such magnitude radicalized significant numbers of young Mayas. Emeterio Toj, Pablo Ceto, and Domingo Hernández Ixcoy from El Quiché had already joined the EGP by that time. Cruz and Miguel Sisay and Felipe Vásquez Tuíz, among others from Santiago Atitlán, joined the ORPA. More commonly, Mayas who were active in opposition organizing and who were willing to support the armed insurgency did so in more subtle ways, by providing logistical support, food, or medical attention to area combatants. Some activist Mayas, to be sure, wanted nothing to do with armed insurrection, but others, including people active in Maya-focused organizing, moved close to the Ladino-led revolutionary movements in the early 1980s. When they did so, however, they wanted to do it on their own terms.

111

Protesting State Terror: CUC and *Ixim* Respond to Panzós

Activists' many and diverse reactions to the 1978 massacre in Panzós tell us much about Maya organizing at that moment. The responses of CUC and *Ixim*, in particular, reveal important differences between these organizations and their strategies. At the same time, they provide evidence of a shared understanding of the violence directed at Mayas. As state targeting of the pueblo maya became increasingly blatant, CUC infused its activism with Maya symbolism. Some Mayas in racially focused organizing simultaneously called for revolution. As always, though, differences in thinking and strategy, if blurred in practice, continued to complicate efforts by clasistas and culturalistas to find common ground.

The Committee for Peasant Unity, CUC, emerged from clandestinity only weeks before the Panzós massacre, timing its public appearance with Labor Day marches in the capital on May 1, 1978. Following the May 29 massacre, CUC leaders and members again took to the streets, joining unionists and students in massive protests on June 1 and 8.[1] A list of dozens of their protest signs and slogans, included in *Ixim*'s June/July 1978 issue, shows how the Left framed its concerns in the wake of the killings. A few organizations did include references to Maya identity in their protests, with signs pledging solidarity with "*hermanos indios*" (brother indios) and "*mártires kekchíes*" (Q'eqchi' martyrs), for example. But CUC's official language again reflected careful adherence to the Left's position on ethnicity: CUC was among the majority of organizations that paid tribute to undifferentiated campesinos. In a paid announcement in the press, too, CUC condemned the killings with careful language, calling for unity among "all the workers of the countryside" in defense against army repression.[2] They referred to Q'eqchi' victims as "campesinos" and "honest workers" rather than indígenas, reflecting their intention to build a multiethnic campesino organization connected to the leftist popular movement. CUC did condemn "discrimination" in its statement—a term that was likely understood as referring to Mayas in particular— and asserted the massacre victims' historic rights to lands that they had worked for over a century, but in print they did not explicitly refer to the dead in Panzós as indigenous. Though it was an organization led by Mayas and whose members were mostly Mayas, CUC seemed consciously to take care not to appear too "indígena."

Yet this careful rhetoric was an imperfect reflection of what took place on the ground. If we look beyond the official statements of the organization, more complicated positions on identity come through. Shortly after the Panzós massacre, for example, one CUC spokesperson expressed an explanation of the violence in Panzós that was quite different from CUC's official position. He gave the following address at an USAC roundtable on state violence held on June 20, 1978. This CUC member (unnamed) saw the indigenous identity of the victims of Panzós as something *not* to be ignored; rather, the fact that the victims were Mayas helped him to interpret the massacre for himself and his audience. He situated the killings as part of a pattern of exploitation of Mayas since the Spanish conquest:

> We will try to give you a picture . . . of what it is like to be an Indian in this context of repression, exploitation, and discrimination. The Panzós massacre is not an isolated incident. It is one link in a larger chain . . . a continuation of the repression, the dispossession, the exploitation, the annihilation of the Indian, an inhuman situation that began with the Spanish invasion. . . . It is enough to mention the massacres that occurred in the colonial epoch, the slow massacres that took place when they forced Indians and poor Ladinos to work in the coffee fields. It is enough to mention the massacres that have been committed by the right since the fall of Arbenz, the thirty thousand or more dead during the last twenty-five years. . . . Our history has been this, and even more, because there are more that have been forgotten, buried, existing only in the heart.[3]

The interpretation reflected in these comments, writes Greg Grandin, "saw colonialism and racism" not as Ladinos tended to, "not as . . . residues held over from Spanish rule that continued to deform social relations in the countryside—but as the central contradictions of national history, the fundamental conditions of an unbroken chain of exploitation and repression."[4] It was an understanding of Panzós, in fact, that shared much in common with that of Mayas writing for *Ixim*.

Ixim published an explicit and Maya-focused condemnation of the Panzós massacre, labeling the killings "ethnocide." The editors dedicated the entire June/July 1978 issue—all thirty pages of it—to the massacre. The front-page headline read "Massacre in Panzós: Another Night in the History of Cowardly Dispossession, Blood, Death and Exploitation against the Indio in Guatemala," and had its largest letters dripping blood. *Ixim*'s editorial, like the CUC member's explanation, linked the massacre to a four-hundred-year history of violence since the conquest, placing the beginning of the story with the arrival of Pedro Alvarado in 1524. Since the conquest, they asserted, "the massacre of indios has been continuous and [has taken place] in the most diverse ways." Panzós was not an isolated case, they argued, but "a link in the chain of problems that daily confront the indio . . . not only is he discriminated against, abandoned, but also dispossessed [of land] and massacred."[5]

The *Ixim* issue contained firsthand reporting. Immediately following the massacre, two *Ixim* writers from Quetzaltenango traveled clandestinely, with the help of priests, nuns, and Q'eqchi' activists, to Alta Verapaz to interview survivors and witnesses. "I don't know how we did it," remembers one of them, "how we had the daring to cross the police and army lines." They managed to get into the hospital in Cobán to talk with victims and their families, he remembers, and his attempt a quarter century later to describe the bullet wounds they saw was choked by tears.[6] What the two learned in Alta Verapaz was portrayed in all its horror in the pages of the publication. A hand-drawn graphic on the front cover depicted soldiers firing from the rooftops of the Panzós municipal building and church into the crowd of campesinos, dozens of them lying dead in the plaza. Lengthy articles detailed the history of land struggles in the area and what had happened on May 29. They produced vivid sketches of weapons and "exploding" bullets used against the campesinos, the ten-centimeter exit wounds these produced in bodies, and soldiers dragging dead bodies into mass graves.[7]

Thirty-eight national press articles and paid advertisements protesting the massacre were reproduced in *Ixim*'s pages, including CUC's statement and others from student organizations, university associations, unions, and the Catholic Church. The activists behind *Ixim* published their own work in a section headed "The Pueblo Indio Repudiates, Condemns, and Analyzes the Massacre of Panzós." Again Panzós was placed in a long history of violence against Mayas, specifically that related to land dispossession. The *Ixim* writers singled out the liberal regime of Rufino Barrios in 1871 as the beginning of massive land loss, followed by post-1954 militarization of the countryside, a time, they charged, when army officials, national police, and local authorities illegally took title to lands belonging to Mayas.[8]

The civic committee Xel-jú published a declaration in *Ixim* condemning the massacre of "our indigenous kekchí brothers," pledging material and moral solidarity with them "in this crucial hour of our existence," when "extermination" seemed to be the government's objective. They explicitly called for agrarian reform. The Coordinadora Indígena Nacional issued a statement, signing it "Indigenous Groups of Guatemala." They insisted that the dispossessed in Panzós were the true owners of the land and that their massacre was only the latest in a pattern of state violence in the highlands—kidnappings, massacres, dispossession—"a systematic repression against all those who demand and struggle for their legitimate rights." These legitimate claims-makers were contrasted with the "barbaric" state and army, an obvious twist on the notion of the savage indio. None of these crimes has been investigated, they charged, but it is clear "who commits these truly savage actions." "Guatemala, oh beautiful Guatemala," they wrote, "land where corn is planted and cadavers are harvested, . . . land of eternal spring, land of eternal Panzós."[9]

Despite the seemingly endless history of oppression that they recounted, the *Ixim* editors insisted that the situation did not have to— nor could it—continue. The victims of Panzós, moreover, would not die in vain. Even endemic violence could not eliminate the indio, they wrote: "The total extermination of the indio has not been achieved. . . . [H]e rises from his ashes like a phoenix. . . . Panzós, the death of your sons is the seed that will germinate tomorrow and whose fruit will give us strength to walk toward our liberation."[10]

The *Ixim* issue protesting state violence in Panzós placed its authors squarely within the opposition movement calling for an overthrow of the state. Yet that last phrase, "walk toward our liberation," captures a fundamental distinction between the ideologies of CUC and *Ixim*, before and after Panzós. Activists in CUC, though many (the spokesperson just mentioned and interviewees) interpreted state violence as purposefully directed against Mayas, aimed to effect change through multiethnic alliances with the broad oppositional movements in Guatemala. Activists with *Ixim* expressed the desire that indígenas themselves provide the solutions to the problems suffered by the pueblo maya. The indio must be "the architect of his own destiny," argued Victoriano Alvarez, a K'iché lawyer in Quetzaltenango and the civic committee Xel-jú's candidate for mayor in 1978. Thousands are becoming educated, he wrote in *Ixim*. "We have brains, intelligence, will, imagination. . . . These attributes were given to men precisely so he could construct his own destiny. . . . We . . . must forget about calling others, the non-indigenous, to solve our problems. . . . [I]t would be an indignity for us, los indios de Guatemala, if others do what we ourselves can and should do. . . . It would negate our glorious origins."[11]

CUC and Ixim had significant philosophical differences, then, even as their concerns overlapped. CUC focused on campesinos as a class, usually

115

without distinction, because it was dedicated to multiethnic organizing. Mayas in racially focused organizing championed Mayas as the leaders of the indigenous pueblos. This is not to say that CUC was unconcerned with rights of Mayas. Neither were *Ixim* activists unconcerned with issues affecting campesinos, in Panzós or elsewhere. Land issues were central to the claims set out in *Ixim*, as was violence against the social classes "dispossessed of the three elements of man: land, capital, work."[12] Should Mayas celebrate national independence, they asked in August 1978, when they have no real economic or political independence, "when land claims are met not with land but with machine-gun fire, [when] capital and work demands are met with accusations of Communism?"[13] On the first anniversary of *Ixim*, its editors noted with satisfaction that the periodical was "most read" in the countryside.[14] But their writing style and content show that *Ixim* was directed largely at people like themselves: regarding the problem of land claims being met by violence, they asked their readers, "what do *profesionales indios* say about this?"[15]

The issue of who would speak and act for the pueblo maya arguably became the central concern for activists in the racially focused Maya opposition movement, as CUC and the revolutionary Left grew in strength in 1979 and 1980. Alongside escalating counterinsurgency violence against indigenous communities, the guerrilla EGP and ORPA both published statements on the "ethnic-national question," but theory was not enough. The practical implications of revolutionary positions on identity were at the heart of negotiations and disagreements among Mayas inside and outside of the guerrilla movements, CUC, *Ixim*, and the Coordinadora Indígena Nacional, shaping alliances and factions alike.

116 ▨▨▨ Race and Revolution in Practice

Differences delineating various forms of activism by Mayas were expressed forcefully in the late 1970s, while at the same time Maya clasistas and some—not all—culturalistas became more closely tied, an improbable outcome directly related to escalating violence. Figures such as Ricardo Cajas and Victoriano Alvarez continued to advocate Maya-led activism in the pages of *Ixim*, but both allied with the multiethnic opposition movement. (Others, such as Jerónimo Juárez, complain that after the Panzós massacre, the periodical *Ixim* and the Coordinadora Indígena

Nacional became unjustly dominated by the revolutionary minded among them.) In the *Ixim* issues of late 1978 and 1979 activists demanded that indios find their own *camino*, or path, while they routinely condemned state violence and repression against campesinos and leftist organizers and advocated revolution. In September 1978, a month after Victoriano Alvarez's "indio as architect" essay quoted previously, *Ixim* editors published another piece by Alvarez, this one from a newspaper column in *La Nación/Quetzaltenango* on violence. It was a lengthy and detailed article arguing that the causes of violence in Guatemala were multiple: economic, social, cultural, political, and structural. Racism since the conquest had relegated the indio to an inferior status, Alvarez asserted, but "now there are mestizos among the oppressed as well," non-Mayas among those without economic or political power. He advocated "total change . . . [in] politics, economics, society, culture, because . . . the causes of the violence . . . are embedded in the structure and superstructure in which we live." "There is no choice," he asserted, "but to achieve the Guatemalan National Revolution."[16]

In the pages of the newspaper *La Nación/Quetzaltenango*, Alvarez advocated political opposition to the state after systematically recounting how the interests of the people—this time not racially defined—and the government had become divorced from each other. It was a call not for clandestine insurgency, but rather "open and public thinking and action, in the full light of day." He continued to assert the need for political independence, but this time in multiethnic terms: arguing that people must act for themselves rather than follow others like "robots," he urged his fellow Guatemalans—not just indígenas, but *nosotros los guatemaltecos*, "we Guatemalans"—to find their own paths rather than mimicking foreign models of change. He criticized the Right and the Left. Regarding army recruits, he said that they were made into fanatics for a nationalism they did not understand and made to hate Communism without knowing what it was. Criticizing the violence and dogmatism of the "extreme Left," Alvarez argued that revolutionaries embraced a worn-out ideology that did not reflect Guatemala's reality and lived "obsessively immersed" in a schema of class struggle. Nonetheless, he placed Mayas like himself fully within the opposition, which by 1978 placed them de facto in league with the guerrillas: Guatemala's struggle pitted the government on one side, Alvarez asserted, against the "workers, campesinos, students, indígenas, and other popular sectors" on the other.[17]

117

Alvarez's ability to make these kinds of statements in the "full light of day"—and survive—is evidence that Maya intellectuals, especially in Quetzaltenango, were considerably less vulnerable to state repression than were campesino activists. As one activist Maya put it, the army hesitated to wake "the sleeping giant" that the indigenous movement represented in Quetzaltenango.

▓▓▓ A *Movimiento Indígena* Defined

The relatively privileged position of Xela-area activists, their ability to speak to area Mayas, and the resources they could bring to the struggle made them potentially valuable to the Ladino-led revolutionary Left. In the late 1970s, the guerrilla organizations developed and maintained contacts with such activists, people who by that time were being labeled the "movimiento indígena" (indigenous movement). The use of the term signifies that a firm distinction was being made by the late 1970s between those Mayas inside and outside of the Ladino-led revolutionary groups. Mayas in the guerrilla groups—people like Emeterio Toj, Pablo Ceto, and Domingo Hernández Ixcoy—by the definition of the late 1970s would have been outside the "movimiento indígena." But because they had been part of earlier efforts, had been involved in insipient pan-Maya activism, they became key figures in a process of negotiating with those in the movimiento indígena who were sympathetic to the revolutionary struggle.

In the years following the Panzós massacre, a core group of Mayas from CUC, the Coordinadora Indígena Nacional, and people associated with *Ixim* and the Maryknolls' Centro Indígena held a series of talks about the role of Mayas in the revolution, prompted in part by the success of the Sandinista revolution in nearby Nicaragua in 1979 and advances by the guerrilla Farabundo Martí National Liberation Front (FMLN) in neighboring El Salvador. Revolutionary victory seemed possible, activists recall. A unified struggle involving the popular Left and the indigenous movement seemed all the more imperative and in 1980 and early 1981, according to some participants, achievable.[18]

Domingo Hernández Ixcoy described meetings around that time between leaders of CUC (by then many of them were part of the EGP) and revolutionary-minded movimiento indígena activists in various locations—the Centro Indígena in the capital, San Andrés Itzapa, San Martín

118

Jilotepeque, Sololá, and Patzicía. Both sides, he explains, saw the need for coordination. Those in CUC and the EGP wanted to strengthen relations and incorporate the movimiento indígena more formally into the revolutionary struggle because the participation of everyone was needed, he said.[19] For their part, some Mayas in racially focused organizations sought greater contact with CUC. "The Coordinadora Indígena Nacional," remembers Hernández Ixcoy, "was seeking a means . . . by which everyone could join the popular revolutionary war." But CUC had to make concessions too, they insisted, had to take up the concerns of the movimiento indígena "as policy, as part of [revolutionary] strategy."[20]

Pablo Ceto argues that by early 1980 CUC was open to the issues that motivated the indigenous movement, since two years of discussions and "indigenous expression" had followed the Panzós massacre.[21] Emeterio Toj similarly explained how CUC's thinking had evolved. Before the Panzós massacre, he said, the idea of rights specifically for the indigenous pueblos was not a central part of CUC's thinking. But pointing to Panzós as a catalyst, Toj claimed, "we started to recognize that the war was mainly against indígenas. We were not saying that they [the state and army] were not also killing [Ladino] workers, but mostly the dead were indios. . . . We realized that the pueblo indígena was the one [hardest] hit, the enemy of the system."[22] There was ample evidence to support such a conclusion. Another shocking example unfolded in broad daylight at the Spanish embassy.

▓▓▓ The Spanish Embassy Massacre and the Declaration of Iximché

The Guatemalan military brutally repressed campesino activism in the department of El Quiché in the mid- and late 1970s, especially in the northern Ixil region, an area where CUC had a large membership and many people supported the EGP. Between 1975 and 1978, state forces kidnapped and disappeared a reported twenty-eight campesinos from the small Ixil communities of Cotzal, Chajul, and Nebaj.[23] In October 1979, army forces kidnapped and executed another seven agrarian leaders from nearby Uspantán.[24] Soldiers reportedly raped and disappeared others from Chajul, including women and children. CUC activists from the area traveled to Guatemala City to protest the violence before Congress,

119

—39—

agarrada

a-ga-rra-da

a e i o u
ga   go gu
rra rre rri rro rru
da de di do du
rada a e i o u   rra

EGP literacy training manual used in the Ixil area, with a lesson drawing on the word for grabbed or kidnapped. Photo by Jean-Marie Simon.

although they were denied access to legislators. Led by CUC activist Vicente Menchú, the father of Rigoberta Menchú Tum, the group made their rounds of sympathetic organizations in the capital. Some fifteen of them stayed overnight in the city at the Maryknoll Centro Indígena.[25]

On January 31, twenty-seven of the activists, mostly Maya members of CUC, occupied the Spanish embassy—which they considered sympathetic to their plight—to call attention to the violence. Guatemalan security forces reacted by firebombing the embassy. According to testimonies received by the UN-sponsored Truth Commission, as the inferno enveloped the building, the national police and security forces made no attempt to assist the people inside. The ambassador suffered burns and barely escaped;[26] all of the others in the building except two burned to death, a total of thirty-seven people. The sole CUC activist who survived the fire, Gregorio Yujá Xona, was taken to a hospital to be treated for severe burns, "guarded" by the national police. Armed men kidnapped Yujá Xona from the hospital, tortured him, and killed him.[27]

The Guatemalan state immediately moved to discredit the CUC activists, the Spanish ambassador, and religious supporters of the opposition. State officials announced that the dead in the Spanish embassy were subversives disguised as campesinos and that they had started the fire themselves. (It is likely that some of the CUC campesinos may have had links to or been members of the EGP, but they were unarmed in the occupation and sought only a meeting with the ambassador.) Government officials questioned the motives of the Spanish ambassador himself in allowing the protestors into the embassy.[28] An article in *Diario Impacto* later claimed that one woman killed in the fire may have been an (unnamed) Belgian nun in disguise, who "entered the Spanish embassy disguised as an indígena, accompanying a powerful [*fuerte*] group of people who appear to have exploded incendiary bombs."[29] The *Revista Militar* claimed that the embassy had been occupied by "a guerrilla commando, dressed in indigenous dress from El Quiché, who were [*sic*] following the Sandinista example in the taking of the National Palace in Nicaragua on August 22, 1978."[30]

The response of activist Mayas to this latest round of violence was confrontational and symbolic. On February 2, Emeterio Toj summoned people in Santa Cruz to go collectively to recover the bodies of the dead for burial; five buses of Mayas in traje and sombreros made their way to the capital, an event that was covered on the radio and prompted a large demonstration of support in Guatemala City.[31] Twelve days later CUC and the EGP organized a protest at the Iximché ruins in Tecpán, Chimaltenango. An estimated two hundred people from various parts of the country converged at the site, with CUC—like the Coordinadora Indígena Nacional before it—claiming that all of the country's ethnic

121

Maya woman with CUC *Boletín*. Anonymous. Source: Dutch Committee in Solidarity with the People of Guatemala, in Fototeca Guatemala, CIRMA.

groups were represented there.[32] Invitees from unions and the church came, as did leftist politicians and the international press. There was no national press coverage of the event.

Ricardo Cajas from Quetzaltenango addressed the gathering at Iximché as a representative of the Coordinadora Indígena Nacional, at the request of CUC. He remembers not knowing exactly what to expect when he got there. Cajas describes being instructed by CUC organizers to go to Tecpán, and from there he was sent to the ruins of Iximché. As he was walking to the site, he recalls, Pablo Ceto came along in a car and picked him up. He was told where to go if the army arrived and told where a car would be waiting for him. When Cajas arrived at Iximché, he noticed that the guard of the site had been tied to a tree by the activists. People were armed. It was a moment of enormous tension.[33]

Cajas describes being greatly moved by a banner that had been hung at the site: "For every indio who falls, thousands of us are rising up." "I'll never forget it," he said. "The word *indio* was still taboo, but to see this . . ." He does not remember what he said in his speech, but people remarked afterward that it was *muy encendido*, that is, inflammatory, provocative. "There was great anger for the Spanish embassy massacre. It was almost a declaration of war by the indígenas," he recalls. Summing up the historical evolution of Maya oppositional activism to that point, he explained that "we were no longer there to discuss, we were each there to act, each in our own capacity."[34]

Shortly after the embassy fire, CUC and EGP members had again gotten together with activists from the Coordinedora Indígena, the Centro Indígena, and writers for Ixim. Together they drafted the Declaration of Iximché in a three-day meeting in San Andrés Itzapa, Chimaltenango. The statement is a testament to their ongoing differences, but at the same time, reflected the progress of discussions about multiple forms of oppression, and the need for revolution. In the words of Miguel Alvarado, a K'iche' physician from Cantel, Quetzaltenango, Iximché represented "an awakening of consciousness for Ladinos and indígenas, . . . a united proclamation demanding a space in the . . . revolution."[35] Together the protestors proclaimed their condemnation of the latest massacre and their support for armed struggle.

The Declaration of Iximché is an intriguing document. Presented as a statement from "the indigenous peoples of Guatemala before the world," it was read aloud at the site by a young K'iche' woman who was also from Cantel. She, too, had been educated at the Socorro school

123

for indigenous girls and after graduating, worked there as a teacher; as a student she had played in the Socorro marimba band, had been active in reinas events, and was closely involved in CUC.[36] The contents of the statement that she read, along with the Iximché site's symbolism, signaled a new moment for CUC itself. At the same time, it was a turning point for the movimiento indígena participants, since they were explicitly allying themselves with the campesino movement and the armed Left, especially the EGP. This embracing of a popular class-based struggle, however, neither negated nor eliminated their Maya-specific demands.

The proclamation combined an appeal for Mayas to rise up together with non-Mayas to fight exploitation and repression, with a long and detailed account of the history of Maya struggle and rebellion since the conquest. It mixed the fundamental concerns of CUC with issues that had filled the pages of Ixim. It urged Mayas to join the popular struggle to combat economic injustices, pitifully low salaries for campesinos, and high prices for basic agricultural inputs, while decrying the long history of racist violence against the indígena, forced military recruitment of Mayas, forced sterilization, and even the cultural violence of state-sponsored folklore. Throughout the piece it is readily apparent which passages came from activists with long histories in multiethnic opposition movements and which came from the more narrowly defined movimiento indígena. For the moment, though, at the site of Iximché and in the closure of the declaration, activist Mayas stood together, their respective demands intertwined. "To end with all these evils," they declared, "we must fight allied with workers, poor Ladino peasants, committed students . . . and other popular and democratic sectors, to strengthen the union and solidarity among the indígenas and poor Ladinos, since the solidarity of the popular movements with the indigenous struggle was sealed with the loss of life at the Spanish Embassy. The sacrifice of those lives has brought us now closer than ever to a new society, to the dawn of the indio."

The participants' specific demands were economic, cultural, and political: "For a society of equality and respect, so that our pueblo indio can develop its culture now broken by the criminal invaders; for a just economy where no one exploits others; with communal lands as in the times of our ancestors; for a land without discrimination; so that all repression, torture, . . . and massacres may be ended; . . . that we all have the same rights to work; that we no longer serve as objects of tourism."

124

While stating that they knew they would be considered "subversives" for such an alliance, the participants committed to it nonetheless, pledging that "our pueblo indio will continue to rise up, step by step until our final triumph." Their justification was based in shared losses: "The blood of the indio and poor Ladinos covering the path . . . has fortified our hope and our struggle." The declaration concluded with the familiar call of the *Popol Vuh*, "May all rise up, may all be called, may not one or two groups among us be left behind the others!"[37]

This is not to say that the activists from the movimiento indígena felt themselves to be equals in the protest at Iximché. It was orchestrated by CUC and the EGP, and Ricardo Cajas, for example, apparently made his way to the gathering without knowing precisely where he was going or even that he would be asked to speak. No one, he conceded, was taken more by surprise than he by the scene at Iximché, with its "reclaiming of consciousness" by the Left.[38]

José Manuel Fernández Fernández, who has studied the development of CUC, writes that the fact that the Left was dealing more explicitly with the question of Maya specificity was "a symptom of a rupture in ideological control."[39] It seems less a rupture, perhaps, than a controlled and limited process. CUC leaders and EGP members Emeterio Toj and Domingo Hernández Ixcoy explain that while the Left began with Iximché publicly to incorporate the ideas coming from the movimiento indígena, they were less able or less inclined to incorporate the leaders themselves. "In 1980," says Hernández Ixcoy, "I think that the leadership of the EGP realized that they had to allow space for demands—not for indígenas, but for their demands. They began to see that they had to incorporate more clearly the question of cultural claims. . . . They spoke for their demands, but didn't incorporate leaders . . . , it was virtually not allowed."[40]

Emeterio Toj put a more positive spin on the issue, as he tends to do. CUC leaders were Maya, but high-level EGP leaders were Ladinos, he explained, and this did not change with time. "But we Mayas managed to enrich the political thinking, the ideology of the EGP. . . . In the beginning we couldn't talk openly about indigenous questions, it was impossible, that wasn't the discourse. The struggle was economic, the question of classes. But little by little, with our presence . . . the EGP was acquiring more of a Maya character [*fue coloreandose de Maya*], began to incorporate *lo Maya*." Toj saw CUC's protest at Iximché as a reflection of that.[41]

After Iximché, the EGP began to publish statements on Maya iden-tity, what it termed the "ethnic-national contradiction," and explicitly addressed the role of Mayas in the revolution. The following piece by Mario Payeras appeared in the EGP's *Revista Compañero* in early 1981, a year after the events at Iximché:

> The revolutionary popular war, and the ethnic affirma-tion of indígenas in the process of this war, today offer the only alternative and future solution to the ethno-cultural complexity of our country. . . . In our country, there will be no revolution without the incorporation of the indigenous population in the war, and without their integration with full rights into the new society, a society which indígenas must help to build. . . . Their role as producers of the wealth gives indígenas both strength and rights: strength to wage the war, and an undeniable right to participate in the con-struction and leadership of the new society.[42]

"In practice," Toj said, "we were the ones who gave life to [these ideas]." But still, Toj explained, the space for "leading" on Maya-specific issues was very limited, and restraint was required. "If you crossed the line," Toj recalled, "you were called a culturalista, indigenista. . . . You had to be very careful not to cross the line."[43]

For some people close to the EGP, events like the CUC gathering at Iximché and the EGP's statements on the "ethnic-national question" seemed to be opportunistic manipulations of ethnicity for political gain. Jesuit priest and EGP member Ricardo Falla, for one, sees the issue of eth-nicity on the Left as highly problematic. There was probably something "authentic" about identity as indígenas for some on the Left, he notes, but still, ethnicity was potentially dangerous. "The idea is a *chicle*," he remarked. Ethnicity could take whatever shape its proponents desired.[44]

126

▓▓▓ The ORPA and Activism in Santiago Atitlán

The Revolutionary Organization of Peoples in Arms, or ORPA, was the guerrilla army described by Guatemalans as the most attuned to the complexities of Maya identity. Rodrigo Asturias, the son of novelist Miguel Asturias, was the main ORPA leader (he adopted the nom de guerre

Gaspar Ilom, the indigenous hero of his father's fictional *Men of Maize*), and he wrote on the theme of racism in the late 1970s, in essays known as "Racismo I" and "Racismo II." Other ORPA leaders, too, frequently addressed issues of racism and discrimination when they gathered people together in Maya communities like Santiago Atitlán and delivered revolutionary speeches.[45]

State repression was brutal around the Lake Atitlán region. In Santiago Atitlán, as elsewhere, virtually all forms of social organizing became suspect in the eyes of the army. Lists of leaders "marked" for army reprisal first circulated there in May 1979, containing the names of the primary school director, teachers, and local priests, including Father Stanley Rother.[46] The army posted soldiers around town during the annual festival in July 1979. ORPA made a visit to the community in June 1980 and "seemed to have the sympathy of the people," wrote Rother. Afterward army soldiers appeared "in force. . . . walking around in groups of three or four, standing on the corners watching everything."[47] As Rother continued in a letter of September 1980, "Since then we have had strangers in town, asking questions about the priests, this catechist or that one, where they live, who is in charge of the Cooperative, who are the leaders."[48]

Father Rother soon noted the involvement of local activists with ORPA: "I am aware that some of our younger catechists are working with those that are preparing for a revolution. They are young men that are becoming more and more conscientious about their situation and are convinced that the only option for them is revolt."[49] Several of them, most obviously the broadcasters at the radio Voz de Atitlán, became vocal critics of the growing repression and violence. Their actions would not be lost on the army.

Gaspar Culán, who had left the seminary and married just before ordination, worked as the Voz de Atitlán director. One of his radio addresses gives a sense of what "consciousness-raising" in Santiago Atitlán meant in 1980, as army repression grew; his words coincided quite closely with ORPA's revolutionary discourse of economic and racial equality. Culán offered a Scripture-based program broadcast in Tz'utujil called the *Word of God*, which involved reading and analyzing Biblical texts. During a broadcast in 1980, he used the program to condemn the violence that hung over residents of Atitlán and the suspicion, distrust, and hate the army was sowing in the community through its use of local informants. He deplored economic inequality and racial

127

discrimination and the concentration of area lands in the hands of the rich and powerful. Culán asked his listeners:

> What do you think? . . . In the readings we learn that God created man, [but] not to be persecuted by death. . . . We are all now under the threat of death, death stalks us; . . . we are losing our being, . . . we are losing our life.
>
> We cannot speak, seek a better life, because death will follow us, will come between us, destroy us. The question is, who . . . has brought death among us? The only thing the enemy wants is that we fight among ourselves, that we separate, that we hate each other. . . .
>
> Dear brothers, let's think. Are we living in real justice? Are we all equal as the Scripture says? Is there no discrimina-tion? That's not true, among us there are poor, and besides being poor . . . we [Tz'utujiles] are discriminated against. Why? Because all are not equal. . . . God says, live with equality and without discrimination, but that is not what we are doing, there is no justice, there is no equality.
>
> Think a little more deeply: do all of us have goods, . . . lands, thousands and thousands of *cuerdas* of lands in our hands? In whose hands are the great quantities of land, . . . while others have none? . . . [Few] people have almost all the lands and the poor have nothing. That is why there is extreme poverty in our families. . . . Think and reflect because God asks you to exercise love, peace and justice.[50]

With ORPA present around the Lake Atitlán area, Culán was calling for residents to resist army violence and to unify in support of revolutionary change. Repression made heeding such a call exceedingly difficult. By September 1980, several local leaders had gone into hiding, and activists cancelled literacy classes and all but the smallest group meetings in the community.[51] The army virtually occupied Santiago Atitlán when they set up a permanent base on the outskirts of town, in October 1980, part of which was on the church's farming cooperative. Within a week of the establishment of the camp, soldiers disappeared five Maya activists, includ-ing Voz broadcaster Gaspar Culán; he was "stalked by death" as he had pre-dicted, dragged from his home on October 24, 1980, and not seen again.[52]

Other kidnappings in Santiago Atitlán followed in rapid succession. *Orejas*—"ears," or informants—infiltrated community groups and the church. Other residents, sometimes under duress, pointed out to the army the houses of activists. "Those who studied, women [activists], were marked," remembers one woman, a community health worker, "those who were in groups, tried to learn to read and write. . . . You didn't go out in the evening. When the lights went out, it was known there would be dead."[53]

Ten days after Culán was abducted, on November 3, 1980, soldiers broke into the radio station, searched files, stole tape recorders and typewriters. It was part of a pattern of repression against radio schools across the country. The diocese of El Quiché reported that six Catholic Church–sponsored radio stations in Guatemala were searched around that time, one was taken over by the army, and three were closed.[54] The Voz de Atitlán fell silent, and the members of its board of directors fled. The army captured four of the board members in the town of Antigua, and they were kidnapped and disappeared. Only one body was found, gruesomely tortured. The young man had small burns covering his body. His captors had cut his fingers off and gouged out his eyes.[55]

Some activist Mayas stayed in the community but left their houses to sleep, residents recall. They asked Father Rother to open the church each night, and hundreds slept inside.[56] On the night of July 25, 1981, in the midst of a military roundup in the community, Rother locked the church doors against the army with a reported six hundred young people inside to protect them from forced recruitment. The priest himself was shot and killed by Guatemalan army forces just two nights later, after midnight, July 28, 1981.[57]

In late October of 1981, the army focused on what was left of the group of young Maya activists in the community. They rounded up the remaining members of the radio association and literacy project, including Felipe Vásquez Tuíz (the protestor in the queens' photo with his fist in the air), along with other lake-area residents. They were taken to the military camp, interrogated, and kept in holes in the ground.[58] After fifteen days, the army apparently was satisfied that it had secured a degree of collaboration and began a public relations offensive. They called in the press and lined up the "confessing subversives" for photographers.

The front-page headline of *Prensa Libre* on November 10, 1981, read "Campesinos Disclose How They Were Recruited for ORPA; The Army

129

Has at Its Base Those Who Turned Themselves In." The caption under a photo of the Voz de Atitlán members read, "Tzutuhil indígenas who formed a literacy association . . . and promoted the Voz de Atitlán, closed for transmitting programs against the government." The article that accompanied the photos claimed that three hundred members of "subversive groups" in the Sololá area—those listed were CUC, ORPA, the EGP, and the Communist Party PGT—had sought refuge with the army and had acknowledged being "duped" by the guerrillas. The army claimed that one was said to have been kidnapped by ORPA when he was drunk, another forced to join under threat of death. They had turned to the army, the article asserted, for protection and collaboration.[59]

The "ex-subversives," according to the press article, accused members of the church and community groups of organizing antigovernment activities. The article detailed the establishment of the Voz de Atitlán and accused its broadcasters specifically of airing programming that aided the insurgency. The lengthy piece mentioned the "subversive" *Pensemos juntos*, the literacy training guide developed by Mayas discussed in chapter 2 (one of its authors was disappeared around that time). Comments attributed to one of the Voz broadcasters, Juan Atzip, claimed that the literacy workers themselves were "humble," uneducated indígenas: "Of course, we are people who . . . completed [only] the second year of primary school. For that reason, we never thought that those programs contained antigovernment ideas." "We only want to live in peace, work in peace," Atzip continued, in a statement similar to others that would be orchestrated by the government and army in the ensuing months and years. "We don't want trouble, we don't want Guatemalans to kill each other."[60] Most of the captives were then released one by one, with the exception of two young women who were accused of being "subversive" members of CUC. Their actual involvement with the campesino organization is unclear, but they had been working with the Voz de Atitlán's literacy program in the neighboring community of San Juan La Laguna. The two women were held at military bases in Santiago Atitlán and in the department of San Marcos for a year after their capture, forced to wash clothes and cook for the soldiers.[61]

Five months after the mass roundup in Santiago Atitlán, the army allowed the Voz de Atitlán to go on the air again. Permission was granted in the form of a letter to three of the members of the radio association, among them Juan Atzip, quoted in the newspaper just previously. Sent from the office of the minister of defense, the letter stated that under the leadership of the three specified members of the board, "the Voz de Atitlán . . . can go on the air with its regular programming."[62]

The programming permitted, however, was far from regular, and literacy and consciousness-raising programs were eliminated. Several of the radio broadcasters, including Felipe Vásquez Tuíz, then president of the board, refused to cooperate with the army and its new format. He went into hiding in Quetzaltenango for a few days, then returned to his wife and two small children in Santiago Atitlán. Three months later he was arrested in front of his fellow broadcasters, taken to the local jail, and beaten. When his family asked why he was being held, the army reportedly said that Vásquez Tuíz represented the radio and that the Voz de Atitlán broadcasters would "take turns" in prison. He was not released. He remained in the local jail for three days and then was disappeared.[63]

Miguel Sisay, after studying at the Instituto Indígena Santiago and working in campesino organizing, at the Voz de Atitlán, and finally in ORPA, saw all of these efforts as part of one idea, one large effort to help the community. But it was violently repressed:

> All of these expressions were shut down, there was no way
> to develop them. Literacy training . . . was shut down, any
> free expression of opinion was shut down, they interrupted
> the radio, killed people, tortured others. It was a horrible
> thing. . . . Everything was . . . cut short, verdad, and every-
> one went his own way. . . . At the end of 1980 and
> the beginning of 1981 practically my whole generation . . .
> disappeared [from Santiago Atitlán], . . . went to the moun-
> tains [guerrilla], many of my school friends, my childhood
> friends . . . died in the war, died in combat.[64]

A woman close to Felipe Vásquez Tuíz argued that he had just wanted to improve the situation people were living in, to help them to read and write, defend their rights, and that his participation in ORPA was an extension of it: "He liked to organize groups, share with people who needed things— even though we were those *gente pobre* [poor people], too. His parents were illiterate. He was one of the first to go to school . . . one of the first professionals from the pueblo. They were the guides for the future. But they were cut down."[65]

An activist Maya who was part of Antonio Pop Caal's "radical" Cabracán remembered Felipe Vásquez Tuíz as someone dedicated both to the "cultural struggle" and to the revolutionary Left. They spent time together in Santiago Atitlán, he recalls, one night talking about culture and identity the whole night through, the next night sitting on the beach in nearby San Pedro La Laguna with members of the guerrilla talking about the revolution.[66] Some say that in ORPA, there was room for both.

The group developed a strong presence around Quetzaltenango, attracting Mayas like Alberto Mazariegos from nearby Olintepeque. Like Felipe Vásquez Tuíz, Mazariegos was someone active in Catholic Action's youth group and cultural organizing in the early 1970s; he was remembered as always first to arrive at queens' events and festivals with his marimba. Again like Vásquez Tuíz, he joined ORPA in the late 1970s. He made his choice while well aware of the misgivings that some Mayas had about participation in the Ladino-led guerrilla movement:

> At that time some indígenas, especially the academics who were already professionals, . . . believed that we [ourselves] were capable, that it was time to build a movement like all of those by our ancestors, . . . the uncountable [historical] armed struggles of our pueblos. But for us [in ORPA], we believed . . . that it was worth sacrificing our indigenous claims, putting the needs of "indígenas y no-indígenas" [Mayas and Ladinos] first. . . . Despite the fact that we knew that the majority of those suffering were indígenas, at the moment we needed to build strength.[67]

"There were many discussions," Mazariegos continued. "We were with people in meetings, in activities that indígenas held, and it was a theme of discussion. . . . [Some said] we can't support a struggle that isn't ours, we can't go on being used . . . we don't need interlocutors."[68]

Mayas like Vásquez Tuíz and Mazariegos (who survived the war and was later elected to Congress) saw Ladino revolutionaries as compañeros rather than interlocutors. Others in the movimiento indígena, however, remained unconvinced.

"Pueblo against Pueblo"

*I dare say that the militares understood the ethnic component
and how to manipulate it better than the revolutionaries. They
understood it was a very serious issue . . . and that they had to
disarticulate it, prevent indigenous support for revolution.*
                                    —Domingo Hernández Ixcoy, 2002[1]

E meterio Toj Medrano of Santa Cruz del Quiché wore many
hats over the course of the 1960s and 1970s: he had been an
AC catechist, radio broadcaster, and someone involved in
pan-Maya discussion groups since their inception. He was a CUC founder
and an EGP guerrillero. Beginning in the late 1970s, the EGP gave him a
new task: to strengthen connections between the revolutionary Left and
the movimiento indígena and to bring the organizing networks around
Quetzaltenango more fully into the opposition movement. While working
as a radio broadcaster earlier in the decade, Toj had provided Jesuits and
Ladino university students with access to the Maya countryside. His role
for the EGP was similar. Since he had maintained connections with Mayas
in racially focused organizing, he was ideally positioned to bridge divisions
between the revolutionary opposition and the movimiento indígena.

As Miguel Alvarado remembers, Toj had "a special task, to organize
indigenous intellectuals so they would not be a counterrevolutionary
threat, but rather a force . . . to strengthen the revolutionary struggle."[2]
In discussions with area activists, Alvarado recalls that Toj talked both
of revolution and problems specific to Mayas. He said that the pueblo
indígena had no alternative but to organize itself as a body and join
forces with the popular, revolutionary struggle. "The main theme of
the meetings was how . . . indígenas could organize as their own force,
and as their own force, participate in the popular struggle. . . . [Just like]
unionists, women's groups, the indígenas also had to take part. It could be

133

done, it was feasible because we were interested."[3] As Alvarado explains further, "We were conscious of the injustices that existed in our country, and that a struggle for revindication of the rights of indígenas was needed, that we couldn't do it as indígenas [alone], but had to work with Ladinos . . . , conscientious revolutionaries. We had to do it together because that was the history of Guatemala."[4]

Area Maya activists had, in fact, been working in roles supportive of the revolutionary movement since it emerged. Activists in Quetzaltenango explained that they provided fleeing or injured guerrilleros or CUC members with places to hide, often in their own homes. They provided food, money, clothing, medical attention, and transportation. A woman working at a local health post that received aid from the international organization CARE managed to pass some of the products to the guerrilla, her husband recalls, through the Alvarados in Cantel, through a local Catholic parish, and through Emeterio Toj. Others helped in other ways, passing information, for example, between the armed movement and area Mayas.

After the Spanish embassy massacre and the Declaration of Iximché, the revolutionary groups were looking for a more formal commitment from the movimiento indígena and full incorporation. Emeterio Toj believed that the professional class in Quetzaltenango had to be incorporated on its own terms, though, so that they could make the revolutionary struggle their own. He felt it was vital that the guerrilla "incorporate their knowledge, their political power. . . . The strategy was to invite them, and that they would decide how to collaborate, the form in which they could make the revolution theirs."[5]

In practice there was considerable disagreement over the roles activists from the movimiento indígena would play. The EGP was not willing to grant any privileges to professionals, one activist remembered, and expected them to be like everyone else, low-level recruits, a fact that did not go over well with the indigenous movement. There was distrust, Toj explained, and no room for leaders.[6]

Ricardo Cajas describes a meeting in Patzicía when activists met specifically to negotiate the position of Mayas in the revolutionary movement. Jesuits came, and CUC and EGP members. "They came to say that the *cristianos* [those affiliated with the church] were already taking on a role," Cajas remembers, "through [the organization] Justicia y Paz. The *universitarios* are in, labor is in it. . . . Now what part are the indígenas going to take?"[7] Domingo Hernández Ixcoy remembers the meeting as a moment when the EGP took what he believed was a radical and not entirely successful position, demanding that those in the movimiento indígena either formally enter the revolutionary movement or be cut off from it. An intense discussion ensued, Ricardo Cajas recalls. "We indígenas don't necessarily have to stop being indígenas to be revolutionaries," Cajas and others declared. They believed that the CUC and EGP rhetoric like that at Iximché was not enough. "We support revolutionary resistance," they said, "but why won't the Left [more fully] take up ethnic claims? Their [the leftists'] position was that they would discuss it when they took over the government. We said no, we have to discuss it now, before."[8]

They finally agreed that those in the movimiento indígena would go on discussing the matter alone. The others left. There was no one remaining among them from Patzicía, Cajas recalled, to justify their presence in the meeting hall, so they hung banners indicating that they were from APROFAM, a family planning organization, in case the army came. "We were worried about the army," Cajas remembered, "but [also] concerned that the very Left could become our adversary as well." It did not happen that way, he says, but they were worried nonetheless.[9]

Amid growing tensions over leadership roles, the Guatemalan state delivered a severe blow to relations between the revolutionary movement and activists in the movimiento indígena. On the afternoon of July 4, 1981, Emeterio Toj was captured, cornered by four armed men in Quetzaltenango, thrown into a car, and taken to the National Police. Toj was interrogated and beaten, his head covered with a *capucha*, a rubber hood used in torture. He was transferred to the local army barracks for similar interrogation under torture, then moved to the army base in Huehuetenango. There he was kept bound in an excruciating position and placed in a bread oven, he later told human rights investigators. He was repeatedly beaten, given electric shocks, and drugged, kept from eating and sleeping, and threatened with the kidnapping and rape of his wife and daughters.

135

His captors, Toj explained to me, wanted him to reveal the names of his contacts in the Quetzaltenango-area indigenous movement. His defiance was still apparent a quarter century later. He made a vow, he said, that "not a single name of those hermanos I worked with in Los Altos [Quetzaltenango area] would leave my mouth. . . . When you are captured, you no longer matter. What matters is what is outside, the others." His captors asked over and over, he said, "'Where are your compañeros? Who are your compañeros?" That's what they asked me a thousand times." No one in Quetzaltenango was captured, he said, because he revealed no one.[10]

As Toj was recounting this episode, his conflicted feelings about the EGP and the movimiento indígena were obvious. He chose the revolutionary struggle, he explained, because it was the only viable option, but even as an EGP member he remained committed to the indigenous struggle. "The war connected us," he said, speaking of himself and the armed revolutionary movement. "It wasn't a matter of devoted friends [carne y uña], it was done out of necessity. But you knew who your brothers were, it's more genuine," he said, referring to those in Xela. "I've never had the chance to tell them," he added, choking up. It was not for the sake of the EGP that he did it, that he withstood unrelenting torture without talking, but to save those lives.[11]

After fifteen days of torture, Emeterio Toj was allowed to bathe and clean his wounds and was flown to a military base in Guatemala City. There he was again bound, beaten, and questioned daily about his contacts, his activities, and the work of certain Catholic priests. His wounds were infected, and he could no longer stand or sit up. "My body couldn't hold itself up, and I fell . . . to the floor . . . so they began to interrogate me in that position," he told the CEH Truth Commission.[12]

Toj's pride in remaining silent about his contacts in Quetzaltenango is accompanied by a more painful acknowledgment that he did go along with the army's wishes in other ways. The army recognized what they had in their hands. Rather than kill their captive, they saw potential value in keeping Toj alive, and he became their weapon in a round of psychological warfare aiming to divide Mayas in opposition groups from their Ladino counterparts.[13] They untied him and again let him bathe, allowed him to eat regularly, even gave him a radio and let him exercise. They arranged to have him meet several members of the US House of Representatives who were on a fact-finding mission. Toj cooperated when he met these visitors, he said, telling them that he was "formerly in CUC . . . and that he did not want to continue." His answers, he believed, gave the army officials a certain confidence that they had won him over.[14]

In time his captors introduced Emeterio to someone they presented as a "psychologist" who would be in charge of his detention. He was given reading materials on the counterinsurgency struggle, among them a lengthy statement by a former Jesuit priest and EGP member, Father Luis Pellecer.

Father Pellecer had been kidnapped in Guatemala City a month prior to Toj's abduction, beaten unconscious in the street, and taken away by unidentified armed men. The priest suddenly made an appearance 113 days later, September 30, 1981, at a press conference held by the Guatemalan government. Foreign dignitaries were invited, and members of the national and international press were in attendance. The conference was broadcast on television throughout Guatemala and El Salvador shortly after its recording. Pellecer, tended by Guatemala's interior minister and the president's secretary of public relations, read an hour-long formal statement in which he denounced his membership in the EGP and in the Jesuit order, criticized the church for supporting socialism, and condemned liberation theology as promoting violence and being based on hatred of the wealthy. He claimed to have "realized that he had taken a mistaken path" and said he therefore had staged his own kidnapping.[15]

The validity of Pellecer's comments was immediately questioned by members of the Jesuit order in Central America, who claimed that his remarks were clearly made under duress. The fact that he was beaten unconscious during his abduction raised obvious questions about his "self-kidnapping." His behavior and speech in the press conference were abnormal, witnesses noted, he made incorrect statements regarding his own background and education, and evidence of torture was apparent. He appeared, for example, "to have an entirely new set of teeth."[16]

While the press conference was not believable to those close to Pellecer, it was viewed as a success by the government and was a model that Emeterio Toj was expected to emulate. He was forced to watch a tape of it repeatedly, and with his "psychologist," Toj had to write a press conference confession of his own. He was told that if he did not cooperate his family would suffer the consequences.[17]

The government presented Emeterio Toj to the press, diplomatic corps, and "special invitees" gathered at the National Palace on October 22, 1981, with the prisoner once again seated next to the interior minister and the president's secretary of public relations. It was three weeks after the Pellecer event and 110 days after Toj's own capture. Like Pellecer, Emeterio Toj renounced the insurgency and claimed to have voluntarily turned himself in to the army. While Father Pellecer's comments had focused on the Catholic Church and priests' roles in supporting socialism and revolution, Emeterio was given a different but similarly critical task: to stress the issue of racial discrimination and oppression by the revolutionary Left.

137

Emeterio Toj Medrano, with Guatemalan government officials.
Source: *El Gráfico*, October 23, 1981.

The army understood quite keenly, Toj argues, the tensions that underlay relations between the guerrilla armies and the indigenous movement. They apparently sought to use Toj to fan the flames of discord. As Emeterio claims, "They [the government and army] had long been managing the indigenous matter. They knew well . . . how risky it would be to awaken, stir the pueblo. . . . They had found the mechanisms, the way to influence [*mediatizar*] this struggle, and this is not recent, this comes from way back, when they co-opted la Malinche, and they have managed it throughout history, they know, they aren't stupid. The basic soldier might be stupid and maybe the low-level officer, but there are strategists who know very well what they are doing."[18] In particular, Toj asserts, the army recognized the danger of a revolutionary movement that could win over the Maya: "At the high levels, they knew well the implications of the incorporation of the indígena into the struggle. They knew, and they had to prevent it, a thousand ways. One of the ways, as in my case, was to use the same people to put out the fire. . . . They are Machiavellian. They use all the symbols at their disposal to manipulate, to impede the struggles of the pueblo, to kill the hopes of the pueblo, to turn pueblo against pueblo."[19]

139

Emeterio Toj Medrano. Source: *El Gráfico*, October 23, 1981.

To a degree, Emeterio Toj gave his captors what they wanted. The guerrilla armies, he asserted in a statement he read aloud to the press, were "oppressive and discriminatory." He described himself as a founder of CUC, which was characterized in the press conference, surprisingly, in terms starkly differentiated from the EGP. As the army well knew, this was in 1981 a false separation. CUC was portrayed explicitly and benevolently as a Maya organization, "an indigenous movement aiming to dignify the campesinos." Toj described peaceful objectives of the organization, which were *not* to fight against the government, but to find ways to deal with the difficult problems confronting Maya communities. He explicitly mentioned another of CUC's objectives: to end the discrimination that had always existed against the indígena.

In a detailed presentation lasting forty-five minutes, Emeterio went on to condemn and denounce the EGP. He was leaving the revolutionary movement, he announced, because the EGP had infiltrated CUC and was using the organization and its members, diverting them from their path and pushing them into violence against the army. He raised the touchy issue of the guerrillas' inability adequately to supply their Maya recruits and supporters: the campesino was expected to fight against a well-equipped army, but with only sticks and machetes at his disposal. Toj had come to understand, he claimed, that "for the EGP, we indígenas are no more than cannon fodder, for them that is our historic function." He went on to repeat the familiar characterization of the indígena as a peaceful political bystander and none too bright: "We Guatemalan indígenas only want peace, work, and food, give us that and we will make the land produce as we have done until now," he said. Like the captured Voz de Atitlán activists would do less than three weeks later, he described himself as having "limited intellectual capacity," proof of which was that he had gone to primary school only as an adult (though several newspapers took note of his perfect Spanish and "fluid narration"). He exhorted his fellow Mayas not to support subversion, not to accept the offers of subversive groups, which trick them into violence. He finally—as instructed—asked permission to make the same plea to his fellow K'iche's in their own language.[20]

Shortly after the press conference, in early November 1981, the army took Emeterio Toj on a speaking tour. One stop was none other than Santiago Atitlán, where he had to meet with the radio broadcasters of the Voz de Atitlán. He arrived when the "subversives" rounded up by the army in late October were still being kept at the military barracks, some of them in pits dug in the ground. Army officials brought the imprisoned Voz directors—freed momentarily from their holes—together to listen to Toj denounce the guerrilla. One official, he recalls, waved the literacy guide *Pensemos juntos* in the air, calling it subversion. "'Look at the work of the guerrilla! Look at these things that are soiling, dirtying the fatherland!'" Emeterio had to say that he was from CUC, but that he was "repenting." It was difficult for him. "I tried to signal that what I was saying wasn't true," he told me.[21]

Emeterio was taken around by the army to other communities as well, speaking to K'iche' audiences in their own language. He was forced to address residents of Chupol, El Quiché, from a helicopter, broadcasting with a bullhorn a message about cooperating with the army. "This is Emeterio," he had to say to the community, which would have been familiar with his name and voice from his radio work. "Don't be afraid. The army won't do anything." Again, he felt guilty recounting this to me. He tried to speak in monotone, he said, in an unnatural manner so that no one could understand him, or so listeners would sense that he was insincere.[22]

The final strange episode of Emeterio's capture occurred at the end of November. Toj had to speak to his own community of Santa Cruz del Quiché, his army captors decided. He told me that it was the final straw, and that he could not do it. The night before his scheduled trip to Santa Cruz, he escaped from the army barracks in Guatemala City, after nearly five months in captivity. By that time, he said, he was allowed to walk freely around the barracks; guards were accustomed to him. He claims that he saw an opportunity when the guards were not looking and slipped out.[23]

Emeterio boarded a bus and in a panic, he said, tried to decide where to go. (He had a bit of money for bus fare, which he had earned by writing letters for the guards.) He considered contacts from CUC who lived in the capital, friends from the church, and friends from Quetzaltenango. He was unsure where to turn, since he had publicly condemned the EGP. Who would believe he was not a traitor? He remembered where a CUC collaborator had a tire shop, and he went there and asked for money and clothes. The man was shocked to see him, Toj recounted, and was both frightened and skeptical: "*Vos,* they say you're with the army." It was a huge blow. Nonetheless, the CUC contact gave him clothes from Sololá, where indigenous men wear *traje.* He did not want Toj to stay with him, so they sought out another CUC

141

activist living in the capital, the same young woman from Cantel who had read the Declaration of Iximché following the Spanish embassy massacre. She was out of town. Desperate and without options, Emeterio spent the night—barely sleeping, he said—hidden in the tire shop where he had gone in the first place.

The next day, a friend from El Quiché learned of Toj's escape through the CUC network in Guatemala City, and by afternoon Toj made contact with Domingo Hernández Ixcoy. Hernández Ixcoy in turn connected him with Gustavo Meoño, a Ladino who had been part of the student group Cráter and was by then an EGP commander. Soon Toj was with Meoño in the capital. The EGP gave him a gun, he said, and accepted him back "as a friend." Meoño decided—apparently without consulting the rest of the EGP leadership—that they would make a public proclamation to "demoralize" the army by announcing that Toj had been rescued, that the EGP had "achieved the escape of compañero Emeterio Toj Medrano." With Toj's own voice they recorded an announcement and sent it along with a statement from the EGP to radio stations and newspapers in Guatemala City. Thus, Toj himself announced to the nation on December 2 that his rescue was "another demonstration of the incapacity . . . of the army of assassins of [Romeo] Lucas García."[24] "The Popular Revolutionary War," an EGP statement asserted, "had extended practically to the entire country. Our Guerrilla Army of the Poor is striking . . . the repressive forces not only in the mountains and campesino areas far from the capital, but also in the main departmental seats including the capital of the country."[25]

The army countered with an announcement that Toj had come to them freely and had been free to go. Officials said that he had provided valuable information that led to successful counterinsurgency operations and claimed that he had agreed to return to his guerrilla contacts to inform on their activities.[26] They even announced that the infiltration plan had been discovered and that Toj's execution by the EGP was imminent.[27] Yet Toj's escape was a blow to the army, and one former officer recounted to the UN-sponsored Truth Commission that it made many in the military distrustful of the so-called conversions of leftists.[28]

The entire episode was costly not only for Emeterio, but more broadly for connections between revolutionaries and the movimiento indígena. Before Toj's kidnapping, "we were all with him," said one Quetzaltenango-area activist, "here in Xela indígenas had begun to move."[29] Seeing Toj on television in the hands of the army, however, raised alarm. His escape deepened suspicions. And certain of the assertions in his "confession," activists said, rang true. Talks with the guerrilla had been producing considerable resentment. The very type of discrimination Toj condemned in his press conference infuriated activist Mayas; even Toj admitted that for him there was a grain of truth in what he said about racism on the Left.[30] All of the guerrilla commanders were Ladinos and the combatants indígenas, activists complained. In meetings with the guerrilla, they asserted, Ladinos would send Mayas for wood, as if it that were their role. "We said no," one activist explained to me. "In truth, the class struggle will leave us in the same conditions, because they [on the Left] don't value indigenous identity. It was the same as in the universities, everywhere . . . only class struggle, only socioeconomics."[31]

Emeterio Toj "came to us and maintained contacts," said Ricardo Cajas, referring to the period before Toj was captured. "Every time he came to my house, the discussion went like this: 'Emeterio, they are using us. There is no ethnic revindication. Where are indigenous rights, where is the right to indigenous autonomy?'" "We always collaborated," Cajas explains, but the final aim, massive incorporation of Maya activists, was never achieved because they could not get past these issues. "We weren't convinced that it was a struggle of indígenas," he said. The Left could incorporate indigenous campesinos but had much more difficulty with "organized groups, groups that were questioning, discussing" the arguments and shortcomings of the would-be revolution.[32]

When they were forced to choose sides, said Domingo Hernández Ixcoy, a majority of Mayas in the movimiento indígena in fact joined the efforts of CUC and the armed revolution. "[But] those who did not trust CUC left the Coordinadora," which then fell apart. He felt that the CUC/EGP ultimatum had been a mistake. Rather than respect the autonomy of the racially focused movement and forge alliances, the revolutionary Left cut them off.[33]

A broad collection of popular, indigenous, and revolutionary organizations did take steps to join forces in 1981, in particular through a group called the January 31 Popular Front (FP-31). Leaders including Domingo Hernández Ixcoy helped found FP-31, naming it for those killed at the embassy on that date the year before.[34] But real unity proved elusive and

143

repression devastating.[35] Hernández Ixcoy said that ultimately the Left turned on the movimiento indígena as traitors. They preferred "indios who didn't think," Domingo said, "indios who didn't question."[36]

▨▨▨ A Pueblo Armed and Divided

The splits between the movimiento indígena and the Ladino-led guerrilla armies have been the subject of rumor, intrigue, and suspicion. Mayas estranged from the Ladino-led guerrilla formed several small revolutionary groups, partially armed and largely or entirely made up of Maya leaders and members, many with experience in the EGP or ORPA. Accusations circulated about guerrilla reprisals, including executions, against those Mayas who formed separate guerrilla groups or factions. They remain rumors, unsubstantiated by the UN and Catholic Church truth commissions.

In various guises—Nuestro Movimiento, Movimiento Indígena Revolucionario, Movimiento Indio Tojil, Movimiento Revolucionario del Pueblo-Ixim (a group that split from ORPA, and not to be confused with the periodical *Ixim*)—revolutionary-minded Mayas with roots in racially focused organizing called for an end to both exploitation of the poor and discrimination against Mayas as the key to liberating Guatemala. One without the other, they argued, would result in an incomplete revolution. Observers have noted, however, that like the Ladino-led guerrilla movement, revolutionary Maya-only groups generally failed to give both of these forms of oppression their due. "They never tackled the question of class in its full dimension," says Domingo Hernández Ixcoy, "just as CUC mentioned the ethnic question, but never developed it."[37]

The Movimiento Indígena Revolucionario, or MIR, seems to have been borne out of the conflicts that arose in Patzicía, when those distrustful of CUC and the EGP broke away from the Ladino-led Left and formed their own revolutionary organization. As Ricardo Cajas explains, MIR "was not very well known, but it was our effort to say, okay, if the popular organizations have an armed guerrilla wing, then we will have an armed guerrilla wing as indígenas. . . . In the movement MIR we said, 'We are going to die, but with an indigenous voice, not used.'"[38] Miguel Alvarado describes MIR as having members from the departments of Quetzaltenango and Chimaltenango, some from Huehuetenango and San Marcos. "But there weren't many of us . . . , perhaps a hundred people in the western highlands," about one-fifth of them armed, he said. According to Alvarado, several members had belonged to ORPA, and they had a good working relationship with the group.[39]

MIR and other splinter groups, Alvarado claims, were seeking equality, not vengeance of Mayas against Ladinos. "What we sought was a better standard of living for all Guatemalans, indígenas or Ladinos, a relation of equality," he said. "With equality, discrimination . . . would disappear."[40] This idea, in fact, was not that different from that expressed in statements by the EGP. But what differed significantly was leaders' definition of equality.

The Left did not look upon the all-Maya groups favorably, notes Alvarado. In his words, they "always saw us with 'bad eyes.'" They wanted indígenas to participate with them, he said, but on their terms. "For them, the indigenous struggle was put aside." That was what concerned Mayas, he said, what many disagreed with. "They [Mayas] left these [guerrilla] organizations because they seemed not to meet their goals for a complete indigenous revindication. So we were seen as counterrevolutionaries, because we believed in our own indigenous struggle. . . . That was basically the essence of the problems."[41]

Miguel Alvarado had been in the urban front of the EGP and the urban front of ORPA, he said, but left those organizations for an all-indigenous movement. "What destroyed everything," Alvarado said, "was that they always gave more opportunities to Ladinos . . . , didn't base assignments or opportunities on merit. For example, a Ladino would come from the capital, who knew nothing of the pueblos, the *aldeas* [small villages] in the heart of the struggle. . . . When they arrived, they would inevitably be made leaders, superiors, occupy privileged posts without knowing [the region]. This bothered, disgusted many indigenous combatants. . . . It was the downfall of everything. Indígenas deserted . . . because there was no justice."[42]

Writing in the early 1980s, Guatemalan academic and former EGP member Arturo Arias published an account of the development of indigenous movements in the 1970s. In it he directed considerable animosity at Miguel Alvarado, whom he labeled the "frontrunner" of the "orthodox indigenistas."[43] Arias portrayed the "indigenous bourgeoisie," personified by Alvarado, as standing in the way of the revolution and suggested that ties existed between them and the US Central Intelligence Agency, which at the time was courting indigenous groups in Nicaragua to gain

145

their support against the Sandinista revolution. These perceptions were shared by others in the EGP.[44] When I asked Alvarado about Arias's characterization of the indigenous movement, he diplomatically noted that "as a beginning, as one of the first documents to deal with this theme, [Arias's work] is very good. But as an accurate document? . . . They portrayed us as counterrevolutionaries, that was completely false. It was perhaps more a subjective fear of many Ladino revolutionary leaders than a real danger."[45]

As Ricardo Cajas saw it, the misrepresentations and fears went two ways. "I think many [Maya] leaders at the time were more afraid of the guerrilla than the army. The guerrilla knew where we were, we had been collaborating with them. The army . . . didn't know much about us, since we had kept the Coordinadora in secrecy."[46] "We wanted to make known that we weren't against the revolution," Cajas said, but wanted to insist at the same time that Mayas not be used or denied their identity as they saw it. Discrimination was a pattern on the Right and the Left, he insisted. The guerrilla "wasn't cruel like the army, but had the same tendency" of discrimination against Mayas.[47]

A Maya Republic?

Relations between the Ladino-led insurgency and revolutionaries within the movimiento indígena went from bad to worse when an organization calling itself the Movimiento Indio Tojil, in alliance with the Movimiento Revolucionario del Pueblo-Ixim, published a document in the early 1980s entitled "Guatemala: From the Centralist Bourgeois Republic to the Popular Federal Republic."[48] Its (anonymous) authors expressed the familiar argument for a multisided revolutionary struggle against oppression of the poor and of Mayas. "A revolution cannot be selective," they wrote, "where some forms of oppression are destroyed and others conserved, where some are considered urgent and others deferrable."[49] But what was new and radical about the Tojil document—and vehemently denounced by activists on the Left—was an explicit assertion of Maya nationhood and a call for political independence: "Guatemala is not a nation but a society, . . . an institutionalized collectivity kept unified by the coercive force of state institutions. . . . Guatemala . . . is a bourgeois authority that dominates a multiplicity of nationalities and claims to be

146

a nation—'single and indivisible.'"[50] For the pueblo maya, they asserted, "the 'Guatemalan nation,' in the sense of community, does not exist; if it does exist, they do not consider it theirs, nor do they feel themselves included in it, but rather consider themselves its victim."[51]

A revolution, the Tojil document asserted, had to reverse Ladino bourgeois economic and political domination. "For the pueblo indio the revolutionary struggle is simultaneously social and national," they argued. A revolution had to attack not just the present government and its capitalist system, but the centralized state structure itself.[52] They called for the establishment of a federalist system with a semiautonomous Maya nation or nations within Guatemala; whether it would include one Maya nation or a plurality of naciones—K'iche', Mam, Q'eqchi', and so forth— was left somewhat open. But their preference for unified Maya action was apparent: in asserting a "panindiana" identity, they argued, by speaking in terms of "'nuestro pueblo,' 'nuestra gente,' 'nuestros connacionales,'" they could take colonialist terms, "apolitical denominations given by their oppressors," and infuse them with political content.[53] Their proposal: a Maya Popular Republic in partnership with a Ladino republic, equal partners in a Guatemalan state.[54]

Technically, the relationship proposed by the Tojiles amounted not to separation from the Guatemalan state, but semiautonomy for Mayas and Ladinos within that state. A total separation would not be advisable nor feasible given the economic and political realities of Guatemala, they argued, nor could it be the basis for political stability. They characterized their proposal as a "viable and moderate" alternative.[55] Each republic would have legislative and administrative autonomy in the areas of economics, culture, and politics; they would share common responsibilities relating to the military, finances, and foreign policy. All would be Guatemalan citizens; unity of the country would be assured by "agreements and compromises freely consented to by both parties, and never again by the force of one and the subjugation of the other."[56] The Tojiles argued that this was the formula for political stability because it maintained ethnic diversity within a single decentralized state.[57]

It is not difficult to see why other activists were alarmed by the proposal, with its assertion of distinct Ladino and Maya republics. Moreover, the integrity of the single state of Guatemala did seem to be at issue for the future: the Tojiles indicated a desire eventually to achieve greater unity between their republic of "Mayas of the East" (in Guatemala) and the "Mayas of the West" (in Mexico). "That is to say that the Mayas

147

of Guatemala consider it their historic destiny to be more connected to their *connacionales mayas* who fall under the jurisdiction of other States."[58] Despite these intentions, the paper set out to convince Ladino revolutionaries that the proposed relationship was in their interest. The Tojiles argued that just like Mayas, the *proletariado ladino*—Ladino urban and rural workers—had an ambiguous relationship to the "Guatemalan nation" as it existed, since that system exploited, repressed, and marginalized them. It had to be recognized, they insisted, that the claim of a single Guatemalan nation, which was in fact a bourgeois nation, was key to the capitalist system that revolutionaries struggled against. It was up to revolutionary Ladinos to "revise their traditional models of interpretation and organization of Guatemalan society," to envision, if they could, a nation *not* dominated by Ladinos.[59]

The Tojil document addressed the positions of the Ladino-led guerrilla armies explicitly:

> There are some revolutionary organizations . . . that acknowledge the "ethnic and cultural" complexity of the country, but that still are not clear regarding the type of national order that would reign in the postrevolutionary society. These organizations seem to have surmounted the bourgeois colonialist version of Guatemalan reality, but due to an ideological block they suffer, or . . . due to their colonial interests that they must defend, they return over and over to . . . racial discrimination, cultural oppression; they also return to solutions in terms of "necessary national integration of the indigenous ethnicities."[60]

The Tojil position wholly rejected that integration. Furthermore, it contested the Left's characterization of the Tojiles and others in indigenous movements as counterrevolutionary, by setting out an alternative definition of socialism: "The indios believe that socialism cannot be reduced to only the socialization of the means of production, but also state structures . . . . [They] also believe that socialism does not consist in socializing particular forms of life and in the standardization of certain national characters, but in the recognition and free expression of said differences. . . . The mode of socialist thinking of the pueblo indio differs from the mode of socialist thinking of the pueblo Ladino."[61]

It was urgent to deal with these issues, they argued. Otherwise, "sooner or later, there will be a fight among socialists." They argued that it would pit those like the Tojiles, who sought a new state structure, against the Ladino-led revolutionaries who wanted to overthrow one centralist state but implant another. The bourgeois Ladino Right, they asserted, wanted the indio only as a symbol of national folklore and persecuted him culturally and as a class. "At the moment," they continued, "it appears also that the Ladino Left . . . wants him as a proletarian class . . . and uses his revolutionary potential; but for lack of historical vision and political myopia, it negates him and obstructs him as a nation with a right to self-determination."[62]

The document ended with the following notes: "Some indios will find the present document to be very daring/impudent [atrevido] and will oppose its content. But their opposition is the same as that of the Roman slaves who trembled and protested the announcement that they would lose their chains and their condition as slaves." The opposition of Ladinos, on the other hand, was to be expected. "Their opposition is the same as that of the bourgeoisie when the proletariat demands that they disappear as a dominant class and be reborn. . . . In other words, for the Ladino to accept these demands, he would practically have to stop being Ladino-colonizer and transform himself into a new social and national being."[63]

The Tojiles considered themselves to be revolutionaries. Moreover, they criticized Maya activists only concerned with culture: "At the present, there are various 'studied' indios who approach/interpret [abordan] the pueblo indio in the same terms as the colonizer and repeat the same mistakes": they "obfuscate their political nature," reducing their identity to only "one of its aspects (culture, history, language, etc.)." The Tojiles offered a class-based critique of those indígenas who had "fully assimilated the colonial bourgeois interpretation of the Guatemalan reality," criticizing students, professionals, and businessmen who benefited from cozy relations with the bourgeois Ladino state.[64]

149

The debut of the Tojil position is remembered by interviewees—without exception—as something radical. It stands out in their memories and serves as a marker in their attempts to reconstruct this history. As its authors predicted, the Tojil position was not universally embraced as a viable option by activist Mayas, although parts of it had appeal.[65] Arguably the importance of the document relates not to the popularity of its proposals, but to the fact that its publication allowed the revolutionary Left to portray—wrongly—the explosive idea of a Maya "nation" as the goal of all activist Mayas who disagreed with them.

The fight between the Tojiles and the Ladino-led Left came sooner rather than later. Leaders, including Mayas such as Pablo Ceto, attacked the Tojil paper.[66] Ceto, like Arturo Arias, accused its authors of being counterrevolutionaries tied to the CIA. The Tojil document did mention the indigenous struggle in Nicaragua and the problems that indígenas experienced with the Sandinistas, who, they wrote, "completely ignored everything related to the fundamental political and cultural rights of the indigenous and black ethnic groups, despite the fact that they had been fighting . . . against the Somoza dictatorship."[67] But the accusations of links between the Guatemalan indigenous movements and the CIA are almost certainly unfounded. The movimiento indígena expressed extreme anti-US sentiment, condemning US economic imperialism and involvement in Guatemalan counterinsurgency.

To the end, many activists in the movimiento indígena felt themselves part of the revolutionary opposition, although their battle lines were at times drawn not only against the government, but against the guerrilla as well, at least politically. Before publication of the Tojil paper, the Ladino-led revolutionary Left wanted the movimiento indígena to join its struggle, but could not accept the leadership terms and autonomy Maya leaders insisted upon. After the separatist sentiment emerged in the Tojil document, the Ladino-led revolutionary movements turned fully against the Maya revolutionaries. Domingo Hernández Ixcoy notes the tragic irony of what happened next: while division plagued the opposition, the state made no differentiation among them. The army did not ask whether they were Ladinos or indígenas, EGP, ORPA, or Movimiento Tojil, clasistas or culturalistas; repression against them was indiscriminate. As Hernández Ixcoy put it, the state crushed them all.[68]

150

▓▓▓ Counterinsurgency, 1978–1983

The UN-sponsored Truth Commission in Guatemala wrote that state violence spiraled in the early 1980s until it reached levels that were "unimaginable." The strategy of the Romeo Lucas García regime (1978–1982) was to "eliminate" the social movement, urban and rural.[69] A military zone was created in each of Guatemala's departments, and all over the country increased repression crippled activism. We have seen that the army shut down Mayan language radio schools or forced them to abandon "antigovernment" programming and arrested, tortured, and disappeared their directors. It crushed or co-opted cooperatives and killed their leaders. Campesino organizing was forced underground. Government repression and violence led many Catholic priests to leave their posts. By 1982, there were only thirty-eight priests left in the diocese of Sololá (where Santiago Atitlán is located), a drop from sixty just three years earlier. The entire diocese of El Quiché closed its doors in 1980 due to severe repression and the killing of several priests. The total number of priests in Guatemala fell by half in two years, with six hundred priests in 1979 falling to three hundred in 1981.[70]

The Maryknoll Apostolic Center and the Center of Integral Development that had operated for ten years in Huehuetenango were subjected to surveillance, harassment, and violence. Lists of local activists began circulating in 1976, and in 1977 state forces started to disappear and kill leaders attending their programs. Mounting violence forced the Maryknolls to close the doors of their centers in late 1979. According to Father Jensen, Maryknoll estimates that of the fifteen hundred students who passed through its programs, state forces killed a staggering four hundred to five hundred in counterinsurgency terror.[71] As state violence decimated the ranks of educated Mayas, Instituto Indígena Santiago alumni were also prominent among the dead and disappeared. A Santiago publication expressed the institute's understanding of violence directed at its own: "Many young alumni of the Instituto Indígena Santiago were assassinated for their high level of consciousness of the reality their people live and for their commitment to their communities."[72]

The army sacked the office and student quarters of Maryknoll's Centro Indígena in the capital, accusing its affiliates of links to the guerrilla EGP. Soldiers stole files containing information about community organizers, recalls Father Jensen, who was then head of the center. Following the Spanish embassy massacre, he feared that it was becoming more a danger than a sanctuary. The army kidnapped one staff member, and another went into hiding. The Maryknolls surreptitiously destroyed the center's remaining files and closed the house in the spring of 1980. Jensen himself fled the country. Its founder, Father Jim Curtin, estimated that more than eighty people associated with the Centro Indígena were assassinated.[73]

When General Efraín Ríos Montt took over the government (1982 –1983), authorities claimed that repression was lessening, and it was marginally true in Guatemala City. But the army was killing far greater numbers in the countryside. The army intensified its scorched-earth

151

Civil patrollers with prisoner, Chichicastenango, El Quiché. Photo by Jean-Marie Simon.

campaign, completely destroying hundreds of villages and displacing hundreds of thousands of rural residents. The army militarized the coun-tryside to an extent previously unseen, establishing mandatory (though officially voluntary) "civil self-defense patrols"—antiguerrilla militias—in nearly every Maya community and requiring their participation in rural terror. The army's own figures indicate that by the end of 1983, 1.3 million Maya men took part in the patrols, nearly 17 percent of the Guatemalan population.[74] The army resettled Mayas from destroyed com-munities—those who were captured or turned themselves in—into army-controlled "development poles" and "model villages," often on the very ashes of their ruined pueblos. It was a concerted and effective effort to "drain the sea" in which the insurgents swam.[75]

While aiming to achieve firm control of the countryside, Ríos Montt pursued a public relations campaign regarding Mayas, aimed at national and international opinion. He created a Council of State purportedly to address issues of Guatemalan "national identity." The council had thirty-four members, with ten Mayas (and ten alternates) from eleven ethnic groups

152

included as "ethnic councilors." Ríos Montt and the "ethnic councilors" took part in Día de la Raza celebrations in 1982.[76] He impressed President Ronald Reagan as being "totally dedicated to democracy in Guatemala," and Reagan famously complained to a reporter that Ríos Montt, the focus of intense criticism from human rights groups, was getting a "bum rap."[77] The Guatemalan Council of Bishops disagreed: "Never in our national history," they wrote in May 1982, "have such grave extremes been reached. The assassinations now fall into the category of genocide."[78]

May All Rise Up?

When I go to political gatherings and meet compañeros again, we say to each other, you're still alive! But while we're embracing we look over each other's shoulders. Is someone seeing this?

—Q'eqchi' woman activist, 2002[1]

The politics of opposition and counterinsurgency shifted in the 1980s and early 1990s as opponents of the state took their offensive underground, and in some cases, to the international level. As they did so, the gulf widened between the main guerrilla armies, joined in the umbrella Guatemalan National Revolutionary Unity, or URNG, and revolutionaries in the Maya-only movements, especially the sector advocating nationalist separation.[2] Meanwhile, the Guatemalan state and army, secure in their grip on the countryside, marched down "constitutional corridors" and professed allegiance to democracy.[3]

Under civilian president Vinicio Cerezo, who came to power in 1986, the Guatemalan government and a weakened URNG faced each other across a negotiating table. Negotiations stopped and started repeatedly for the next seven years with little progress, but in the mid-1990s, preliminary peace accords were finally drafted with the mediation of the United Nations. With civilian input channeled through a newly created Guatemalan Assembly of Civil Society (ASC), the parties hammered out an official end to thirty-six years of civil war in 1996. One of the agreements—the Accord on Identity and the Rights of Indigenous Peoples—dealt explicitly with Maya rights to official recognition, freedom from discrimination, the use of language and dress, and a degree of autonomy at the local level. Yet a national referendum on legislation to implement the agreement went down in defeat three years later.[4] The post-accords "peace" has been fraught with unresolved

155

conflicts, and political activism continued to be met by state repression. As the epigraph suggests, legacies of the past—histories of activism, mixed with the trauma of violence and loss, fear and distrust—remain a tangible part of the present.

▨▨▨ Activism on the International Stage

The intensification of counterinsurgency from 1981 through 1983 was brutally effective, both in urban Guatemala and in the countryside. By certain measures, state terror succeeded: it largely disarticulated the broad and loosely unified opposition movements ignited by outrage against the Panzós and Spanish embassy massacres. In 1981 public protest became prohibitively dangerous, and the documentary record from 1981 to 1984 is virtually absent all but the most radical opposition voices, those who opted for revolutionary movements. Even clandestine organizing became unviable within Guatemala. The Guatemalan army destroyed the revolutionary movements' "safe houses" in the capital and relentlessly attacked, in massacre after massacre, the communities believed to support them in the highlands. Most guerrilla leaders fled to exile in Mexico and Nicaragua. Guatemala's revolutionary offensive was waged after 1982 primarily at the international level, in alliances with what were known as solidarity movements in Europe and the United States and in the international media.

The war had reached a stalemate: the guerrillas could not effectively fight the army, and the army could not wholly defeat them, at least not politically. In that context, polarization among organized Mayas was palpable. This was the case for Mayas involved in the multiple revolutionary movements in the early 1980s, and when repression eased somewhat, between Mayas who worked alongside the revolutionary Left in human rights organizations and those who pursued a safer agenda focused on cultural identity. In some respects, the disagreements reflected familiar points of contention from the 1970s, but this time the context and outcome were different: where state violence had at crucial moments pushed activist Mayas together in the earlier period, a politics shaped by near defeat drove them farther apart.

In the early 1980s, the Ladino-led revolutionary Left sharpened its criticism of the Maya-only opposition movements. At the same time, however, they adjusted to changed circumstances by giving more prominence to Maya-specific issues. The shift (which exasperated the Maya-only movements) was more than opportunism, no doubt linked to the realities of state genocide against Mayas. At the same time, however, URNG leaders were aware of growing international concerns about indigenous rights. It is safe to assume that guerrilla leaders were cognizant of the visual and emotional power in international circles of a revolutionary struggle with an indigenous face. In search of material and political support abroad, the Ladino-led guerrilla armies emphasized the state's targeting of the pueblo maya and focused attention on Maya support for and participation in the revolutionary movement.[5]

I, Rigoberta Menchú

Rigoberta Menchú Tum was the Maya opposition figure who became most well known in international solidarity circles in the early 1980s. Menchú was in her early twenties at the time, a K'iche' from Chimel, Uspantán, an area of El Quiché with considerable campesino mobilization—revolutionary and otherwise—and, not coincidentally, extreme state repression.[6] Menchú was part of the area's radicalizing catechist movement of the 1970s and a CUC activist, along with the rest of her family. (The Menchú Tum family was torn apart by the violence of the late 1970s and early 1980s: army soldiers tortured and killed her brother in late 1979; her father Vicente Menchú was among the CUC activists burned to death in the Spanish embassy massacre in January 1980; her mother was captured, raped, and killed less than three months later; and two of her sisters joined the EGP as guerrilla combatants.) Menchú kept working with CUC in Guatemala through 1980, helping to organize a massive strike among coastal sugar and cotton workers in February and widespread mobilization in the capital on May 1 (Labor Day) of that year, and the next. She finally fled to exile in Mexico.

From Mexico in late 1981, Menchú along with Domingo Hernández Ixcoy traveled to Paris with a delegation of the January 31 Popular Front (FP-31).[7] In Paris Menchú met anthropologist Elisabeth Burgos-Debray, who recorded her testimony and compiled the famous narrative *I, Rigoberta Menchú: An Indian Woman in Guatemala*, first published in Spanish in 1983 and in English in 1984. The original title in Spanish is more apt, since Menchú in the narrative powerfully recounts her path toward participation in CUC and in the multiethnic revolutionary opposition: *Me llamo Rigoberta Menchú y así me nació la conciencia*,

157

Labor Day, May 1, 1980. Banners proclaim that "the woman is present in the people's struggle" and tally the dead in Panzós and in the Ixcán, northern El Quiché. Anonymous. Source: Dutch Committee in Solidarity with the People of Guatemala, in Fototeca Guatemala, CIRMA.

"My Name Is Rigoberta Menchú and This Is How My Consciousness Was Born."

Controversy about the Menchú narrative emerged (mostly in the United States) in 1999 when anthropologist David Stoll published a critique charging that in the autobiography Menchú misrepresented certain events.[8] While the episodes of violence and brutality Menchú narrated did in fact happen, Stoll conceded, she was not always an eyewitness. These accusations set off a firestorm of criticism ("Rigoberta Lies!") with detractors expressing shock and dismay that in recounting her story Menchú could have had a political agenda. Criticisms focused on Menchú's connection to the revolutionary Left, particularly CUC and the EGP, and reduced the memoir to guerrilla propaganda.

Menchú was quite candid in the narrative about her connections to the revolutionary Left, though she contrasted the choices made by her sisters to go to "the mountains" (combat) with her own decision to "organize the people." "My life does not belong to me," she said, "I've decided to offer it to a cause. They can kill me at any time, but let it be when I'm fulfilling a mission, so I'll know that my blood will not be shed in vain. . . . The world I live in is so evil, so bloodthirsty. . . . The only road open to me is our struggle, the just war." She frequently spoke of a collectivity when referring to the Guatemalan conflict: "We opted for the just war." She described the *people's* struggle, the *people's* armies, the *people's* handmade weapons. She then clarified the relationship between revolutionary combat and political organizing: "We all contribute in different ways, but we are all working for the same objective."[9]

A reading of *I, Rigoberta Menchú* clearly reveals Menchú to be more than a symbolic voice for the armed Left. Greg Grandin argues that what makes the text so compelling is the story of her own "progress into political awareness [as it] merges with the revolutionary momentum of society as a whole." He observes that Menchú's "engagement with ideas clearly outstripped whatever orientation she might have received from organizers. . . . It is . . . rooted in her personal grappling with the dilemmas of history and her own particular experience of power and powerlessness." Widespread social mobilization becomes more understandable, in fact, when we consider how people like Menchú and a radicalizing liberation theology shaped oppositional organizing in Guatemala. As Grandin writes, what made the era's organizing "so potent a threat in a place as inhumane as Guatemala in the 1970s was not just its concern with social justice but its insistence on individual human dignity. This combination of solidarity and insurgent individuality is the heart of Menchú's memoir."[10]

Without detracting from that individuality and Menchú's unique role in the history of oppositional organizing in Guatemala, I do want to consider at the same time how *I, Rigoberta Menchú* fit with the goals of the revolutionary Left.[11] Menchú's gripping account, read around the world, seems to have added credibility to the guerrillas' claim to represent a Maya struggle for justice.[12] The work also gives a glimpse, especially in its odd introduction by Burgos-Debray, of tensions developing among Maya activists abroad.

The actual degree of EGP involvement in producing *I, Rigoberta Menchú* is somewhat unclear. Arturo Arias recounts that Menchú's talents as a narrator were noted by an ORPA contact, who mentioned her to the EGP representative in Paris, Arturo Taracena.[13] Taracena in turn arranged introductions between Menchú and Burgos-Debray, a Venezuelan and the wife of leftist intellectual Régis Debray. (At least part of the taping of Menchú's testimony took place in Taracena's apartment.) The manuscript was apparently approved by an EGP commander, but there is disagreement as to which one it was: Burgos-Debray claims that the commander in chief of the EGP, known as Rolando Morán, approved the manuscript, while Taracena asserts it was Gustavo Meoño.[14] Recall that Meoño was the same EGP commander who orchestrated the announcement of Emeterio Toj's EGP "rescue" in 1981. In at least one instance, the EGP imprint on Menchú's narrative—most likely Meoño's—is unmistakable. As I reread the narrative after conducting the research for this book, a passage leapt off the page: when Menchú was describing her father's membership in CUC, she mentioned Emeterio Toj by name. "My father was with many compañeros," said Menchú, "with Emeterio Toj Medrano and others who've since been murdered, and some who are still alive."[15] With CUC leaders in hiding in the early 1980s, singling out Toj by name was a dangerous move that would have been inexplicable if not for the fact that the EGP was (untruthfully) claiming to have rescued him from the army's clutches just months before.[16] Burgos-Debray later acknowledged that the work was "supposed to help the movement in solidarity with Guatemala's guerrillas."[17]

Menchú's task, then, was to make the Guatemalan conflict understandable to an international readership and to elicit empathy and support for the revolution. This is something that she and EGP leaders would likely have agreed on, though none of the parties could have expected the enormous impact her story would have.

As for the introduction to the text, Burgos-Debray speaks for herself rather than for Menchú. Heavy-handed, ironic, and misleading, it is also quite revealing of its author's (and perhaps the EGP's) views on ethnicity and Maya-focused organizing. Burgos-Debray begins by leaning on familiar and patronizing interpretations of Mayas when presenting Menchú to readers: "The first thing that struck me about her was her open, almost childlike smile. Her face was round and moonshaped. Her expression was as guileless as that of a child and a smile hovered permanently on her lips."[18] But readers soon got the message that despite appearances, this was a mobilized, articulate indígena: "I later discovered that her youthful air soon faded when she had to talk about the dramatic events that had overtaken her family. . . . I very soon became aware of her desire to talk and of her ability to express herself verbally."[19]

Menchú began her own narrative by positioning herself as an indigenous woman, but also as part of a community of "all poor Guatemalans" engaged in a multiethnic struggle for justice. "I'd like to stress that it's not only *my* life, it's also the testimony of my people," she said. "The important thing is that what has happened to me has happened to many other people too: My story is the story of all poor Guatemalans. My personal experience is the reality of a whole people."[20] In the text's introduction, however, Burgos-Debray characterized Menchú as a spokeswoman for the indigenous population. It is a strategic but problematic framing, and Burgos-Debray seems to have felt the need to clarify for readers which Mayas could and could not legitimately play such a role, differentiating Menchú from those advocating a separate Maya struggle. As she does so, though, Burgos-Debray claims for Menchú the basic demands voiced by Mayas in the organizations she herself is condemning:

> Rigoberta Menchú is . . . issuing a manifesto on behalf of an ethnic group. . . . As a popular leader, her one ambition is to devote her life to overthrowing the relations of domination and exclusion which characterize *internal colonialism*. She and her people are taken into account only when their labour power is needed; culturally, they are discriminated against and rejected. Rigoberta Menchú's struggle is a struggle *to modify and break the bonds that link her and her people to the Ladinos.* . . . She is in no sense advocating a racial struggle, much less refusing to accept the irreversible fact of the existence of the Ladinos. She is fighting for the recognition of her culture, for acceptance of the fact that it is different and *for her people's rightful share of power.*[21]

Again, these aims as expressed by Burgos-Debray shared much in common with those of members of various Maya opposition and revolutionary groups that likewise stressed problems of "internal colonialism" and discrimination, and called for Mayas to have a role in shaping society and a degree of power. Yet the editor simplified the positions of the array of Maya opposition groups that existed in the early 1980s (and were at the time lobbying for support in Europe), focusing exclusively on the most radical, the Tojiles, and their call for Maya autonomy. She warned readers that these "indigenists" were not to be confused with true revolutionaries—the four guerrilla groups of the URNG, the families of the disappeared, and the trade unions: "The Indians [read "indigenists"] too have their European supporters, many of whom are anthropologists. I do not want to start a polemic and I do not want to devalue any one form of activism; I am simply stating the facts."[22] Of course, Burgos-Debray was not starting a polemic in 1982, but continuing one with a decade-long history. The "facts" were a simplified version of more nuanced positions and complex historical relationships among organized Mayas.

"A part to the indígena"

It was easy to portray (all) Maya revolutionaries outside the Ladino-led URNG as separatists because activists advocating separatism *were* prominent on the international scene, writing, establishing links to solidarity organizations in Europe and the United States, and searching for funds. From the materials I could gather, it appears that the Tojil line of argument was amply and disproportionately represented at the international level. The German NGO Infostelle recently donated its archive from the period to the research institution CIRMA in Antigua, Guatemala. Among the collection are position papers similar to those by the Movimiento Indio Tojil discussed in the last chapter, but with names that vary; sometimes they claim to represent the K'iche' ethnic group, other times the pueblo maya or *nación maya* collectively: the "Maya-Quiché Nations" from the "Land of the Maya-Quichés" (1982); the "Movimiento Indio of Guatemala," writing from the "Land of the Mayas" (1983); and simply the "Movimiento Indio" (1983).[23]

The materials illustrate how their authors tried to position themselves internationally; they also reveal tensions between the Maya-only revolutionary groups and the URNG. One document apparently from 1982 (as indicated in a margin note) argues that financial support from international solidarity groups should flow directly to Mayas rather than exclusively to the four armies of the URNG. The authors asserted that it was Mayas who were being massacred, who were suffering, who were being attacked as "subversives." The authors pointed to the problems of discrimination suffered at the hands of the Ladino Left and claimed to be shut off from access to resources. They insisted that they did not advocate cutting aid to the "four groups of the Left," but that solidarity groups should also "give a part to the indígena, who has neither voice nor vote."[24]

Other correspondence details ongoing violence in indigenous regions of the country, while simultaneously sending a message about the existence of

162

Maya "nations," as the Tojiles asserted. Unlike most human rights reports of the period, these accounts prominently included victims' ethnic identification and at the same time, the "nations" to which they belonged: "*nación Cakchiquel*," "*nación Mam*," "*naciones Kekchí y Pocomchí*."[25] Another document echoed the Tojil argument that Maya socialism is different from Ladino socialism, calling for "the reconstruction . . . of Maya socialism." Again a separate Maya nation was explicitly on the agenda of the Movimiento Indio, vital to its continued existence: "¡Patria Maya o Exterminio!" (A Maya Nation or Extermination!)[26]

The URNG and Mayas advocating autonomy at this point were in direct contention, not just theoretically, but over political and financial support. The Tojil demands were completely unacceptable to revolutionaries in the URNG, who ostensibly fought for the creation of a new state; they would not acquiesce to that state being divided in two. Support for Maya-specific groups, moreover, could directly cut into their own sources of funding. The URNG assailed the Maya revolutionaries as "counterrevolutionary." Like Burgos-Debray in her portrayal of "indigenists," they homogenized all Maya-only groups and reduced their demands to just one: a Maya nation. That "nation" was not a legitimate demand, asserted one of the URNG groups, the PGT, because Mayas had never been unified: "The large Indian mass is constituted by various small minorities, whose particular most distinctive feature consists of a multitude of languages . . . so fragmented that we cannot identify [them] as a nation. . . . They were neither unified nor communal in the past, much less so after the ravages of conquest. . . . [T]hey can only be unified effectively into Guatemalan society through the revolution."[27] The EGP conceded the need for ethnic consciousness but continued to argue that ethnic-specific claims would endanger the central struggle, class conflict. Without being fully grounded in "revolutionary class politics," they warned, "the revolutionary process runs the risk of becoming distorted, turning into a four-centuries-late liberation struggle which today can have no revolutionary content. *The main danger is that the national-ethnic factors will burst forth in detriment of class factors.*"[28]

The rigid posturing both of the Tojiles and the URNG had the effect in the 1980s of nearly eliminating middle ground, silencing those Mayas who called for a revolution that would grant sufficient attention both to class exploitation and discrimination against Mayas. This latter position, though it had been voiced in various forms in the 1970s, was only expressed again in the mid-1980s after multiple fractures within the EGP.

163

Into the Breach

The EGP fractures of the 1980s were related to what many saw as its failed strategy in the western highlands, which left area Mayas unprotected and vulnerable to army massacre. The high-level guerrilla commanders were mostly in exile in Nicaragua in 1982, but two who remained in Guatemala—a Ladino known as Camilo and the EGP's only high-level Maya commander, an Ixil whose nom de guerre was Milton—accused the leadership of abandoning the people. They formally split from the EGP and formed an autonomous organization. (Both were killed in 1983.)[29] A second major rift developed between the National Directorate and EGP leader Mario Payeras, who also criticized the EGP leadership's rigidity and failure to change course after the massive loss of civilian life at the hands of the state following a "triumphalist" guerrilla offensive in the early 1980s. When Payeras was ordered back to Guatemala in January 1984 (a move he believed may have been a setup for assassination), he and numerous others left the EGP. The splinter group became know as the "contingent" and in 1986 formed Octubre Revolucionario, "Revolutionary October."[30]

Most of the men and women who broke from the EGP with Payeras were Ladinos, but Domingo Hernández Ixcoy and four Maya women also went with him.[31] (At the time of the Payeras rupture, Rigoberta Menchú was in Guatemala with the internal refugee settlements called Communities of Population in Resistance, or CPRs, and she did not join the "contingent.")[32] From outside the EGP, the splinter Revolutionary October advocated a more "democratic" revolutionary movement, with the popular masses—Maya and Ladino—"as protagonists." As the group wrote in 1987, "We consider that the participation of the indios in the process of their liberation—which is that of the Guatemalan society at large—requires revolutionary democracy."[33]

Domingo Hernández Ixcoy, along with a K'iche' from Santa Cruz named Francisca Alvarez and the other Mayas in the "contingent," organized a working group of Mayas in exile called Ja C'Amabal I'b. The name, which translates as "the House of Pueblo Unity," reveals their goal of continuing a revolutionary struggle by Mayas while countering arguments for separation. In position papers presented in Mexico, Nicaragua, the United States, and Europe, Hernández Ixcoy and Alvarez argued that Mayas who were (or had been) part of the revolutionary Left needed to speak out about their concerns, visions of society, and aspirations. Ja C'Amabal I'b rejected both extremes in the debate about Maya identity and revolution, those of the URNG and the Tojiles. Their position papers (drafted by them and apparently reviewed by Payeras) were at once in dialogue with the main guerrilla armies, Mayas inside and outside the separate and separatist revolutionary movements, and the international indigenous rights movement more broadly. Their positions bring to mind the kinds of discussions that took place in the mid-1970s.

The URNG groups, Hernández Ixcoy and Alvarez believed, had not gone far enough in putting theoretical ideas about ethnicity into practice. At the same time, they denounced what they termed the "ethnopopulism" of the separatist Mayas. They wrote that ethnopopulism was an understandable reaction to the state's integrationist indigenismo, but that its exaltation of ethnic qualities and virtues led invariably to racism and discrimination in reverse.[34] They criticized its ahistoric and romantic notion of Mayas and their location outside of class struggle. Showing a keen awareness of the recent history of Maya organizing, Hernández Ixcoy and Alvarez pointed out that "in political and organizational terms, this tendency produces sectarianism and deep distrust that isolates them from other social and political sectors that fight against exploitation and oppression."[35] Hernández Ixcoy and Alvarez were more generous than others on the revolutionary Left in their critique of Maya-only organizing, but came to a similar conclusion: "Despite the intentions of its defenders," they wrote, "this position favors the counterinsurgency and bourgeois project as they try to divide the struggle of the oppressed from that of the exploited."[36]

Ja C'Amabal I'b put forward what its members called an alternative "new thinking," although again, variations of these positions had been debated in the 1970s. Hernández Ixcoy and Alvarez stressed the need for Mayas to "find the path to our liberation," but insisted on "realistic solutions" rather than separation from non-Mayas. For Hernández Ixcoy and Alvarez, the solution lay in class solidarity and unity among Mayas, in partnership with Ladino campesinos, and in a more open and democratic revolution.[37]

The influence of an incipient international indigenous rights movement is apparent in their positions, though they adopted its provisions with qualifiers. Hernández Ixcoy and Alvarez acknowledged indigenous

165

calls for autonomy as legitimate; probably not coincidentally, they did so at an international symposium entitled "State, Autonomy, and Indigenous Rights" in Nicaragua in 1986. There they defended the much-maligned autonomy demands of other Maya activists, yet they cast them not as demands for separation, but for the self-determination that they argued had to be central to a truly democratic system: "Autonomy is a right," they asserted, "a just demand, and an expression of the new revolutionary democracy."[38] In other words, a certain degree of autonomy was to be part and parcel of a new participatory revolutionary society. In the same address they defended "special" rights for Mayas, but placed them firmly within the revolution: "We affirm that the struggle of the indios for their liberation, although it takes diverse forms and has its own specific demands apart from the oppressed pueblos, must form part of the great historical flow [caudal] of the Guatemalan revolution, be a decisive part of it."[39]

These calls for multifaceted change, with Mayas in partnership with Ladino activists, would be picked up by a reinvigorated opposition movement in the 1990s as Guatemalans grappled with the challenges of ending decades of armed conflict. Yet in the 1990s the context shifted yet again. During Guatemala's long and rocky peace process, the definition of "indigenous rights" became more and more narrow, with "special" rights—and those who championed them—set apart from the broader claims-making advocated by Hernández Ixcoy and Alvarez, and by Mayas in human rights and other multiethnic opposition groups. It was an outcome linked to the polarization of the 1980s, but also to the very logic and resources of the international indigenous rights movement.

166

▓▓▓ War by Other Means: Negotiating Rights in the 1990s

With much of the opposition leadership in exile and the insurgent threat "contained," President Efraín Ríos Montt in 1983 nonetheless called for a continuation of military rule to "consolidate" Guatemala. The Army High Command had other plans and forced him from his post in August of that year. Jennifer Schirmer's interviews with Guatemalan military officers help to illuminate military strategy.[40] The army sought to continue the "pacification" campaign, one officer told Schirmer, but at the same time, gradually "return Guatemala to a regime of legality."[41] An Air Force colonel explained that "one must run down constitutional corridors."[42] As General Héctor Gramajo elaborated, the war was to be continued, but waged by other means: "Our strategic goal has been to reverse [Karl von] Clausewitz's philosophy of war to state that in Guatemala, politics must be a continuation of war. But that does not mean that we are abandoning war; we are fighting it from a much broader horizon within a democratic framework. We may be renovating our methods of warfare but we are not abandoning them. . . . We are continuing our [counterinsurgency] operations [against] international subversion because the Constitution demands it."[43]

In accordance with their desire to appear more democratic in their "methods of warfare," Guatemala's armed forces supported the election of a civilian president, scheduled for 1985. Officers left their government posts, while the military orchestrated the political "opening." An intelligence analyst explained to Schirmer that newly elected civilian president Vinicio Cerezo was told, "You have been given the freedom to act, but to act only within the [army's National] Plan." As he continued, "If civilians occupy their assigned places, then the success [of the plan] is assured."[44]

Under such circumstances, the militarization of Guatemala was not undone with a return to civilian rule. Yet opposition groups appropriated what political space they could.[45] Prominent among the opposition were groups with large memberships and links to the Left, generally referred to as *populares*, or the "popular movement." A number of these groups were Maya led and focused on rights violations largely directed against the indigenous population, but the popular movement as a whole was explicitly multiethnic; many of its leaders and members had experience in CUC, the EGP, and ORPA. In the mid- to late 1980s, such groups continually denounced repression and brought international pressures to bear on the Guatemalan state. The Mutual Support Group for Families of the Disappeared (GAM) and the widows' organization National Coordinating Committee of Guatemalan Widows (CONAVIGUA), founded in 1984 and 1988, respectively, condemned ongoing government violence and pressed for information on the disappeared. The Council of Ethnic Communities Runujel Junam "Everyone United" (CERJ), founded in 1989, protested forced participation in the civil patrols in Maya communities and forced military recruitment.

Maya women in particular led these organizations, with women such

167

as Rosalina Tuyuc of CONAVIGUA becoming prominent spokespersons for the reemergent oppositional Left. Like elsewhere in societies under state terror, women in Guatemala started these efforts with searches for their own family members. CONAVIGUA soon became an association addressing critical problems of subsistence for women whose husbands had been killed, then grew into a large human rights organization denouncing all types of rights violations. Tuyuc explained that Maya women needed to express their experiences as women, as Mayas, and as class victims of government killings and rape. "It shouldn't be the men who speak for our pain and certainly not the government who speaks for what we suffer: illiteracy, misery, poverty, illness, repression. It is we women who must tell the world about the reality we live in."[46]

Around the same time, in the late 1980s and early 1990s, Mayas who took on the name "Mayanistas" (re)entered public debate. Their focus contrasted with that of Mayas in the popular movement like Tuyuc: they mostly set out culturally oriented demands, stressing issues of language, dress, and self-determination for the pueblo maya. Their most prominent spokesperson was Demetrio Cojtí Cuxil, a Kaqchikel from Tecpán, Chimaltenango. In the 1970s Cojtí had contributed to *Ixim: Notas Indígenas* (using a pseudonym), was involved in the annual Seminarios Indígenas, and worked in the Christian Democrats' Institute of Socioeconomic Development, IDESAC, in earthquake relief efforts. During the height of the violence he studied in Belgium, earning a doctorate in communications in 1980. He returned to Guatemala and took teaching positions in 1983 at the University of San Carlos and the Jesuit Rafael Landívar University.

Cojtí's absence from the country and subsequent academic positions seem to have allowed him to reengage questions of Maya identity and indigenous rights in the late 1980s as somewhat removed from the politics of the 1970s, despite having been closely involved in the activism unfolding in that period. While state repression continued against the activist sector in the late 1980s, Cojtí carefully positioned himself and the Mayanista movement that solidified around him as distant from the opposition struggle. In rooting their demands, Mayanistas emphasized the work of Adrián Inés Chávez, for example, especially his scholarship on the *Popol Vuh* and contributions to Maya linguistics. At the same time they downplayed a history of political activism.

In Cojtí's accounts of the rise of pan-Mayanism, he points to the Panzós massacre as a moment when generalized state terror against Mayas began. But his reference to the violence of 1978 did not implicate

Mayanistas in the social mobilization that followed. He argued, on the contrary, that the Mayanista movement was "too young" to take a position in the growing conflict, although he and most of the Mayas in the movement were of the same generation as the other protagonists of this study. In historicizing the Mayanista movement, Cojtí does recount the formation of a group called the Movement in Solidarity Assistance and Action (MAYAS), which he describes as arising in place of the controversial Movimiento Indio Tojil at the international level. It was made up of Mayas, he writes, "who accepted the necessity of social change but not the perpetuation of colonialism in a new society for which they fought."[47] He even attributed to MAYAS the Tojil document discussed in chapter 6, but at the same time depicted that organization as almost apolitical, as *apart* from the real conflict. Cojtí positioned MAYAS (and by extension, Mayas in general) *between* the state and the guerrilla and therefore not part of the opposition. "The members of the movement," Cojtí wrote, "were between two fires, that of the guerrilla and the army. Mayanism was moderate."[48] Rather than being part of the conflict, MAYAS, Cojtí argued, could learn from it and develop their own positions: "This period . . . allowed [MAYAS and future Mayanistas] to analyze and theorize the Maya question, and verify that both the guerrilla organizations and the Guatemalan state used Mayas as combatants for their war. It was verified that the Marxists . . . in their thinking . . . neglected anticolonialism, and . . . that the national army was racist to a pathological degree for the magnitude of genocide effected against the Indian."[49] Downplaying the fact that the Tojiles (or MAYAS) did in fact advocate revolution (Cojtí instead used the more palatable term *social change*), he supplied a sanitized history for the 1990s movement. Charlie Hale argues that in setting out these positions, Cojtí created political space for organized Mayas whose demands in the 1990s could be tolerated by the state, with some of them even granted at little socioeconomic or political cost.[50]

169

In 1990 indigenous rights had considerable cachet in Guatemala due to the approaching Quincentennial of Columbus's arrival in the Americas and the International Labour Organisation's new Convention on Indigenous and Tribal Peoples (ILO 169), which was adopted internationally in 1989 (and passed in Guatemala in 1995). In that context, Cojtí and the Mayanistas launched a successful effort to put their demands for the pueblo maya on the national agenda. On October 16, 1990, the Permanent Seminar of Maya Studies sponsored the "Forum of the Pueblo

Maya and the Candidates for the Presidency of Guatemala," held in the capital. Mayanistas set out their proposals and engaged the candidates in debate about Maya identity and rights.[51] The fact that presidential candidates from six political parties (and representatives from two more) agreed to attend the event reveals much about the high profile of such issues at that political moment in Guatemala. It also suggests, as Hale would argue, that politicians perceived the Mayanista agenda to be relatively unproblematic.

At the forum, Cojtí gave a speech that would serve as the basis for Mayanista demands from that point forward. His arguments in that speech are strikingly similar, in fact, to positions put forward by the Tojiles in the early 1980s, with the important difference being that Cojtí dropped calls for revolution. Like the Tojiles, Cojtí described internal colonialism, where Ladinos dominated Mayas economically, politically, and culturally, as justification for Maya separation. He condemned a pattern of Ladino monopolization of the state and a political division of the country that kept ethnic communities fragmented. He deplored assimilationist policies. He set out the right for Mayas to exist as a people. Like the Tojiles had done, he called for the restructuring of administrative divisions in Guatemala to reflect linguistic and ethnic boundaries, and the recognition of limited territorial and political autonomy. "We also have the right . . . to civil and political equality," he argued, "like every Guatemalan . . . [although civil and political rights] must be exercised through our culture . . . and not . . . after a forced ladinization. . . . These are the rights of the pueblo maya which point toward a different direction, not toward assimilation but toward . . . autonomy."[52]

By including the phrase "like every Guatemalan," Cojtí softened the impact of the call for autonomy, setting its limits within the boundaries of the state. (Recall that the Tojiles had done so too, despite how their position was characterized.) Cojtí at the same time called specifically for a set of culturally focused rights: to ethnic and cultural identity, to use and preservation of languages, to cultural integrity, and to control over education for Mayas.[53] Arguably, the specificity and limited nature of this list gave the Mayanista agenda much of its political power, even while real self-determination was sidelined. The Guatemalan government was not about to concede to the establishment of any significant degree of Maya autonomy. Forum participant and future president Jorge Serrano Elías, for example, called Cojtí's presentation a "brilliant exposition," but said he was grateful that (as the Mayanista speakers had charged) the political parties did *not* represent the aspirations of the "Maya nation." Serrano, like the PGT quoted earlier, denied the existence of any singular Maya nation and painted a picture of fragmented ethnic groups vying for power. "Gentlemen," Serrano said, "thank God the political parties do not represent these aspirations, because we are not called to [do] that, we are called to represent the aspirations of all the nations of Guatemala."[54] But limited autonomy in certain matters identified as specifically affecting indigenous communities *could* be discussed. Moreover, the Mayanista package of demands closely mirrored the rights set out in international human rights instruments such as ILO 169. As Guatemalan peace negotiations proceeded, the Accord on Identity and the Rights of Indigenous Peoples addressed many of these issues, including rights to "cultural integrity," dress, and language use. It was an agenda that could be advanced and discussed in 1990 without raising issues of more fundamental economic or political reform.

Cojtí and the Mayanistas were extremely important figures in evolving debates about Maya identity and rights in the 1990s.[55] Together they made indigenous rights issues a topic of everyday conversation in Guatemala, a tremendous accomplishment. The rights they focused on—including the right to bilingual education, the right to speak Mayan languages in government institutions, the right to wear traje—are crucial to the quality of life for many Mayas, a key part of efforts to end discrimination and, especially in the case of bilingual education, essential to breaking cycles of poverty. Yet this history shows that such rights do not reflect the range of issues deemed vital to and demanded by Mayas. As Maya journalist Estuardo Zapeta asked, which issues should and should not be considered "specific" to Mayas? Kay Warren summarized Zapeta's point this way: "The real question is what national issues—education, health, justice, and social security—*do not* affect indigenous communities. Reforms that single out one ethnic community and not others are deeply paternalistic."[56] In the process of negotiating "indigenous rights," broader issues of concern to many Mayas were rendered nonindigenous and in effect, so were their proponents. Regarding Mayas in the popular movement in the early 1990s, Demetrio Cojtí asserted that they were Mayas in fact but not in word or deed.[57]

The issue was complicated in yet another way. In a place like Guatemala, where a "peace" process coincided with continuing high levels of political repression, a focus on certain delimited rights as "indigenous" had far-reaching consequences. Significant amounts of political pressure and

171

monetary assistance from abroad became tied to rights labeled "indigenous" in the 1990s. Those resources and a certain level of political protection that came with them were unavailable to activists—Mayas or Ladinos—advocating a broader range of demands. The tragedy of the process was this: The divisions so important to counterinsurgency, divisions among Mayas, became exacerbated through a peace process where one form of activism was sanctified and supported and another form, in the eyes of the state and army, remained suspect.

A similar pattern had played out a decade before. In the early 1980s, publication of the Tojil position artificially narrowed the demands that were identified with the pueblo maya; almost immediately the diverse positions of activist Mayas were boiled down into one (in that case, easily caricatured, easily rejected) proposal for separation. In the early 1990s, the positions of the Mayanistas—similar to those of the Tojiles—were again characterized as representative of the demands of the pueblo indígena. This time, in a political context more attuned to "indigenous rights," some of the demands could be met.[58] Other components—real autonomy, for instance—again could be easily dismissed.[59]

As these processes unfolded, "indigenous rights" in Guatemala became a subject of much discussion and study, though the demands of Mayas in the popular movement were granted little space in it. (Detailed studies by Bastos and Camus are important exceptions.) That is not to say that activist Mayas outside the Mayanista movement did not help shape debates on rights for Mayas; they did. In fact, many Mayas on the Left took up ethnic concerns to a greater degree than before, with their treatment of Maya identity becoming pronounced and fine-tuned.[60] While some saw this as opportunistic, the heightened focus probably reflected multiple influences besides strategic and monetary calculations. The war itself drew attention to Maya experiences, as unthinkable numbers of activists lay dead or disappeared, and hundreds of indigenous communities lay in ruins. Marxist ideologies were shaken by these realities and by the global collapse of socialist regimes. Finally, as in the past, Maya populares learned from and reacted to other activists' culturally focused demands.

As usual, Mayas on the Left did not simply replicate these demands. As they had done since the 1970s, in the early 1990s they continued to treat Maya-specific claims in tandem with issues of class, arguing against an interpretation of the rights and needs of Mayas that excluded or downplayed economic needs. As the leftist Maya umbrella group Majawil Q'ij expressed in 1991, "The constitution of the republic speaks of rights . . . but the indigenous pueblo only knows pain and suffering: is it our right that the children cannot go to school, that they only eat tortilla with salt, the recent [1990] massacre at Santiago Atitlán? . . . Is it a right that the pueblo indígena is obligated to be in the development poles, in the model villages? It is not possible that one speaks of our rights while the pueblo continues going hungry."[61]

CUC reemerged on the public scene in 1986 and likewise reshaped its political message in the Quincentennial moment. Like Majawil Q'ij (to which it belonged), CUC in the early 1990s combined ethnic and class concerns in its statements. When CUC commemorated its fourteenth anniversary in 1992, it declared that "the threats against the Mayas continue" and specified the ethnicity of each victim on a list of individuals recently subjected to violence, precisely as the "Movimiento Indio" had done ten years earlier. In 1992 CUC wrote that the Maya New Year was "an opportunity for us, the indigenous pueblos, for deep reflection over what it is and what it means to be Maya. . . . We salute all those of us who are [Maya] and feel the Maya blood in our being, with a desire to deepen and live more than ever that which we are. We rise and walk with the wisdom and thought of our ancestors."[62] At the same time, CUC insisted that culture could not be separated from socioeconomic and political reality. CUC raised the issue of Mayas no longer wearing traje (they had changed their position on this one!) but argued that the problem was connected to economics and politics. It was not merely the case that people no longer wanted to use traje, they argued. Traje was expensive to make and out of reach for the poor, and it continued to be politically dangerous to wear.[63] (In counterinsurgency thinking, which persisted during the peace process, community-specific dress marked Mayas from certain areas as "subversive.") Similarly, Majawil Q'ij argued that formal recognition of cultural aspects of identity was necessary but insufficient and that Mayas' human rights broadly defined, including communal rights to land, had to be respected: "It has taken five hundred years for them to recognize our values," they asserted in 1992. "How much longer will it take before they recognize us as human beings and as peoples?"[64]

As always, the positions of these groups developed in response to each other, though relations were strained by the close association between Maya populares and the revolutionary Left, along with the narrowly defined "indigenous rights" discourse and the considerable resources tied to it. In October

173

1991, Mayas of Guatemala's popular movement, led by Rigoberta Menchú, sponsored the Second Continental Meeting of the Campaign of 500 Years of Indigenous, Black, and Popular Resistance, an explicitly multiethnic regional congress to plan collective responses to 1992 commemorations. They reportedly failed, however, to consult the Mayanistas in planning the event, and as Kay Warren writes, some in that movement "found political and personal dilemmas in [the event's] framing of social conflict and possibilities for change."[65] The Mayanistas in turn reenacted a dispute from the mid-1970s, leaving meetings in Quetzaltenango in protest of what they considered an agenda with too great a focus on issues of class struggle.

Activist Ricardo Cajas had identified that previous moment in Santa Cruz del Quiché as the occasion when the indigenous movement split in two, when the clasista and culturalista camps became clearly differentiated. As we have seen, the distinctions made in the earlier period did not in practice preclude tactical—if strained—alliances among Mayas in the late 1970s and early 1980s, when activists responded collectively to the state's most egregious violence against the pueblo maya. But the subsequent all-or-nothing positions, those staked out in 1982 and in the early 1990s, made broad-based social action by Mayas more difficult and less successful than it had been before.

Granted, during the tension-filled peace process, Mayas from different organizing experiences did come together in a number of ways. They got behind Rigoberta Menchú's candidacy for the Nobel Peace Prize in 1992, and they formed an important part of the public's rejection of President Jorge Serrano's attempt to take dictatorial powers in 1993. Most significantly, activist Mayas from over one hundred organizations took part in COPMAGUA, the Coordination of the Mayan Pueblo of Guatemala, founded in 1994 as part of the Assembly of Civil Society, an institution that facilitated the indirect participation of civil society members in crafting a settlement to the war. Like other ASC sectors, COPMAGUA was charged with the task of drafting positions on the accords under discussion by the government and URNG, and the group managed to reach consensus on an important proposal that served as the basis of the Indigenous Rights Accord. But while that was an important—even unprecedented—accomplishment, it was ultimately unsuccessful. Real compromise among Mayas was elusive during the peace process. The defeat of the Indigenous Rights referendum in 1999 can be explained in part by logistical problems and widespread political disillusionment. It is difficult not to conclude, however, that the limited rights the measure contained—mostly cultural issues championed by the Mayanistas—were not enough to win the solid support of more activist Mayas or to get a majority to the polls.[66]

▨▨▨ May All Rise Up?: The Twenty-First-Century Maya

Guatemalan army officers expressed concern over the reemergence of Maya activism as the peace process unfolded. As one officer explained to Jennifer Schirmer in the early 1990s, "[The Maya movement] for the next five to six years will *only* be run by Mayan intellectuals and academics, but in the medium term of twenty to twenty-five years, if it succeeds in homogenizing the differences within the Mayan community and creates conditions for leadership, [it] could become a political movement that forms the basis for a new political party in the twenty-first century."[67] During the long peace process, Mayanistas did continue to dominate debate about Maya rights. The army officer's comment that the movement would be "only" run by these intellectuals in the short term suggests, again, that their claims-making was viewed as manageable and unthreatening. Only with a significant degree of unity between Mayanistas and activist Mayas involved in broader efforts could they pose a dilemma as a "political movement," a long-held preoccupation of the Guatemalan government and army. "Now, everyone's Mayan, or ethnic, or whatever they call themselves," complained another officer.[68]

In one sense, these officers can rest easy: Mayas will almost certainly not "homogeniz[e] their differences." Mayas are a population diverse in all respects—economically, politically, culturally, and linguistically—and their demands have long reflected that diversity. But arguably, Maya diversity has at times served as a strength rather than a weakness by drawing attention to a range of concerns—cultural, economic, and political. As former ORPA member and later congressional deputy Alberto Mazariegos asks, "Why necessarily do we want indígenas to have . . . only one form of thinking, when we are located across the social structure?"[69]

Rigoberta Menchú Tum, winner of the Nobel Peace Prize in 1992, has used her position as a Nobel laureate to try to bridge some of the

175

distance between Mayas of different political persuasions, and among Guatemalans more generally. Working through the foundation she established, Menchú has repeatedly argued for unity "as our ancestors recommended."[70] She refers, like many before her, to the call of the *Popol Vuh*, "May all rise up, may no one be left behind." Menchú is not calling for homogeneity, however, and explicitly reaches out not just to Mayas in the cultural movement *or* the popular movement, but to all Mayas, and in fact, to Guatemalans in general. In doing so, she counters calls for Maya separatism while still asserting that Guatemala is a "plurinational" country. Guatemalan national unity, she argues—reminiscent of points made in *Ixim*—"does not mean that we abandon the specificity of the indigenous pueblos, [but] recognize that this is a plural-national, pluriethnic country." At the same time, "there cannot be a single representative of the indigenous pueblos," she writes, "because we group ourselves in many ways. The representation should be plural, respecting the different manners of seeing things."[71] The goal that Menchú and her foundation have stressed is not the creation of some singular Maya entity, but political participation of Mayas in all their diversity.

Yet even at the end of the 1990s, a time of careful probing into Guatemala's dark past, a history of diversity among activist Mayas remained an uncomfortable subject. In the aftermath of genocide, experiences of extreme state terror continued to shape how Mayas remembered the past and how they mobilized—or not—around claims in the present. The Catholic Church and UN-sponsored truth commissions produced powerful, highly detailed historical reports on over three decades of repression and conflict. But the history of activism itself—in all its diversity—has not been widely discussed.

Otilia Lux de Cotí is a K'iche' woman who first entered this narrative as a teacher and adviser of Amalia Coy Pop, the 1978 reina indígena from San Cristóbal Verapaz. In July 1978, when the young Coy Pop was abruptly dethroned for protesting against the Panzós massacre, Lux helped her publicize what had happened in San Cristóbal. Twenty years later, the same Otilia Lux was part of the three-member committee heading the UN Truth Commission's investigation into the civil war. In 1998 she addressed a large crowd gathered to hear the Truth Commission's conclusions. At that weighty moment Lux sought to speak for Guatemalan Mayas. She offered listeners a starkly different narrative of Maya participation in the conflict than the one set out so famously fifteen years earlier in Menchú's account of the "people's war." "In the name of the Maya, living and dead," Lux pleaded, "we ask the God of gods and all Guatemala to pardon us, because we became involved in an armed conflict that was imposed on us and that was not ours."[72]

Otilia Lux acknowledged Maya participation in the war, yet in the same breath distanced Mayas—all Mayas—from ownership of the era's struggles. Carlota McAllister witnessed the speech and described the "loud and lengthy cries for justice" in the auditorium, packed with Mayas, every time mention was made of army violence; some Mayas, McAllister asserted, did feel "that the war was theirs." McAllister raises a perplexing question: In the context of an inquiry into historical truth, why was Maya political engagement unspeakable?[73] With the shock and horror that came of counting the war's dead, it seems, came a desire on the part of Lux and many others to distance the pueblo maya from any part in the conflict aside from that of its victims.

Like other Mayas who came of age in the 1960s and 1970s, Otilia Lux would be no stranger to the political struggles of the war period. Despite her words, she would be aware of a complicated past that is masked by characterizing Mayas as bystanders. Part of the explanation for her position was certainly political; part may be related to a disturbing sense that genocide somehow requires apolitical victims. The indígena Lux evoked is familiar, a mainstay of Ladino racial thought and a figure conjured up in times of need by Mayas.[74] But does that racialization continue to have a place in Guatemala? Can Mayas afford to rely on the apolitical indio if the process of reconstructing society is to be more than "war by other means"?

Events since that moment do suggest that Lux's posturing was strategic. In the years since Lux's speech her rhetoric has not matched even her own actions, just as it did not accurately reflect the diverse and complicated Maya roles in the civil war. Lux, like many Maya leaders, has taken an active part in working to shape a postconflict Guatemala.[75] In an interesting twist, her political positions and goals came to overlap, in fact, with those of Rigoberta Menchú. In 2007 the two women helped to create a new political party, Encuentro por Guatemala (EG), loosely translated as "Together for Guatemala." Menchú was the party's (unsuccessful) candidate for president that year, while the more moderate Lux was elected to Congress.

It is tempting to interpret the Lux and Menchú "encounter" as evidence that the rigidities and divisions produced by extreme violence and by the peace process itself are lessening, that working relationships among Mayas of different political persuasions are again becoming viable. If Guatemala in the twenty-first century no longer seems an "eternal Panzós," problems facing the pueblo maya remain formidable. But at this juncture, the eternal call to action remains a question: May all rise up, leaving no one behind? The history of Maya activism is fraught with complications and tensions among indígenas, conflicts over strategy and aims, feelings of guilt and pain. But—as both Lux and Menchú might agree—it is also a history that is full of possibility.

Notes

░░░ Introduction

1. *El Gráfico*, July 30, 1978. The young people's communities were listed in the photo's caption. They came from Soloma in Huehuetenango; Quetzaltenango, Cantel, and La Esperanza in the department of Quetzaltenango; Nahualá and Santiago Atitlán, Sololá; Chichicastenango, in the department of El Quiché; and San Sebastián, Retalhuleu. Among them were speakers of K'iche', Q'anjob'al, and Tz'utujil, three of the twenty-one Mayan languages spoken in Guatemala. Departments are administrative areas similar to provinces or states.

2. The war itself began in 1962 and lasted over three decades, making it the longest running of the Cold War–era conflicts in the region between repressive military or military-controlled governments and armed revolutionary opposition movements. The bloody conflict left over two hundred thousand dead and "disappeared" (this generally involved kidnapping, torture, killing, and official denial that the person had ever been detained) and over one million displaced, out of a population in the early 1980s of less than seven million. The war was formally brought to an end in 1996 with the signing of peace accords between the Guatemalan state and revolutionary guerrilla armies. The fundamental problems that fueled that war—inequality and landlessness, subjugation of Mayas and the poor, obdurate resistance to reform on the part of the economically and politically powerful—remain largely unresolved.

3. On the Panzós massacre, see Comisión para el Esclarecimiento Histórico (CEH), *Memoria del silencio*, 6:13–23. See also Grandin, *Last Colonial Massacre*, and Sanford, *Buried Secrets*. National press coverage was extensive. See Guatemalan newspapers *El Gráfico*, *La Nación*, *La Tarde*, *El Imparcial*, and *Diario de Centro América*, June 1–4, 1978. For overall figures on the violence, see CEH, *Memoria del silencio*, "Conclusiones y recomendaciones." For discussion of "Acts of Genocide," see CEH, *Memoria del silencio*, section 2, vol. 3, paragraphs 849–1257, and Oglesby and Ross, "Guatemala's Genocide Determination." Maya communities on a national map were famously assigned colored pins by the army, white indicating areas that were judged to be free of "subversion," pink indicating a low-level guerrilla presence that

required the elimination of local leaders, and red signaling wholesale (actual or potential) support for the insurgency and justifying massacre. As geographers Liz Oglesby and Amy Ross explain, army assessments reflected calculations about both ethnicity and a history of activism: "The army was not simply killing Mayans; it was killing Mayans *in particular places* where social organizing was most intense." The CEH findings on genocide accounted for these complications and thus "avoided reifying the racial dynamics of the violence." "By situating its argument in the concrete geographies of genocide in Guatemala, linking both historical and territorial dimensions of violence and resistance, the CEH avoided framing Mayans as passive 'victims' of state violence. Mayans *were* victims of horrible crimes, but at the same time, thousands of people in the hard-hit communities were also participants and protagonists in broad struggles for political and social change" (Oglesby and Ross, "Guatemala's Genocide Determination," 21 and 30). The guerrillas, too, committed massacres of civilians, thirty-two of which were documented by the CEH. These were sometimes in retaliation for cooperation with the army. The CEH found state forces to be responsible for 93 percent of documented acts of violence and the guerrilla armies to be responsible for 3 percent (CEH, *Memoria del silencio*, "Conclusiones y recomendaciones").

    4. *El Gráfico*, July 30, 1978. The use throughout the declaration of the term *indio*—a label typically holding negative connotations of dirtiness, laziness, backwardness—was a purposeful act. In the 1970s indigenous activists adopted the term, challenged to do so by Q'eqchi' intellectual Antonio Pop Caal in his December 1972 article in the journal *La Semana*, "Replica del indio a una disertación ladina." For more on the term *indio* and on Pop Caal, see chapter 3 of this book.

    5. For more on race and ethnicity in Guatemala, see chapter 1.

    6. A note about interviews: I spoke with just over one hundred people in twenty communities over the course of this study, most of them Maya activists, women and men, who came of age in the 1960s and 1970s. Interviews were mostly conducted in Spanish, which as Rigoberta Menchú pointed out decades ago, tended to be the language of pan-community activism itself (Burgos-Debray, *I, Rigoberta Menchú*, chapters 11 and 12). In a few cases, a daughter or son translated for me when a parent was a monolingual Mayan language speaker. Men tend to dominate this retelling, and they held the most prominent roles in activism in the 1970s. But Maya women were a constant and important presence, even if their efforts are not as visible; many were also less inclined than their male counterparts to discuss this history in detail. For more on gender in activism by Mayas, see chapter 4. My profound thanks to all interviewees for making this study possible. Most interviewees gave permission for me to use their names when discussing this history. I

have done that in many cases, especially when interviewees have continued to be public activists, when they themselves have written publicly in their own names, or when their names have been previously published in the press or in other studies. For other interviewees, for reasons of privacy and safety, I have withheld names or used first names only. Except when quoting from secondary sources in English, Spanish translations are mine.

7. These remain especially sensitive questions revolving around tensions within Maya communities and can touch on uncomfortable issues of acquiescence to or even collaboration with a violent state. For the most part, Maya activists were not inclined to discuss such tensions with me, an outsider, in any detail, and efforts to explore this subject with Mayas outside of oppositional organizing were not fruitful. Several authors have written about Mayas seeking distance from the violence. See especially Montejo, *Testimony*.

8. Destruction of the historical record of these years happened in many forms. As repression intensified, activists themselves burned their papers, records, publications—anything that could link them to reformist movements, most of which were seen as "subversion" in the eyes of the army. One former member of a guerrilla group, now an academic, recounted with dismay fire-crackers being made in Mexico (where many Guatemalans were in exile) out of materials produced by the Guatemalan Left. Important documentary evidence from the 1970s and early 1980s does exist, though, enhanced by materials now being sent back to Guatemala from NGOs abroad. See the collection in the Archivo Histórico at the Centro de Investigaciones Regionales de Mesoamérica (CIRMA), in Antigua. In addition to the extensive materials at CIRMA, I relied on records and publications from Catholic Church sources, local municipal archives, nongovernmental organizations, the Hemeroteca of the Archivo General de Centro América (AGCA), and on newspapers housed in the Hemeroteca of the Biblioteca Nacional de Guatemala. (The press was generally uncensored in the 1970s but became increasingly vague in its coverage with the rise in repression in the latter part of the decade and in the early 1980s.) I also consulted records of institutions such as the Instituto Indígena Santiago, the Instituto Nuestra Señora del Socorro, and the Sociedad El Adelanto. Whenever possible I brought written sources—newspaper articles, photographs, publications of other kinds—to the attention of interviewees, which enriched discussions and jogged memories.

9. Interview with Juana, September 10, 2002, Soloma, Huehuetenango.

10. Ibid.

11. Ibid. She referred to her speech as a "discurso de golpe," "a speech dealing a blow."

12. It took time and effort—along with financial and logistical support from area priests—for young people to travel even between Soloma and the

departmental capital of Huehuetenango in the 1970s. A former Maryknoll priest, Thomas Melville, describes the journey from the city of Huehuetenango to the northern region of the department, which probably took around four hours in the 1970s: it was a drive "over a twisting dirt and gravel, one-lane mountain road, climbing from 5,400 feet at Huehuetenango out through Chiantla into a series of switchbacks and hairpin turns to an altitude of just over 10,000 feet at Paquix. The road then continued across an 11-mile-wide quasi-moonscape of volcanic rock outcroppings and patches of grass nibbled by a few scrawny sheep here and there, past Capzín and its 800-foot sheer drop-off, down through another series of switchbacks to tiny San Juan Ixcoy. Then came a straight (almost) run to the ring of mountains around San Pedro Soloma" (Melville, *Through a Glass Darkly*, 30). Today the road is much improved. The sheer cliffs and hairpin turns still make the trip to Soloma a hair-raising journey (for me), but the road now has two lanes and is paved.

13. Interview with Juana, September 10, 2002, Soloma, Huehuetenango. The Guerrilla Army of the Poor (EGP) was one of several leftist revolutionary groups operating in the highlands in the 1970s and 1980s. The EGP, formed by Guatemalans exiled in Mexico, first entered Guatemala in early 1972 and by 1974 had a presence in indigenous communities in the Ixil region of northern El Quiché and in the capital, through universities and secondary schools. While Ladino led, it soon began to recruit heavily among rural Mayas in the departments of El Quiché, Huehuetenango, Alta Verapaz, Sololá, and Chimaltenango and became the largest of the guerrilla armies. The Revolutionary Organization of Peoples in Arms (ORPA), also with significant numbers of Mayas among its ranks, was formed in the late 1970s and operated in and around Quetzaltenango, San Marcos, and Sololá. The Rebel Armed Forces (FAR) was a guerrilla group organized in the 1960s that initiated the insurgency and was active mostly in the eastern part of the country. A fourth guerrilla army was made up of a wing of the Guatemalan Workers Party (PGT), the Communist Party of Guatemala. These four joined together in 1982 in the umbrella Guatemalan National Revolutionary Unity, or URNG. Small splinter guerrilla groups formed in the early 1980s, several of them Maya-only movements. See chapters 6 and 7. For all of these revolutionary groups, see CEH, *Memoria del silencio*, 1:172–83.

14. As detailed in later chapters of this book, the few studies of Maya political engagement published in the 1970s and early 1980s seemed to share the Left's frustration with Mayas calling attention to indigenous identity, and a focus on Maya-specific issues was generally construed as counterrevolutionary. See Falla, "El movimiento indígena," and Arias, "El movimiento indígena en Guatemala." Due to repression, fieldwork examining political differentiation among indígenas was nearly impossible in the 1980s and early 1990s, and studies of the violence rested on assumptions of Mayas as apolitical. For portrayals of Mayas'

experiences of violence and terror, see Carmack, ed., *Harvest of Violence*; Montejo, *Testimony*; and Smith, ed., *Guatemalan Indians and the State*. For the view that Mayas wanted nothing to do with either state forces or the insurgency, see Stoll, *Between Two Armies*, and Le Bot, *La guerra en las tierras mayas*. During the 1990s peace process, scholars published important work on the rise of a culturally focused indigenous rights movement, but the scope of these studies allowed authors to raise few questions about more diverse organizing by Mayas, connections between cultural concerns and demands for socioeconomic change, or the roots of current indigenous struggles. See Cojtí Cuxil, *Políticas para la reivindicación de los Mayas*; Fischer and Brown, *Maya Cultural Activism*; Nelson, *A Finger in the Wound*; and Warren, *Indigenous Movements and Their Critics*.

15. See McAllister, *The Good Road*, for a discussion of this tendency to treat past activism by Mayas as taboo, and Hale, *Más que un indio*, for analysis of the "two demons" explanation of the conflict adopted by many Mayas. See also chapter 7 of this book.

16. For new scholarship on Maya participation in political life during the civil war, see McAllister, *The Good Road*, and Grandin, *Last Colonial Massacre*. See also Grandin's "To End with All These Evils." Santiago Bastos and Manuela Camus chronicle Guatemalan indigenous movements from 1986 to 2001, with attention to the historical development of organizing by Mayas and diversity among them. See Bastos and Camus, *Quebrando el silencio*, *Abriendo caminos*, and *Entre el mecapal y el cielo*.

17. Interview with Juana, September 10, 2002, Soloma, Huehuetenango.

18. This topic is addressed in chapter 7. For a discussion of government-sanctioned Maya rights in the 1990s, see Hale, "Rethinking Indigenous Politics in the Era of the 'Indio Permitido,'" and "Does Multiculturalism Menace?"

▨▨▨ Chapter 1

1. For a persuasive argument about the utility of the "conceptual apparatus of race" for studying Guatemala see Hale, *Más que un indio*. See also Smith, "Interpretaciones norteamericanas sobre la raza." An important new body of literature on racial formation in Guatemala includes Arenas Bianchi, Hale, and Palma Murga, eds., *¿Racismo en Guatemala?: Abriendo el debate*; Heckt and Palma Murga, eds., *Racismo en Guatemala: De lo políticamente correcto*; and Casaús Arzú, *Linaje y racismo*, and *Genocidio*. As Appelbaum, Macpherson, and Rosemblatt argue, the many meanings and uses of race should remind us to ask "how historical actors themselves deployed the term" ("Introduction," in *Race and Nation in Modern Latin America*, 2–3). Attention both to racialization and to different and contested meanings of race facilitates a focus on "why different articulations arose, while noting the continuities that have made race and the racialization of . . . identities so pervasive" (Appelbaum, Macpherson,

and Rosemblatt, *Race and Nation*, 9). By focusing on racialization, I do not mean to suggest that race is scientifically valid. Instead I try to understand how powerful and competing ideas of race were created, used, and contested. For more on race, ethnicity, and relations between and among Mayas and Ladinos in Guatemalan history, see the series entitled *Por qué estamos como estamos?* produced by the Centro de Investigaciones Regionales de Mesoamérica (CIRMA). Works include Adams and Bastos, *Relaciones étnicas*; Taracena, *Etnicidad, estado y nación en Guatemala*, vols. 1 and 2; and on the idea of mestizaje (mixing) in Guatemala and Central America more broadly, Euraque, Gould, and Hale, eds., *Memorias del mestizaje*. For analysis of multiculturalism and identity debates in today's Guatemala, see the study coordinated by Bastos and Cumes, *Mayanización y vida cotidiana*.

2. See Hale, *Más que un indio*, for a detailed account of such assumptions and Ladinos' conflicted views of Maya "efflorescence" since the war's end.

3. Lund, "They Were Not a Barbarous Tribe," 175. As we will see in this book, it was the Ladino insistence on cultural erasure and a static, oppressive definition of what it meant to be indigenous that activist Mayas in the 1970s so strongly rejected. In doing so, they built on a long history of indigenous opposition to assimilationist pressures. The language of acculturation was unacceptable to Maya leaders when harnessed to nation-state formation and the Liberal *reforma* of the nineteenth century, and to reformism of the 1920s and 1940s. For more on these processes see the edited volume by Smith, *Guatemalan Indians and the State*. See also Grandin, *Blood of Guatemala*, for a discussion of nineteenth-century K'iche' elites' efforts to shape understandings of race and nation in Quetzaltenango. To resist the Ladino equating of culture with class, K'iche' elites, writes Grandin, "had to embrace a racial definition of indigenous culture so as not to lose their ethnic identity. Ironically, they were less equivocal than Ladinos about the racial content of ethnicity: one could adopt as many defined Ladino traits as possible and still remain indigenous." Grandin argues that "this antiassimilationist, racialist view of indigenous ethnicity still resonates among Quetzalteco K'iche's." In interviews with members of the Sociedad El Adelanto, Grandin found that "for these men, ethnicity was defined by blood rather than culture or class traits. 'We have the blood of Tecún, they [the Ladinos] have the blood of [conquistador] Pedro de Alvarado'" (*Blood of Guatemala*, 143 and 284n41). It is interesting to compare this to a Q'eqchi' Maya campesino petition in 1920 drawing on the language of Liberal nationalism—"liberty, equality, and security of persons, honor, and property"—to secure the "indisputable rights of the Indian" to equal treatment under the law: an end to forced work on public projects, special taxes, and debt peonage. See Grandin, *Last Colonial Massacre*, 28. See chapters 3, 5, 6, and 7 of this book for debates on ethnicity and class among Mayas linked to the agrarian Left later in the twentieth century.

4. The 1940 census used "Blanca y mestiza," "white and mixed," as the nonindigenous category. In 1940 55 percent of the population was classified as indigenous, with highland departments having much larger indigenous representation: Totonicapán, 96 percent; Alta Verapaz, 94 percent; Sololá, 93 percent; Huehuetenango, 87 percent; and El Quiché, 85 percent (Dirección General de Estadística, *Quinto censo de población*). In 1950 53.6 percent of the national population was classified as indigenous, as were over 90 percent of the inhabitants of Totonicapán, Sololá, and Alta Verapaz. El Quiché was listed as 84 percent indigenous, and Huehuetenango 73 percent (Dirección General de Estadística, *Sexto censo de población*). The 1964 census measured for the first time an indigenous minority in Guatemala: 42 percent of the population in that census was classified as indigenous, and nearly 58 percent of the population "no-indígena." Still, twelve of twenty-two departments registered majority indigenous populations, with Sololá, Totonicapán, and Alta Verapaz again above 90 percent (Dirección General de Estadística, *VII censo de población 1964*). Censuses conducted in 1973 and 1981 measured the indigenous population at 43.8 percent and 41.9 percent, respectively. Several authors, Mayas prominent among them, have expressed skepticism at these figures that "officially 'diminish' the Maya presence over the course of the past century" (Lovell and Lutz, "'A Dark Obverse'"). See also Cojtí Cuxil, *Ub'anik Ri Una'ooj Uchomab'aal Ri Maya' Tinamit*; Oxlajuuj Keej Maya' Ajtz'iib' (Maya Linguistic Research Group), *Maya' Chii'*; and Tzian, *Mayas y ladinos en cifras*. For an alternative explanation of census undercounting of rural Guatemalans in general, see Adams, "Some Premodernist Thoughts on the Mayan Population in Guatemala." For a history of the meanings of *Ladino* in Guatemala, see Grandin, *Blood of Guatemala*, chap. 3. There are also small Garífuna and Xinka populations in the country, not categorized as Ladino or indígena.

5. According to the 1940 census, departments with large indigenous populations—Totonicapán, Sololá, and Huehuetenango, for example—tended to have illiteracy rates well above the national average of 65 percent: in these cases 84 percent, 89 percent, and 87 percent, respectively. Illiteracy rates were even higher among women in these departments: 91 percent, 92 percent, and 89 percent, respectively. (There are exceptions to this pattern: Chimaltenango, located near the capital, had a lower than average rate of illiteracy, 58 percent, with 87 percent of its population classified as indigenous.) See Dirección General de Estadística, *Quinto censo de población*, 214–15 and 312–13. Ten years later educational discrepancies related to ethnicity and gender were again stark. The 1950 census, conducted during the reformist "October Revolution," found that 49 percent of Ladinos in the nation could read and write, while only 9.7 percent of indígenas could do so. Broken down by gender, the literacy figures were 14.4 percent for indigenous men, 4.8 percent for indigenous women. In rural areas 33 percent of Ladinos were classified as literate along

185

with 8 percent of indígenas. In urban areas 73 percent of Ladinos were literate and 21 percent of indígenas (Dirección General de Estadística, *Sexto censo de población*, xxxix). For later economic indicators see Steele, "Guatemala."

6. See CEH, *Memoria del silencio*, "Conclusiones y recomendaciones." Again, the war began in the 1960s and ended only in 1996, with most of the killings taking place in the early 1980s.

7. Nelson, *Finger in the Wound*, 35.

8. See, for example, Levenson-Estrada, *Trade Unionists against Terror*.

9. Of the twenty-one Maya linguistic communities in Guatemala, the top four language groups, K'iche', Mam, Kaqchikel, and Q'eqchi' (written as "kekchí" by Pacay and others in the 1970s), account for a little over half of all Mayas. For more on Mayan languages and activism focused on linguistics, see Cojtí Cuxil, *Políticas para la reivindicación de los Mayas de hoy*; England, *Autonomía de los idiomas mayas*; the edited volume by Fischer and Brown, *Maya Cultural Activism*; Garzon et al., *Life of Our Language*; and Warren, *Indigenous Movements and Their Critics*. Walter Little has shown that ideas of "Mayaness" remain limited in Guatemala, with Kaqchikel handicrafts vendors, for example, reluctant to embrace the positions of the 1990s "Maya movement." "Vendors choose political strategies that widen their economic and social options," writes Little. They tend to identify not as Maya, but as indigenous artisans, evoking "both cultural and worker identity orientations," while still marketing their Mayaness to tourists. Little has noted that some, too, do not identify as Guatemalans. As one Kaqchikel vendor put it, "I'm not Guatemalan; I just live in Guatemala" (Little, "Outside of Social Movements," 51–52). The Ladino category is also problematic, considering that there are nonindigenous Guatemalans who opt out of it. A small elite sector prefers to think of itself not as Ladino, but as white or European. See Casaus Arzú, *Linaje y racismo*.

10. Adams and Bastos, *Relaciones étnicas*, 35.

11. The rich scholarship on race and ethnicity in Mexico, Central America, and the Andes offers means for comparison. On Mexico, see Rubin, *Decentering the Regime*; Rus et al., eds., *Mayan Lives, Mayan Utopias*; and Mattiace, *To See with Two Eyes*. For Central America, see Hale, *Resistance and Contradiction*; Gould, *To Die in This Way*; and Tilley, *Seeing Indians*. For the Andes, see de la Cadena, *Indigenous Mestizos*; and Gotkowitz, *A Revolution for Our Rights*.

12. Some (seemingly few) non-Mayas do choose the label "mestizo," or mixed. In his study of Chimaltenango, Hale discusses the quandary faced by one woman when asked how she wanted to be identified. She initially indicated *mestiza*, in a show of solidarity with Mayas. After pondering the choice and receiving a genealogy lesson from her "horrified" relatives, however, she changed her mind and indicated that she was a Ladina (Hale, *Más que un indio*, 167–68). Hale also notes a differentiation between the terms *mestizo* and the

commonly used *mistado*, the latter describing a mixing that is seen as inherently problematic. "Although mistado and mestizo sound like synonyms," writes Hale, "they key into distinct ideological precepts. To refer to someone as a mistado is to foreground an infelicitous mixture of starkly different racial types, with the implication that the two sets of characteristics are destined to be at war with one another, jockeying for dominance within the hybrid body, the 'ladino' side fending off contamination by the Indian" (*Más que un indio*, 172). See also Euraque, Gould, and Hale, eds., *Memorias del mestizaje*.

13. See Taracena's *Etnicidad, estado y nación*, vol. 1, for a detailed analysis of the coexistence of assimilationist ideas and segregationist labor practices. My understanding of developments in state racial ideology owes much to the work of Taracena. See also Taracena, *Etnicidad, estado y nación*, vol. 2.

14. McAllister, "Authenticity and Guatemala's Maya Queen," 105. I'll confess here a fascination with the identity politics that surround pageant queens. For more on Maya and Ladina beauty queens, see chapter 4 of this book. It should be noted that while there is no room for Mayas in the Miss Guatemala pageant, the Ladina contestants do model indigenous traje as part of the contest.

15. Adams and Bastos, *Relaciones étnicas*, 37.

16. González Ponciano, "'Esas sangres no están limpias,'" 16–17. González Ponciano analyzed over six hundred press articles and opinion pieces from the end of the nineteenth through the twentieth centuries, finding a "double stigmatization" of the indígena: he is *laborioso*—hardworking—but because of his inclination to vice, in need of the heavy hand of the finquero. The "hard worker" images included the Indian as obedient, capable, humble, and respectful. These were consistently paired with negative stereotypes such as being stupid, stubborn, lazy, drunk, and swindling.

17. Government *Circular*, November 3, 1876, reproduced in Skinner Klée, *Legislación indigenista*, 34–35.

18. For analysis of the rise of Guatemala's coffee oligarchy and its repercussions in the countryside, see McCreery, *Rural Guatemala*.

19. Asturias, *Guatemalan Sociology*, 103–4. His was one line of thought among many. For an alternative position, see the 1931 essay by Fernando Juárez Muñoz, "El indio guatemalteco: Ensayo de sociología nacionalista," discussed in Adams, "¿Diversidad cultural?" For the broader history of ideas about race and nation in Latin America, see Andrews, *Afro-Latin America*; Appelbaum, Macpherson, and Rosemblatt, *Race and Nation*; Kicza, *The Indian in Latin American History*; and Wade, *Race and Ethnicity*.

20. Asturias, *Guatemalan Sociology*, 78.

21. Quoted in Taracena, *Etnicidad, estado y nación*, 1:108–9.

22. Ibid., 1:125. It was published as *Manuscrito de Chichicastenango: Popol Buj* (Guatemala: Tipografía Sánchez y de Guise, 1927). For more on the *Popol Vuh*, see chapter 3 of this book.

187

23. *El Excelsior*, February 9, 1926, cited in Taracena, *Etnicidad, estado y nación*, 1:125–26.

24. See Decree No. 1996, Ley Contra la Vagancia, May 8, 1934, in Skinner Klée, *Legislación indigenista*, 110–14; and "Reglamento relativo a los jornaleros para trabajos agrícolas," September 24, 1935, in Skinner Klée, *Legislación indigenista*, 118–19. Maya positions on such changes would be closely tied to class status. For contrasting views, see Warren, *Symbolism of Subordination*, 148–51; and Manz, *Paradise in Ashes*, 45–47.

25. For a critique of Ubico's policies related to the "problema indígena," see a speech by the minister of education during the subsequent Arévalo regime, reproduced in Instituto Indigenista Interamericano, *Boletín Indigenista* 5, no. 4 (December 1945): 387–97. Under Ubico, he charged, "the indigenous problem was solved by denying its existence" (cited in González Ponciano, "Diez años," 105).

26. See Adams, "Las masacres de Patzicía de 1944." Hale sets the figure of Mayas killed at some three hundred (*Más que un indio*, 52).

27. "Censo escolar," *Boletín del Instituto Indigenista Nacional*, 1, nos. 2–3 (March –June 1946), cited in González Ponciano, "Diez años," 117.

28. Decree No. 76, March 10, 1944, in Skinner Klée, *Legislación indigenista*, 123–25. Such reforms were limited in scope, fiercely resisted by landowners, and often incomplete in practice. See Grandin, *Last Colonial Massacre*, chap. 1, for a discussion of the limited nature of revolutionary policies as applied in Alta Verapaz and the sharply conflicting interests at play between reformers and landowners. Regarding the 1945 vagrancy laws, Grandin reports that in the municipality of Carchá an average of two hundred "vagrants" a month were arrested in 1946 (*Last Colonial Massacre*, 38).

29. Decree 900, Law of Agrarian Reform, in Skinner Klée, *Legislación indigenista*, 134–35.

30. For the effects of October Revolution reforms see Handy, *Revolution in the Countryside*. For connections to later Maya mobilization, see chapter 2 of this book.

31. Speech reproduced in Instituto Indigenista Interamericano, *Boletín Indigenista* 5, no. 4 (December 1945): 372–87.

32. Ibid. For more on Goubaud, see Adams, "¿Diversidad Cultural?" Goubaud was trained as an anthropologist and stands out among indigenistas of the era as accepting of cultural difference. Adams concludes that Goubaud "opposed racialist nationalisms and was perhaps in favor of a united nation with cultural diversity" ("¿Diversidad Cultural?" 66).

33. Speech reproduced in Instituto Indigenista Interamericano, *Boletín Indigenista* 5, no. 4 (December 1945): 386–97. For more on indigenismo during the October Revolution and the period that followed its overthrow, see González Ponciano, "Diez años."

34. See Instituto Indigenista Nacional, "Guía sociológica: Investigaciones de campo de las comunidades indígenas Guatemaltecas," *Boletín del Instituto Indigenista Nacional* 2, no. 2 (March 1947): 54–105. The IIN prepared at least 114 monographs on Maya communities during the Arévalo administration, with fewer produced during the Arbenz regime. A large number appeared again in the mid-1950s, but this time authored by a very different IIN, one linked to a resolute anti-Communism. See the IIN materials in the collection donated by Silvia Barreno Anleu to CIRMA's Archivo Histórico, Antigua, Guatemala.

35. Constitution of 1945, Article 87, in Skinner Klée, *Legislación indigenista*, 126.

36. Congressional Decree No. 426, September 24, 1947, in Skinner Klée, *Legislación indigenista*, 127–30. These provisions grew from concerns over "inauthentic" production of fashions in the United States inspired by Maya designs. During the Ubico years, what was seen in Guatemala as the "falsification of Maya tradition" by Macy's and Sears resulted in a Guatemalan government statement about Maya textile traditions as "the cultural patrimony of the nation" and the imposition of a trademark for textile exports (personal communication with Jean-François Bélisle, October 15, 2009). See Bélisle, "Macy's vs. Ubico." The debates around these issues during the Ubico regime can be traced in the Archivo General de Centro América, B98/10 leg. 7581, exp. 6683 (1935). During the October Revolution, these concerns found their way into the Constitution itself.

37. Taracena examines such ambiguities during and after the October Revolution in *Etnicidad, estado y nación*, vol. 2.

38. For positions of the opposition party Movimiento de Liberación Nacional, see its "Plan de Tegucigalpa," December 24, 1953, published in Mariñas Otero, *Las constituciones de Guatemala*, 681–730. The plan is discussed in detail in Taracena, *Etnicidad, estado y nación*, 2:50–54. For more on the Catholic Church's anti-Communism, see chapter 2 of this book.

39. See Instituto Indigenista Nacional, "Un dictamen favorable," and "Nuevo reglamento del instituto," *Boletín del Instituto Indigenista Nacional*, 2nd epoch, 1, nos. 1–5 (1955, republished in 1957): 23–24 and 33–42.

40. Instituto Indigenista Interamericano, "Informe del IIN [Guatemala], 1955," *Boletín Indigenista* 6, nos. 1–4 (1956): 58–60.

41. See Instituto Indigenista Nacional, "El museo del indio guatemalteco," *Boletín del Instituto Indigenista Nacional*, 2nd epoch, 1, nos. 1–5 (1955, republished in 1957): 47–50.

42. Decree of April 9, 1959, by Ydígoras Fuentes, reproduced in the newspaper *La Ruta*, April 16, 1974.

43. *Guatemala Indígena* 1, no. 1 (January–March 1961): 5.

44. "En torno a la integración social de Guatemala," *Guatemala Indígena* 1, no. 1 (January–March 1961): 7–30.

45 Instituto Indigenista Nacional, *Por qué es indispensable el indigenismo?* 9.

46. bid., 9–10.

47. Interview with Concepción Ramírez Mendoza, July 6, 2002, Santiago Atitlán. See also the newspaper *Día*, May 27, 2002. The army's murder of her father is believed to have been a mistake, since he was thought by residents of Santiago Atitlán to have been cooperating with the military. According to witnesses, his limited proficiency in Spanish caused confusion when soldiers questioned him, and they linked him to the guerrillas. Ramírez Mendoza's husband's death is more mysterious. People in the community believed him to be an army informant, yet attributed his death to the army because "he knew too much" or was no longer deemed useful. He could have been killed by the guerrillas, too, for his collaboration with the army. The killings were not fully investigated.

48. Interview with Concepción Ramírez Mendoza, July 6, 2002, Santiago Atitlán.

49. *Ixim: Notas Indígenas*, 1, no. 12 (September 1978).

50. Tecún Umán figured in accounts of Guatemalan history in an earlier era as well. See, for example, a textbook by José Villacorta, *Curso de la historia de la América Central para uso de los institutos y escuelas normales*, published in 1915. Tecún Umán was the subject of a poem published in *El Comercio*, Quetzaltenango, August 12, 1911 (both cited in Taracena, *Etnicidad, estado y nación*, 1:126–27nn232–33). Grandin notes that Quetzaltenango K'iche' elites in the early twentieth century developed a "cult" of Tecún Umán, which was then appropriated and militarized by the national state and army. See Grandin, *Blood of Guatemala*, 288–89 n18. For the post-1954 period see Taracena, *Etnicidad, estado y nación*, vol. 2.

51. Vela, "Tecun Uman en la historia y la leyenda." It was one of many such articles appearing in the same period. See *Revista Cultural del Ejército*, 1979 through 1982.

52. Otzoy, "Tekum Umam: From Nationalism to Maya Resistance," 164.

53. Nelson, *Finger in the Wound*, 11.

54. Ibid., 16.

Chapter 2

1. Archbishop Mariano Rossell y Arellano, "Carta pastoral sobre los avances del comunismo en Guatemala." April 4, 1954, in Diócesis del Quiché, *El pueblo y su iglesia*, 33.

2. Interview with Emeterio Toj Medrano, August 24, 2002, Guatemala City.

3. The next chapter focuses on Quetzaltenango and Cobán. There is still a great deal to be learned about these five cases (especially Huehuetenango)

and many others, including areas of Chimaltenango, northern El Quiché, and Baja Verapaz. The remainder of this book will follow activists from the five regions introduced here as area Mayas became involved in broader forms of organizing.

4. Interview with Emeterio Toj Medrano, August 24, 2002, Guatemala City.

5. Local leaders set up agrarian committees throughout the country, with a reported four hundred CALs established within the first month of the reform and more than three thousand set up within four months. See Handy, *Revolution in the Countryside*, 93. State-owned fincas (plantations) were distributed almost immediately, and some eight hundred private fincas were subject to expropriation over the course of the next two years. A total of 17 percent of the country's productive land had been expropriated or was in the process of expropriation by the time of the coup in June 1954, with many more petitions waiting to be considered (Ibid., 93–94). In many cases, however, landowners fought the expropriations and refused to cede their holdings. The *Nunca más* report from the Guatemalan Archbishop's Human Rights Office shows that the reform process was far from smooth: it was marked by abuses by petitioners in some areas, and landowners unleashed a wave of violence that included assassinations of agrarian organizers (ODHAG [Oficina de Derechos Humanos del Arzobispado de Guatemala], *Nunca más*, 3:7–9). For an excellent history of rural organizing during this period in the department of Alta Verapaz, see Grandin, *Last Colonial Massacre*.

6. For studies of the development of Catholic Action and relations between AC and traditional religious practices, see Falla, *Quiché rebelde*; Warren, *Symbolism of Subordination*; and Brintnall, *Revolt against the Dead*. These studies recount tensions between old and new, but some observers have also noted more accommodating relationships developing in some places by the 1970s. See, for example, descriptions of a Sololá community by Maryknoll sister Bernice Kita, in *What Prize Awaits Us*.

7. Father James Curtin, letter to Reverend Eugene Higgins, July 5, 1963, 4, in James Curtin Media, Box 128, Maryknoll Mission Archives, Maryknoll, New York.

8. Interview with Emeterio Toj Medrano, August 24, 2002, Guatemala City.

9. Grandin, *Last Colonial Massacre*, 62.

10. Interview with Domingo Hernández Ixcoy, August 10, 2002, Chimaltenango.

11. Ibid. Seasonal migration to coastal fincas became an economic imperative for many campesinos in the 1960s and 1970s.

12. It was no accident, says Hernández Ixcoy, that the first guerrilla uprisings in the 1960s were in areas where campesinos had been most politicized by the October Revolution and its aftermath and had received—then

lost—lands in the agrarian reform. Prominent among them were the Achí of Rabinal, Baja Verapaz. Interview with Domingo Hernández Ixcoy, March 1, 2002, Chimaltenango. Violence over land and campesino mobilization in San Martín Jilotepeque, Chimaltenango, likewise can be traced to the agrarian reform period and the counterrevolution. The reform, and specifically petitions by San Martín agrarian committees, resulted in the redistribution to workers of area *fincas de mozos*, where landowners had for generations provided *mozos* (resident plantation workers) access to land only in exchange for labor on coastal plantations. With the undoing of the agrarian reform, the state returned the fincas to their former owners. These experiences helped convert San Martín into a hotbed of agrarian organizing, social unrest, and insurgency for the next three decades. See ODHAG, *Nunca más*, 3:7–9.

13. ODHAG, *Nunca más*, 3:13, 70. A Maryknoll publication listed a total of 522 Catholic priests in Guatemala in 1968, with 81 percent of them foreign born. ("5 Year Plan, Maryknoll Fathers, Guatemals-El Salvador Region," 7, 1969, Maryknoll Mission Archives, Maryknoll, New York). Archbishop Rossell reportedly had reservations about such an influx and the decentralization of power that would come with it (ODHAG, *Nunca más*, 3:13).

14. Kita, *What Prize Awaits Us*, xxi.

15. Diócesis del Quiché, *El pueblo y su iglesia*, 72. One of the founders of Guatemala's Christian Democrats in a speech to area priests called the party "the only alternative to Communism."

16. Ibid., 73. Some Mayas would disagree with the view that Catholic Action and the DC represented interests that "sprang from within," seeing them as another example of positions shaped by the Catholic Church itself. See chapter 3 of this book. For earlier peasant mobilization in the area of Alta Verapaz, where the Catholic Church was less prominent at the local level, see Grandin, *Last Colonial Massacre*.

17. William Price, "New Wine in Old Bottles," no date, but from the text, apparently written in 1974 (William Price, Creative Works, Box 33, Maryknoll Mission Archives, Maryknoll, New York), 10.

18. Diócesis del Quiché, *El pueblo y su iglesia*, 44.

19. Manz, *Paradise in Ashes*, 50.

20. Interview with Emeterio Toj Medrano, September 29, 2002, Guatemala City. Some priests began to learn Mayan languages as well.

21. Press article quoted in ODHAG, *Nunca más*, 3:72n47. This was in response to the establishment of cooperatives in the communities of Joyabaj, Chinique, Zacualpa, Chicamán, Uspantán, and Sacapulas.

22. Interview with Emeterio Toj Medrano, August 24, 2002, Guatemala City. Beatriz Manz reports that following Gurriarán's expulsion, "continual political pressure from cooperative activists and Catholic Action mobilization" brought about his return to Guatemala. As Manz writes, "Campaigning

in El Quiché, presidential candidate Julio César Méndez Montenegro, in his quest for votes, promised he would allow Luis back into the country. Once elected in 1966 he was reminded and pressured to fulfill his promise. Luis was told of the promise and did not wait for a letter of invitation from President Méndez Montenegro" (*Paradise in Ashes*, 259n37). Gurriarán was forced to flee again in 1975.

23. *Prensa Libre*, April 5, 1967.

24. *El Gráfico*, December 31, 1971.

25. Diócesis del Quiché, *El pueblo y su iglesia*, 79.

26. Loans by 1971 totaled 334,525 quetzales, with one quetzal equal to one US dollar at the time (Ibid., 78n88).

27. For more on this, see chapter 4. This was one of the few events in which Maya women could readily take on a prominent public role. It was more difficult for young women to lead other kinds of organizing in the 1970s, though not impossible. The Diocese of El Quiché writes of a small group of women in Santa Cruz, "*valientes y decididas*"—brave and determined—who focused attention on the rights and needs of women at the time, airing a program on women's issues on Radio Quiché and traveling to area villages to offer women study sessions. Apparently they were pressured by men in the community to stop. Women in the northern Ixil region, and in Cunen and Uspantán, in contrast, were described as being more involved in politics, protests, and in confronting the army over issues of repression in the 1970s (Ibid., 69–72). The authors attributed the difference to greater machismo in the south.

28. Interview with Domingo Hernández Ixcoy, August 20, 2002, Chimaltenango.

29. Interview with Gregorio Chay Laynez, September 5, 2002, Guatemala City.

30. Interview with Domingo Hernández Ixcoy, August 20, 2002, Chimaltenango. *Rezar* translates into English as "pray," but it also reflects the practice of recitation or rote memorization that was part of highland Catholicism of the 1960s.

31. Ibid.

32. Established in the mid-1960s by Maryknoll sister Marian Peter and a few others, Cráter began as a center in Guatemala City where Ladino secondary and university students could meet with each other and with rural Mayas visiting the capital to attend "social promotion" training workshops that were being held at the Jesuit Rafael Landívar University. (One instructor there was Father Luis Gurriarán). In 1966 Sister Peter took Cráter students to visit Huehuetenango, and in the early 1970s, Jesuits began taking them to work in rural El Quiché. Many young people connected to Cráter became prominent leftist intellectuals, including Myrna Mack Chang, Gustavo Porras, and Gustavo Meoño. Mack was later an anthropologist working with internally displaced refugee communities.

193

Targeted by the Guatemalan military for her work, she was brutally murdered in 1990. Porras and Meoño became leaders of the guerrilla EGP.

33. Interview with Ricardo Falla, November 12, 2002, Santa María Chiquimula.

34. Interview with Domingo Hernández Ixcoy, September 7, 2002, Chimaltenango.

35. Interview with Emeterio Toj Medrano, August 24, 2002, Guatemala City.

36. Interview with Pablo Ceto, September 28, 2002, Guatemala City. *Nukuj* is a K'iche' term that Ceto translated as "preparation."

37. Manz writes that "75 percent of all cultivators lacked sufficient land even for subsistence—the average landholding was 3.4 acres of often exhausted soil, and 22 percent of the peasants had less than two acres of land or no land at all" (*Paradise in Ashes*, 37).

38. For a detailed and moving account of Father Gurriarán's work in the cooperative movement in El Quiché and the colonization efforts he led in the northern Ixcán region, see Manz, *Paradise in Ashes*. Maryknolls led the colonization projects and cooperatives in northern Huehuetenango and in the Petén beginning in the late 1960s.

39. Ibid., 20.

40. Nueva canción refers to the social protest music that became popular in Latin America's Southern Cone in the 1950s, 1960s, and early 1970s, especially in Chile. Shortly after the Chilean coup of September 11, 1973, Victor Jara was arrested, tortured, and then assassinated by Pinochet forces.

41. Manz, *Paradise in Ashes*, 4–5. It is also interesting that one of Manz's Ladino interviewees, a minority among the colonizers, noted the growing Maya mobilization in the 1970s: "We knew from the classes we attended in Uspantán about the big Mayan movement. . . . We knew that Catholic priests and nuns were helping the indigenous people" (Ibid., 66).

42. See Payeras, *Days of the Jungle*; and Manz, *Paradise in Ashes*, for descriptions of the encounter.

43. See Manz, *Paradise in Ashes*, chap. 3.

44. For more on Stanley Rother and the Santiago Atitlán mission, see the collection of his letters, *The Shepherd Cannot Run*. Information about organizing in Santiago Atitlán was gathered through interviews with former members of the radio association Voz de Atitlán, campesino organizers, literacy workers, and families of the dead and disappeared.

45. Interviews with family of Felipe Vásquez Tuíz, June 27 and October 5, 2002, Santiago Atitlán, and interview with Pedro Esquina, July 6, 2002, Santiago Atitlán.

46. Rossell championed Catholic educational institutions for Mayas but was suspicious of public schools. Regarding public education under

Ubico, he commented that "books are too fragile a staircase for our Indians to climb to civilization" (quoted in Grandin, *Last Colonial Massacre*, 80). References to similar preoccupations about public education appear in other Catholic mission documents, such as a 1966 Maryknoll report that lamented that "in the . . . [public] schools . . . of Guatemala City no one was teaching religion even though it was allowed. These are a special target of the Communists, who aim for recruits at between 14 and 19 years of age" ("Maryknoll in Guatemala—El Salvador," 1966, 5, in Maryknoll Fathers and Brothers Archives, Box 128, James Curtin Media, Maryknoll Mission Archives, Maryknoll, New York).

47. Letter from Hermano Manuel Estrada C., Director, Instituto Indígena Santiago, no addressee, October 25, 1974, in Archivo Inaremac, San Cristóbal de las Casas, Mexico. Records from Socorro during a sample year, 1973, indicate that a total of 105 young women were enrolled, coming from small, often remote, communities all over the highlands: Tecpán, Patzún, and Comalapa in Chimaltenango; San Pedro La Laguna (on the shores of Lake Atitlán), Santa Lucia Utatlán, and Nahualá in the department of Sololá; San Francisco El Alto and Momostenango in Totonicapán; Chiché and San Martín Jilotepeque in the department of El Quiché; Santa Eulalia, San Miguel Acatán, and San Idelfonso Ixtahuacán in Huehuetenango; as well as a few from the larger towns of Quetzaltenango and Cobán (Inscripciones, Instituto Indígena Nuestra Señora del Socorro, Antigua, Guatemala).

48. Interview with Juana, September 10, 2002, Soloma, Huehuetenango.

49. Similar dynamics seem to have developed at other regional schools for Mayas, such as the Escuela Nacional Comunal Indígena in Chichicastenango, El Quiché. See Manz, *Paradise in Ashes*, 99.

50. Cruz Sisay was part of a class of twenty-two to graduate from the Instituto Indígena Santiago in 1974, listed in a class seminar report, Instituto Indígena Santiago, 1974.

51. Interview with Miguel Sisay, July 2, 2002, Guatemala City. Miguel graduated from the Instituto Indígena Santiago in 1978.

52. Ibid. Though most of the community's more prominent activists were young men, their tactics, as in this case, often relied on the help of young women.

53. Interview with Pedro Esquina, July 6, 2002, Santiago Atitlán.

54. Ibid.

55. "25,000 campesinos alfabetizados por las escuelas radiofonicas," *La Ruta*, October 4, 1975. The Ministry of Education entered into formal contracts with the radio schools beginning in 1971 and agreed to offer equivalency diplomas for students and to support monthly salaries of literacy workers. As we'll see in later chapters, within a few years the relationship between the state and such radio schools turned confrontational.

195

56. Federación Guatemalteca de Escuelas Radiofónicas (FGER), *Pensemos juntos*.

57. Interview with Marco Antonio de Paz, November 21, 2002, Guatemala City.

58. Interview with Miguel Sisay, July 2, 2002, Guatemala City.

59. Asociación Voz de Atitlán, "La verdad está en la historia," unpublished manuscript, Santiago Atitlán, n.d.

60. Interview with Miguel Sisay, July 2, 2002, Guatemala City.

61. FGER, *Pensemos juntos*, 32–33 and 40–41.

62. The details of these events and excerpts from a radio address by Gaspar Culán are included in chapter 5.

63. In the early 1960s, electricity was available in only two of Huehuetenango's thirty-two municipalities. For conditions and projects at that time, see report by Father James Curtin to Father Eugene Higgins, July 5, 1963, James Curtin Media, Box 128, Maryknoll Mission Archives, Maryknoll, New York. By 1969 there were thirty-two Maryknoll priests in the department, along with four in Quetzaltenango, one in the Petén, and three in Guatemala City ("Maryknoll in Central America," 30). The description of developments in Huehuetenango is drawn primarily from the recollections and writings of priests who worked in the region. Theirs is a valuable viewpoint, but much remains to be learned about and from the local Maya movement. For changing economic circumstances in the early 1970s in a community in the department see Brintnall, *Revolt against the Dead*. For a firsthand description of the violence of the 1980s in another Huehuetenango community, see Montejo, *Testimony*.

64. "Maryknoll in Central America, 1943–1978," Central America MFBA, Box 11, Folder 1, Maryknoll Mission Archives, Maryknoll, New York. The Academy of Mayan Languages (ALMG) differentiates the following linguistic communities in Huehuetenango (language groups were classified somewhat differently in the 1960s): Akateko, Awakateko, Chalchiteko, Chuj, K'iche', Mam, Jakaltko/Popti', Q'anjob'al, and Tektiteko.

65. Price, "New Wine in Old Bottles," 5.

66. Ibid.

67. William Price, "Guatemala: Dare to Struggle, Dare to Win," no date, but from text, written in 1986, 5, in William Price, Creative Works, Box 33, Maryknoll Mission Archives, Maryknoll, New York.

68. Ibid.

69. Father Thomas Melville started the effort for the Maryknolls, and he was followed by Fathers Ronald Hennessey and William Wood. Wood was killed in a mysterious plane crash in 1976. See, too, Manz, *Paradise in Ashes*, for Santa María Tzejá colonizers' strained relations with INTA.

70. The Maryknolls geared these centers toward the goals set out in their five-year plan of 1968: to train students in "social awareness and responsibility" and to "transform this initial awakening into an effective instrument of development." As a Maryknoll report stated in 1975, "It is recognized that this process of making people aware of their dignity and potential is a never-ending one" ("5 Year Plan," 1969, and "Regional Plan," 1975, Maryknoll Mission Archives, Maryknoll, New York). The Maryknoll Center for Integral Development was connected to the training programs at the Jesuit Rafael Landívar University in the capital, with "primary" training taking place in Huehuetenango and more advanced training offered at Landívar.

71. Telephone interview with Father Daniel Jensen, March 30, 2004.

72. Ibid.

73. Ibid.

74. Kita, *What Prize Awaits Us*, 15, 18, and 26. Kita, who worked in a Kaqchikel community in Sololá, writes that the catechists from her community joined a group of approximately ninety men at the Apostolic Center, most of them from Guatemala and a few from Mexico.

75. Price, "Guatemala: Dare to Struggle," 9. Sacred Heart father Luis Gurriarán said practically the same thing in an interview with Manz: "I came to evangelize the Indians of Guatemala, but in the process of getting to know them they evangelized me" (Manz, *Paradise in Ashes*, 52).

76. Price, "New Wine in Old Bottles," 8–9.

77. Ibid., 5–6. Jesuit Ricardo Falla tells of traveling along the serpentine roads of Huehuetenango in a car driven by Maryknoll priest Jim Curtin, probably the person most responsible for the Maryknoll's strong Maya focus. When rounding a bend Curtin nearly hit someone walking along the road. Checking the rearview mirror, Curtin jokingly pointed to the philosophical rift between the two priests. "At least it wasn't an indígena!" (interview with Ricardo Falla, November 12, 2002, Santa María Chiquimula). These positions will be examined in more detail in chapter 3. There seem to have been concerns on the part of some Maryknoll personnel about this privileging of Mayas, and one Maryknoll report labeled the position racist: "Some Maryknollers working in Guatemala have fallen into the racist attitude of lauding the Indian and disparaging the Ladino" ("Mission Leadership Vision, Central American Region," January 1980, Central America MFBA, Box 11, Maryknoll Mission Archives, Maryknoll, New York).

78. "Maryknoll in Central America," 18 and 26. Father John Breen wrote in the regional superior's diary in December 1968 that he found "a lack of unity and direction among the men in Huehuetenango. . . . I find a split as regards trends in theology and mission apostolate approach" (Ibid., 28).

79. See Behrens, "From Symbols of the Sacred," 210–211.

80. "Maryknoll in Central America," 18.

81. Ibid., 19. See also Melville and Melville, *Whose Heaven, Whose Earth?*; Melville, *Through a Glass Darkly*; and Manz, *Paradise in Ashes*, 258n32.

82. "Maryknoll in Central America," 19.

83. Price, "Dare to Struggle," 6.

84. Ibid., 5.

85. Ibid., "New Wine in Old Bottles," 6, 9.

86. Ibid., "Guatemala: Dare to Struggle," 4.

87. A second Maryknoll priest, Father Joseph Towle, was expelled at the same time, along with a Spanish Sacred Heart priest, Father Secundino Varela.

88. For more on the strike, see chapter 3. The organizers almost certainly would have known about a one-thousand-kilometer march on foot by miners from Coahuila, Mexico to that nation's capital in 1952.

89. Price, "Guatemala: Dare to Struggle," 9.

90. Kita, *What Prize Awaits Us*, 48–49.

Chapter 3

1. Guzmán Böckler and Herbert, *Guatemala: Una interpretación histórico-social*, 99–100. These ideas continue to resonate with Maya activists, and the book was republished by Editorial Cholsamaj in 1995.

2. I was not able to treat Chimaltenango separately in this study, though that local history deserves focused attention. Chimaltenango-area Mayas were instrumental in the founding of the campesino organization CUC, and others were behind the creation of the National Integration Front (Frente de Integración Nacional), or FIN, discussed later in this chapter.

3. Interview with Jerónimo Juárez López, July 19, 2006, Quetzaltenango.

4. Ibid., February 15, 2002, Quetzaltenango. For more on the Sociedad El Adelanto, see Grandin, *Blood of Guatemala*, 144.

5. Interview with Jerónimo Juárez López, February 15, 2002, Quetzaltenango.

6. Interview with Isaías Raconcoj, November 13, 2002, Quetzaltenango.

7. Ibid.

8. For a history of Xel-jú, see Cajas Mejía, "Lógica local de participación política maya." Of the five Xel-jú members who won seats in 1974, only two remained on the council three years later; Juárez resigned in protest of the council's lack of transparency and open debate in March 1977. See "Con carácter de irrevocable renunció el concejal 4to. Jerónimo Juárez López," *La Nacion/Quetzaltenango*, March 8, 1977. Xel-jú still exists and won the mayor's post in 1995, with the election of Rigoberto Quemé Chay, who also entered the presidential race in 2002.

9. Bastos and Camus, *Entre el mecapal y el cielo*, 50.

10. It is important to note that not all Xel-jú members or all indígenas associated with Maya-focused organizing in the 1970s sided with opposition movements, revolutionary or otherwise. Some maintained a clear separation from broader organizing efforts and in the 1980s focused exclusively on community development, linguistics, and education. One important result of their efforts was the creation of the Academy of Mayan Languages, ALMG, in 1984, which won official recognition for Guatemala's Mayan languages.

11. Personal conversation with Enrique Luis Sam Colop, January 15, 2002, Guatemala City.

12. Interview with Antonio Pop Caal, January 23, 2002, Cobán.

13. Of Cabracán's eight founders, three were assassinated in the 1980s. Antonio Pop Caal himself was kidnapped and held for ransom in October 2002 and subsequently murdered. His body was found the following December. The crime, not thoroughly investigated, was declared by authorities to be the result of criminal violence rather than political motivation.

14. Another Cabracán founder from Santa Eulalia, Huehuetenango, had also gone to seminary, but then like Pop Caal, rejected the church. As one priest remembered, "Something happened in the seminary. . . . He suddenly turned on the church and came back and was preaching atheism in the parish, and his father was horrified!" (telephone interview with Father Daniel Jensen, March 30, 2004).

15. Pop Caal, "Replica del indio." Pop Caal also delivered the piece before the Congress of Americanists in Puebla, Mexico, in 1974. It was subsequently reproduced in Bonfil Batalla, *Utopía y revolución*, 145–52, and translated into English and published under the title "The Situation of Indian Peoples in Guatemala" by the organization Indigena in Berkeley, California, in partnership with *Akwesasne Notes*, no date.

16. Interview with Antonio Pop Caal, January 23, 2002, Cobán. This changed dramatically in the 1990s. See, for example, the writings of newspaper columnists Enrique Luis Sam Colop in *Prensa Libre* and Estuardo Zapeta in *Siglo XXI*.

17. Pop Caal, "Replica del indio," 43.

18. Ibid. For discussion of a similar use of the word *nègre* as a term of defiance, see Depestre, "An Interview with Aimé Césaire."

19. Interview with Miguel Alvarado, November 7, 2002, Cantel.

20. Interview with Ricardo Cajas Mejía, August 28, 2002, Quetzaltenango, referring to the CUC-organized protest at Iximché, February 14, 1980, following the Spanish embassy massacre. For details, see chapter 5.

21. Price, "New Wine in Old Bottles," 6.

22. Interview with Ricardo Falla, November 12, 2002, Santa Maria Chiquimula.

23. Arnulfo Delgado was a priest who connected Mayas from different areas to each other. He attended seminary in El Quiché and was the priest who drew the reina indígena from Soloma, Huehuetenango, into regional activism. Tomás García was involved in oppositional organizing around Totonicapán and Quetzaltenango. Juana Vásquez was active in reinas organizing, in CUC, including at the international level where she became a spokesperson for the organization, and in the EGP. (She sometimes used the pseudonym Rosario Pu.) She survived la violencia, but her (biological) sister, also active in community organizing and the revolutionary Left, was tortured to death.

24. Interview with Jerónimo Juárez López, July 19, 2006, Quetzaltenango. *La situación* is a term much like *la violencia*, usually referring to repression without clearly saying so.

25. Interview with Ricardo Falla, November 12, 2002, Santa Maria Chiquimula.

26. Telephone interview with Father Daniel Jensen, March 30, 2004. Father Gerardi became central to church efforts in defense of human rights in Guatemala and oversaw the Archbishop's Human Rights Office 1998 report on atrocities during the war, *Guatemala: Nunca más.* He was assassinated by state forces two days after releasing the report. For a gripping study of Gerardi's murder and its aftermath, see Goldman, *The Art of Political Murder.*

27. Father Luis de León V., "Encuentro indigenista de alto nivel en Cobán," *Boletín Misionero Salesiano* 3 (May 1973): 1.

28. Manuscript by Padre Tomás García entitled "Experiencia indígena," in the Biblioteca Parroquial, Santiago Atitlán, no date, 8. This racialist critique of AC contrasts with the criticism of Catholic Action that eventually developed among catechists such as Emeterio Toj, who faulted AC not for its assimilationism, but because it could not go far enough in addressing the needs of campesinos.

29. Attendees came from the communities of Olintepeque, Cabricán, and San Juan Ostuncalco in Quetzaltenango; Momostenango in Totonicapán; Chiantla, Jacaltenango, Barrillas, San Pedro Necta, and Santa Eulalia in Huehuetenango; Nahualá, San Andrés Itzapa, and Patzún in Sololá; Rabinal, Tactic, Cahabón, Carchá, and Cobán in the Verapaces; Santa Cruz, Sacapulas, Uspantán, Chichicastenango, Chicamán, Joyabaj, and Jocopilas in the department of El Quiché; and Tejutla, San Pedro Sacatepéquez, and Comitancillo in San Marcos. List of participants, *Curso de antropología y teología para la actividad misionera en Guatemala,* held November 18–December 13, 1974. Document from the parish archive, Momostenango.

30. Agenda of the *Curso de antropología y teología para la actividad misionera en Guatemala,* held November 18–December 13, 1974. Document from the parish archive, Momostenango.

31. See chapter 4 for more on the church's role in queens' organizing.

32. Interview with Ricardo Cajas Mejía, August 29, 2002, Quetzaltenango.

33. Ibid.

34. Almost no documentation is available about the Seminarios Indígenas, and there is some confusion over their dates and venues. The Catholic Church's *Nunca más* report describes the first of the Seminarios Indígenas taking place in Quetzaltenango in 1972. Demetrio Cojtí Cuxil, a participant in the meetings, writes that they were held first in Tecpán in 1974, then in El Quiché in 1975, and in Quetzaltenango in 1976. Cojtí Cuxil, *Ri maya' moloj pa iximulew*, 97. The last of the workshops, I believe, was held in 1979.

35. Interview with Domingo Hernández Ixcoy, September 7, 2002, Chimaltenango.

36. Interview with Emeterio Toj Medrano, August 24, 2002, Guatemala City.

37. Interview with Ricardo Cajas Mejía, August 28, 2002, Quetzaltenango.

38. Recall that in 1971, Eduardo Pacay from Cobán claimed to speak for the "Maya blood!" *La Ruta*, September 26, 1971. In 1973 the former national indigenous queen América Son Huitz of San Cristóbal, Totonicapán, called on the present-day "*mujer maya, hermana mía*" (Maya woman, my sister) to have pride in her connection to the pre-Columbian past. "Palabras pronunciadas por la Rabín Ahau saliente en el Festival Folklórico de 1973," *Boletín Misionero Salesiano* 8 (August 1974).

39. Interview with Ricardo Cajas Mejía, August 28, 2002, Quetzaltenango. The same debate, whether to use the term *indio* or *Maya*, reemerged in (tense) discussions in the 1990s between groups aligned with the revolutionary Left and those in the Consejo de Organizaciones Mayas de Guatemala, COMG.

40. In Bastos and Camus, *Entre el mecapal y el cielo*, 40. The document indicates that the Tecpán meeting took place in 1974.

41. Interview with Emeterio Toj Medrano, August 24, 2002, Guatemala City.

42. Interview with Ricardo Cajas Mejía, August 28, 2002, Quetzaltenango. Latifundismo and minifundismo refer to inequitable land tenure patterns in Guatemala, where huge plantations (*latifundios*) occupy most arable lands and campesinos are left with "mini" plots inadequate for subsistence agriculture.

43. Interview with Domingo Hernández Ixcoy, March 1, 2002, Chimaltenango.

44. See "*Unidos en la esperanza, presencia de la iglesia en la reconstrucción de Guatemala*," mensaje del Episcopado de Guatemala, July 25, 1976. Reproduced in Conferencia Episcopal de Guatemala, *Al servicio de la vida, la justicia y la paz*, 126–60.

45. Interview with Ricardo Cajas Mejía, August 28, 2002, Quetzaltenango.

The terms *movement* and *unification* are used loosely here. They reflect a new sense at the time that Mayas were confronting the needs of their communities together. The task was very broadly defined, and activists' efforts were not coordinated in a "movement" in any formal sense. Earthquakes have had similar effects on political organizing in other times and places: Miguel Angel Asturias marks the 1917 Guatemala City earthquake as contributing to the downfall of dictator Manuel Estrada Cabrera in 1920, although the class dynamics were quite different than in 1976. "I remember a Guatemala where people dressed in tails and top hat," he said, and "they wore gloves and carried canes . . . . But now suddenly the earth shook and everyone was left out in the street. And it's curious but undoubtedly the earthquake not only shook the earth but also jolted consciences. . . . People from all walks of life suddenly found themselves thrown together in the streets in nightshirts and pajamas. . . . So what was the result? Those who had lived withdrawn, out of touch with the rest of the population, joined the crowd. . . . In 1917 my generation, no longer intimidated by memories of previous reprisals, entered the political arena" (Harss and Dohmann, "Miguel Angel Asturias," 417). Earthquakes in Managua in 1972 and Mexico City in 1985 also come to mind.

46. Interview with Pablo Ceto, June 4, 2002, Guatemala City.

47. Interview with Emeterio Toj Medrano, August 24, 2002, Guatemala City. Demetrio Cojtí Cuxil, from Tecpán, worked at IDESAC at the same time.

48. Price, "Guatemala: Dare to Struggle," 8.

49. Interview with Domingo Hernández Ixcoy, March 1, 2002, Chimaltenango. This view is at odds with that expressed by the Diocese of El Quiché, quoted in the last chapter, that the DC was the means by which Mayas (finally) were able to express and pursue their own interests.

50. Interview with Domingo Hernández Ixcoy, August 20, 2002, Chimaltenango.

51. Interview with Pablo Ceto, September 28, 2002, Guatemala City. The degree to which CUC members in general knew of the organization's relationship with the EGP is unclear. Many CUC leaders, like Ceto, Toj, Hernández Ixcoy, and Gregorio Chay, became EGP combatants or leaders, but many others remained local activists without becoming active in the guerrilla group. In private circles CUC members expressed at least some resentment at their loss of agency to the EGP. Personal communication with Arturo Arias, June 23, 2008.

52. Interview with Gregorio Chay Laynez, September 5, 2002, Guatemala City.

53. See Grandin, "To End with All These Evils."

54. Interview with Gregorio Chay Laynez, September 5, 2002, Guatemala City. Ironically, Chay's first organizing experience in 1977 was in defense of traje. See following.

55. Interview with Emeterio Toj Medrano, August 24, 2002, Guatemala City. Toj added that CUC always fought ethnic discrimination, especially the everyday discrimination faced by Maya women who wore traje. It was not written in CUC documents, he said, was "not in the discourse, but we did it, fought against that type of discrimination."

56. This meeting seems to have been in 1975, though one participant placed it in 1976. The EGP was becoming influential in the department at that time, a fact that the participants would have been aware of.

57. Interview with Emeterio Toj Medrano, August 24, 2002, Guatemala City.

58. Interview with Domingo Hernández Ixcoy, September 7, 2002, Chimaltenango.

59. Interview with Ricardo Cajas Mejía, August 28, 2002, Quetzaltenango.

60. Ibid.

61. Interview with Ricardo Falla, November 12, 2002, Santa Maria Chiquimula.

62. The Centro Indígena also received funding from an association of German bishops, Adveniat, although funds were cut in 1980 due to the dissatisfaction of the Germans with the center's Vatican II–inspired activities. According to Father Daniel Jensen, who was running the program at the time, an Adveniat representative came to the center with one question: "Do you believe in liberation theology?" he asked. Jensen answered in the affirmative. "[With] his pencil," Jensen recalls, "[the Adveniat representative] drew a big X right across the funding request. . . . He never even gave me a chance to answer" (telephone interview with Father Daniel Jensen, March 30, 2004).

63. Interview with former Cabracán member who wishes to remain anonymous, January 24, 2002, Cobán.

64. Interview with Ricardo Falla, November 12, 2002, Santa Maria Chiquimula.

65. *Ixim: Notas Indígenas* 1, no. 1 (October 1977): 2. This passage from the Recinos (1947) translation of the *Popol Vuh* became enormously popular among activists beginning in the 1970s, due in part to the work of Adrián Inés Chávez. For details see chapter 5 of this book. Its call for Maya mobilization was repeated over the next decades by Maya queens, culturalistas, campesino organizers, and revolutionaries alike. A subsequent translation offers a more mundane (and more accurate) interpretation of the passage: "All penitents and sacrificers of the tribes spoke to the others. They roused and summoned one another, all of them. Not even one or two divisions were left out. All of them conversed and presented themselves, then they shared their thoughts" (Tedlock, *Popol Vuh*, 166). Despite recognition that the Tedlock translation

is a better one, the Recinos call for Maya action remains the most commonly used passage from the *Popol Vuh*.

66. *Ixim: Notas Indígenas* 1, no. 1 (October 1977): 3.

67. Ibid., 4.

68. For more on gender and markers of indigenous identity see chapter 4.

69. Interview with Gregorio Chay Laynez, September 5, 2002, Guatemala City.

70. *Ixim: Notas Indígenas* 1, no. 2 (November 1977): 4. Language concerns had a prominent place in the periodical, and writers on these issues were undoubtedly connected to the Maya linguistics movement that became active in the mid-1980s. See Cojtí Cuxil, *Políticas para la reivindicación de los Mayas*; England, *Autonomía de los idiomas mayas*; Fischer and Brown, *Maya Cultural Activism*; and Warren, *Indigenous Movements and Their Critics*.

71. *Ixim: Notas Indígenas* 1, no. 2 (November 1977): 7. By this time, several young Maya men and women from Guatemala, among them Jerónimo Juárez and Antonio Pop Caal, had traveled to international indígenous congresses abroad.

72. Ibid., 8.

73. *Ixim: Notas Indígenas*, April 1978.

74. I believe this was the April 1978 issue. My copy of that issue is missing its cover, but the image is reproduced on another page, no number. It may have appeared on that April cover, or it may have been published the month before. The April 1978 issue was the last one produced at the Centro Indígena.

75. Interview with Ricardo Cajas Mejía, February 15, 2002, Quetzaltenango.

76. Telephone interview with Father Daniel Jensen, March 30, 2004. Such notions of docility, of course, have never matched historical reality.

77. *Ixim: Notas Indígenas*, June/July 1978.

78. Jorge Luis García de León, in *Ixim: Notas Indígenas*, September 1978.

79. *Ixim: Notas Indígenas*, April 1978.

80. *La Nación*, December 12, 1976, and *El Gráfico*, February 14, 1977.

81. For more on the rise and fall of FIN, see Falla, "El movimiento indígena," and Hale, *Más que un indio*, chap. 3.

82. "Indígenas agrupados en el Frente de Integración Nacional apoyan a Lucas," *Prensa Libre*, February 20, 1978, and "El 'FIN' concluyó por dar su apoyo a los candidatos del Frente Amplio: Lucas y Pancho," *La Tarde*, February 21, 1978.

83. *El Gráfico*, February 18, 1978.

84. Santiago Ixbalanqué Rojop, "La politica y el indio de Guatemala," *Ixim: Notas Indígenas*, April and May 1978.

85. *Ixim: Notas Indígenas*, November/December 1978. Additional excerpts reprinted in all remaining issues of *Ixim*.

86. Hale, *Más que un indio*, 90.

NOTES TO PAGES 83–88

Chapter 4

1. The Panzós massacre was preceded by a massacre in 1975 of some thirty indigenous campesinos in Sansirisay, El Progreso, overseen by future dictator General Efraín Ríos Montt, though that massacre was less known publicly.

2. Beauty pageants and questions of gender, race, politics, and identity that play out within them are explored in a wonderful array of contexts— Nicaragua, Tibet, Guatemala, Minnesota, Belize—in the collection edited by Cohen, Wilk, and Stoeltje, *Beauty Queens on the Global Stage*. See also Craig, *Ain't I a Beauty Queen?* for an examination of race, beauty, and politics in US pageantry; and López, "The India Bonita Contest of 1921 and the Ethnicization of Mexican National Culture," for a discussion of the relevance of that contest to changing ideas of Indianness in Mexican nationalism.

3. Marco Aurelio Alonzo, "Los objetivos del Festival Folklórico," unpublished manuscript, no date. Interview with Marco Aurelio Alonzo, January 25, 2002, Cobán.

4. "Rabín Ahau" means "Daughter of the King" in the Q'eqchi' language.

5. For a fascinating discussion of the Rabín Ahau contest, see McAllister, "Authenticity and Guatemala's Maya Queen."

6. Schirmer, "'Those Who Die for Life Cannot Be Called Dead,'" 45.

7. Almost all of the former reinas stayed in their original communities, and residents could often tell me the names of the reinas indígenas of the 1970s in a sequence of two or three. The reina indígena contests of the era may have been "play" or make-believe, as Robert Lavenda suggests in a study of Minnesota pageants, but the fact that people remember them reflects the intensity of that politicized moment (Lavenda, "'It's Not a Beauty Pageant!'" 44).

8. Many exceptions exist. Some men in the communities of Sololá, Santiago Atitlán, Todos Santos, and the Ixil area, for example, wear traditional clothing. Other Mayas in a new class of urban professionals, too, wear "neotraditional" dress. See Hendrickson, *Weaving Identities*. At the same time, representations of indigeneity are not limited to traje, though it is a most visible marker. Language is also important, and many Mayas claim that certain traditions, values, and worldviews also denote Mayaness.

9. In Quetzaltenango, the first reina indígena was elected in 1934, due to efforts by the indigenous Sociedad El Adelanto. The 1934 naming of the reina indígena of Quetzaltenango was "the first time the pueblo indígena of Xelajú [Quetzaltenango] was permitted to take part directly in the fair" (Tzunun M. and Nimatuj I., *Historial del certamen de la belleza indígena*, n.p). For early contests in Quetzaltenango, see also Grandin, *Blood of Guatemala*, chap. 7. An especially Europeanized Indianness was reflected in contests in Cobán, Alta Verapaz. The 1958 India Bonita Cobanera ("Pretty Indian from Cobán"), for example, was a woman of mixed German and indigenous descent, María Elena Winter Flor,

who has been involved in the Folklore Festival since its inception (interview with María Elena Winter Flor, December 8, 2002, Cobán, Alta Verapaz). Rick López has noted that in early "India Bonita" contests in Mexico, the public had difficulty conceptualizing "indias" who were "bonitas," substituting photos of white women in Indian costume ("India Bonita Contest," 301).

10. We see similar parallel pageants established in other locations, including neighboring Belize in the 1940s. In one pageant Richard Wilk explains that "tall, charming, beautiful and dignified Honduran beauties" competed for the title of Queen of the Bay, while Garifunas held a Queen of the Settlement contest emphasizing native dances and indigenous languages and culture (Wilk, "Connections and Contradictions," 220–21).

11. From interviews with spectators and participants in Quetzaltenango, San Cristóbal Verapaz, and Santiago Atitlán.

12. As Arturo Arias noted in his study of Guatemala's indigenous movement in the 1970s, Maya community activists in Santa Cruz del Quiché (including Emeterio Toj) demanded that their pageant winner receive prize money equal to what the Ladina queen received ("Movimiento indígena," 76). Interviews about queen pageants in Santa Cruz conducted with the 1974 reina indígena of Santa Cruz, April 18 and November 4, 2002, Santa Cruz del Quiché, and with former catechists and founders of CUC: Emeterio Toj Medrano, August 24, 2002, Guatemala City; Gregorio Chay Laynez, September 5, 2002, Guatemala City; and Pablo Ceto, September 28, 2002, Guatemala City. In many communities, such as Santa Cruz, Quetzaltenango, Santiago Atitlán, and San Cristóbal Verapaz, students won changes in the winner's title, changing it from *princesa* (or even the diminutive *princesita*) or *india bonita* to *reina indígena*, again on equal footing with the Ladina *reina*.

13. Grandin, *Blood of Guatemala*, 4.

14. Photos of the first fifty reinas indígenas of Quetzaltenango were published in Tzunun and Nimatuj, *Historial del certamen de la belleza indígena*.

15. Similarly, the reina indígena of Santiago Atitlán was renamed Rumam Tz'utjil Pop, "Granddaughter of the King" in Tz'utujil, in 1978. That same year activists campaigned in San Cristóbal Verapaz and in other areas to replace their representatives' cape and crown with adornments specific to their communities—in the case of San Cristóbal, a ceremonial huipil and skirt, a red tape for the reina's hair, a woven belt, and a silver necklace (interviews with Pedro Esquina, Santiago Atitlán, July 6, 2002, and with the 1978 reina indígena of San Cristóbal, Amalia Coy Pop, San Cristóbal, March 17, 2002).

16. The 1973 reina indígena of Quetzaltenango, in her farewell speech, September 7, 1974. Parish archives, Momostenango. Interview with María Elvira, Quetzaltenango, October 7, 2002.

17. Speech excerpts reproduced in *Ixim: Notas Indígenas*, August 1978.

18. Interview with Magdalena, 1977 reina indígena of San Sebastián, Retalhuleu, Guatemala City, August 25, 2002.

19. *La Nación/Sur*, October 14, 1977. Variations of the quotation from the *Popol Vuh* appeared frequently in reinas' speeches, likely due to the influence of K'iche' linguist Adrián Inés Chávez. The expression was used in many other—sometimes contradictory—ways as well. As we will see, these were the final words of the Iximché Declaration in February 1980 protesting the Spanish embassy massacre; CUC subsequently used the reference in its public statements; and the Guatemalan army itself, in its *Revista Cultural*, used the passage to call on all Mayas to rise up to defend the fatherland against subversion. See "Poles de desarrollo," *Revista Cultural del Ejército* (January–February 1985), quoted in Schirmer, *Guatemalan Military Project*, 114–15.

20. Interview with Juana, September 10, 2002, Soloma, Huehuetenango.

21. Interview with Ricardo Cajas Mejía, February 21, 2002, Quetzaltenango.

22. "Reina Indígena de Quetzaltenango electa el 12 de agosto," *Ixim: Notas Indígenas* 1, no. 11 (August 1978).

23. Ibid.

24. See Grandin's *Blood of Guatemala*, "Conclusions" and "Epilogue," for a discussion of widening divisions among indígenas in Quetzaltenango at this time, as "indigenous elites lost the ability to fulfill their historical role as brokers" (223). Similar divisions developed in other communities and show themselves again and again. There were also growing rifts among Maya oppositional activists, as discussed in the remainder of this book.

25. Grandin, *Last Colonial Massacre*, 134.

26. Ibid. Grandin writes that another woman, amid the devastation of army violence in 1982, commented to a Ladino Communist Party organizer that "women can do more than 'throw a handful of beans into water.'"

27. The reina from Santiago Atitlán, who was fifteen years old in 1978, may have been an exception. She did not want to discuss the event with me and deferred most of my questions to the men who had sponsored her candidacy.

28. From a speech by a reina indígena in 1978, as remembered by the 1977 reina indígena of Cantel. Interview with Emilia, reina indígena of Cantel, July 13, 2002, Cantel.

29. Catarina Ortiz Jimenez was the first national indigenous queen in 1971, and a year later América Son Huitz was the first to be given the title of Rabín Ahau.

30. Aurelio Alonzo, "Los objetivos del Festival Folklórico." Interview with Marco Aurelio Alonzo, January 25, 2002, Cobán.

31. From *Prospecto del festival*, printed by the Army Editorial, July 1976.

32. *La Ruta*, August 13, 1972. Arana Osorio earned the gruesome nickname the "Butcher of Zacapa" for his zealous tactics of counterinsurgency.

207

Also in the audience that year were the Guatemalan minister of education, the governor of Alta Verapaz, the commander of the local military base, and the US ambassador to Guatemala, William Bowdler.

33. *La Ruta*, August 2, 1976.

34. *Prensa Libre*, August 7, 1976.

35. Program of the thirteenth Festival Folklórico Nacional, July 23–26, 1981, Cobán AV.

36. In stark contrast to the Guatemalan case, Rick López writes that people in Mexico in 1987 "remembered" (mistakenly) that the India Bonita of 1921 was the first Miss Mexico. While those two categories had been "incompatible" in the 1920s, by 1987 such racial boundaries had been dropped from national memory ("India Bonita Contest," 292). It is doubtful that Guatemalans even today would make the mistake of conflating the racially separate titles of Miss Guatemala and Rabín Ahau.

37. Letter by Padre Esteban Haeserijn, no addressee, November 23, 1974. Haeserijn, the same priest giving the talks on race-based colonialism mentioned in the previous chapter, saw the contests as an opportunity for young Maya women to speak for their communities. Other festival organizers disagreed, and contest rules permit contestants to speak only of "culture." Since the beginning of the pageants, contestants have routinely violated such restrictions. Recently former queens have taken to meeting together, and several have spoken out against the Folklore Festival. Mercedes García Marroquín, elected Rabín Ahau in 2000, denounced the festival in the press; while at the 2001 Rabín Ahau pageant to coronate her successor, she condemned discrimination and accused the festival committee of using Maya women for commercial gain. The candidate chosen as the 2001 Rabín Ahau, Manuela Pol, then refused the crown "*por dignidad*," (out of dignity), and the committee was forced to crown the runner-up (see *Prensa Libre*, May 25, 2001, and July 30, 2001). As Richard Wilk notes, "Pageants as an institution can serve the state's goals of 'domesticating difference,' of channeling potentially dangerous social divisions into the realm of aesthetics and taste. But they can also fail in getting this message across, and can end up emphasizing and exacerbating the very divisions they are meant to minimize or control" ("Connections and Contradictions," 218).

38. McAllister writes that Miss Guatemala, the nation's symbol of idealized beauty, is "invariably among the whitest of the nation's young women." The indigenous queen's "task," she adds, is "to represent what makes Guatemala most distinct: her tradition, her Indian past. Authenticity marks the Maya Queen's particularity as an aesthetic property, subordinate to the truly beautiful" ("Authenticity and Guatemala's Maya Queen," 106).

39. Marisol de la Cadena provides another example of tests of "authenticity" in indigenous beauty pageants in Cuzco, Peru. Contestants (date unknown) "had to prove their indigenous 'racial' authenticity," she wrote. "The judges

required that the participants in the beauty contest pose nude; short legs, small breasts, and scant pubic hair were the physical characteristics that the gentlemen organizers chose as markers of the bodies of *real* Indian women" (de la Cadena, *Indigenous Mestizos*, 81).

40. One queen explained that her family wanted her to attend so they could see her on television! (She didn't go.) I don't have a figure for how many Guatemalan municipalities elected reinas indígenas in the 1970s or a corresponding rate of participation in the national Rabín Ahau contest, but clearly a majority did not take part. The major indigenous municipalities typically held local pageants, and many smaller ones did as well. (There are over two hundred municipalities in ten highland departments with majority indigenous populations.) The national-level Rabín Ahau contest attracted twenty-five participants in 1972, thirty in 1974, and twenty-nine in 1975, when it was televised for the first time. In 1976 there were participants from forty-five municipalities, forty-two in 1977, and in 1978 the government claimed that forty-nine queens participated, though the outgoing Rabín Ahau contested that figure (see following). Participation rates were remarkably high in the coming years of intense repression (sixty-five contestants in 1979; more than forty in 1980; forty-seven in 1981; fifty-six in 1982), with newspaper articles on pageant folklore in those years appearing alongside gruesome accounts of dead bodies and assassinated subversives. In its first thirty-five years (1971–2005) winners of the national indigenous queen pageant came from twenty-five communities in fourteen departments.

41. Rigoberta Menchú expressed these same criticisms in the early 1980s in *I, Rigoberta Menchú*, 204–9. Ricardo Falla, too, commented on the contests in 1978, noting that the state's gesture transferred the tensions surrounding community pageants to the national level, while at the same time—since they named a national queen, not a reina K'iche', for example, or a reina Q'eqchi'—it reinforced the new concept of pan-Maya identity (see Falla, "El movimiento indígena").

42. "El colonialismo cultural: Requiem por los homenajes a la raza maya," *Ixim: Notas Indígenas* 1, no. 8 (May 1978): 4, 5, and 8. There are striking similarities between the authors' 1978 critique and that advanced much earlier by K'iche' elites in efforts to contest class definitions of Indianness. See Grandin, *Blood of Guatemala*, chaps. 6 and 7. See also Guzmán Böckler and Herbert, *Guatemala: Una interpretación histórico social*. Many of the ideas central to this piece had been presented five years earlier in the article by Pop Caal, "Replica del indio a una disertación ladina," *La Semana*, December 12, 1972. Pop Caal did not deny a role in writing "Requiem por los homenajes" but said it was a joint endeavor and the authors will remain anonymous (interview with Antonio Pop Caal, January 23, 2002, Cobán).

43. "Requiem por los homenajes," *Ixim*, May 1978.

44. Ibid.

209

45. Ibid., emphasis in original.

46. See chapter 5.

47. Interview with Fidelina Tux Chub, July 29, 2002, Carchá, Alta Verapaz.

48. *Boletín Misionero: Noticiero Trimestral de la Actividad Misionera de la Iglesia en la Verapaz* [formerly *Boletín Misionero Salisiano*] 25 (October 1978): 4.

49. She did not recall meeting Adrián Inés Chávez and assumed that she had heard the slogan from her priest. Interview with Fidelina Tux Chub, July 29, 2002, Carchá.

50. *Prensa Libre*, June 10, 1978.

51. Ibid.

52. The following account comes from author's interviews with the 1978 reina indígena of San Cristóbal, Amalia Coy Pop, January 24 and March 17, 2002, San Cristóbal; the 1977 reina indígena, Estela, March 18, 2002, San Cristóbal; and others in the community. My thanks to Victoria Sanford for first telling me of this case.

53. Interview with Amalia Coy Pop, January 24, 2002, San Cristóbal.

54. Interview with Estela, 1977 reina indígena, March 18, 2002, San Cristóbal.

55. "Privan de su corona a reina indígena de San Cristóbal AV," *El Gráfico*, July 25, 1978.

56. "Damas de San Cristóbal V., explican lo que ocurrió con la reina indígena," *Prensa Libre*, July 29, 1978.

57. Ibid.

58. Ibid. Controversy surrounding this incident continued at least for another year. For one teacher's defense of the school, see "La verdad del trabajo de la Escuela Normal Regional de Santa Lucía y su transformación," *La Nación Occidente*, May 17, 1979. The author noted that the school could not count on the full support of the authorities because they misunderstood its philosophy, objectives, and activities.

59. *Inforpress*, no. 301, July 20, 1978.

60. *Cha'b'l Tinamit* 2, no. 23 (June 1978): 6.

61. The letter addressed to Lucas García was published in *El Gráfico*, July 25, 1978, and *Prensa Libre*, July 26, 1978.

62. Interview with local activist, November 1, 2002, Comalapa, Chimaltenango. For a description of contemporary speeches by reina contestants in nearby Tecpán, see Demetrio R. Guaján (Raxche'), "Reinas de Tecpán Guatemala," *Ixim: Notas Indígenas*, October 1978.

63. "Solidaria protesta por lo de Panzós; La reina indígena de Xelajú no irá a Cobán," *La Nación/Quetzaltenango*, July 29, 1978. Interview with Teresa, 1977–1978 reina indígena, February 14, 2002, Quetzaltenango.

64. Interviews with Elisa, November 6, 2002, and Norma, November 14, 2002, Quetzaltenango. Interview with 1977 Rabín Ahau, July 12, 2002, San Francisco El Alto, Totonicapán. The 1977 Rabín Ahau also spoke with the local press after the pageant and mentioned her family pressuring her to attend (*La Nación/Quetzaltenango*, August 9, 1978).

65. *El Gráfico*, July 30, 1978.

66. For Mayor Overdick, see "Subversores disfrazados lanzaron a los campesinos a chocar con los soldados," *Diario de Centro América*, June 2, 1978. For General Laugerud, see "'Lo sucedido en Panzós es el resultado de un plan general de subversión,': Kjell," *La Nación*, June 1, 1978; and "Panzós: Conmoción sigue; Presidente señala a los culpables de la Matanza," *El Imparcial*, June 1, 1978. Laugerud, president from July 1974 through June 1978, explicitly placed the blame for the incident on the guerrilla EGP. In doing so, he was not denying that the army did the actual killing; on the contrary, his explanation was that because of suspected guerrilla presence in the region, the guerrilla was responsible for an army massacre of unarmed civilians.

67. Interview with Ricardo Cajas Mejía, February 21, 2002, Quetzaltenango.

68. The infamous case of Rogelia Cruz, the 1959 Ladina "Miss Guatemala" brutally killed in 1968 for suspected guerrilla involvement, should remind us that such symbolic protection had its limits. As Miss Guatemala, Cruz was a symbol even more revered than the reina indígena. She was, nonetheless, murdered by the state she represented for her ties to the 1960s revolutionary group Rebel Armed Forces, FAR. See coverage in the Guatemalan press, January 1968, and Treacy, "Killing the Queen."

69. *New York Times*, December 6, 1982.

70. "Sí se realizará el X Festival Folklórico éste fin de semana," *El Gráfico*, July 28, 1978; and "Festival Folklórico de Cobán está desvinculado de la política," *El Gráfico*, August 1, 1978.

71. *La Nación*, August 1, 1978. The press reported that the outgoing Rabín Ahau urged organizers and the public not to allow partisan politics to enter an "eminently folkloric" event (*La Nación*, August 1, 1978). For her own description of the evening, see the local version of the paper, *La Nación/Quetzaltenango*, August 9, 1978.

72. For military involvement in pageants in Santa Cruz del Quiché, see Carmack, "The Story of Santa Cruz del Quiché," 62 and 66.

73. Movimiento Indio, "Guatemala," January 1983, 7, in the Archivo Histórico, Centro de Investigaciones Regionales de Mesoamérica, Antigua, Guatemala.

74. See chapter 5. Interviews with family of Felipe Vásquez Tuíz, July 2002, Santiago Atitlán. See also CEH, *Memoria del silencio*, case no. 4245.

75. Interview with María Elena Winter Flor, December 8, 2002, Cobán. As mentioned earlier, Winter Flor was India Bonita of Cobán in 1958. She married *cobanero* General Benedicto Lucas García, brother of President Romeo

Lucas García and the Guatemalan minister of defense during one of the most violent periods of counterinsurgency. For a journalist's interview with Benedicto about relations between Mayas and Ladinos, see the documentary film *Memoria del viento*, directed by Felix Zurita and Yvan Patry (Alter-Ciné, Inc. and Alba Films, 1993).

Chapter 5

1. CUC joined student and union organizers, among them the Asociación de Estudiantes Universitarios (AEU), the Central Nacional de Trabajadores (CNT), the Comité Nacional de Unidad Sindical (CNUS), and the Federación Autónoma Sindical Guatemalteca (FASGUA). For press reports, see "Manifestación de repudio hoy," *El Imparcial*, June 1, 1978; "20,000 en la marcha de los paraguas para protestar por matanzas de Panzós," *El Imparcial*, June 2, 1978.

2. *La Nación*, June 4, 1978.

3. In Grandin, *Last Colonial Massacre*, 161.

4. Ibid. For a discussion of ethnicity within CUC, see also Grandin, "To End with All These Evils."

5. *Ixim: Notas Indígenas*, June/July 1978, 2.

6. Interview with former writer for *Ixim*, February 2002, Quetzaltenango.

7. After publishing that *Ixim* issue, they fled Guatemala for a time, staying in Canada for three months and publishing even more detailed and condemnatory articles abroad.

8. *Ixim: Notas Indígenas*, June/July 1978, 21–26.

9. Ibid., 26.

10. Ibid., 2. This is almost identical to the banner carried at the funeral of the assassinated mine workers organizer in Huehuetenango discussed in chapter 2, which took place at the same time, July 1978.

11. *Ixim: Notas Indígenas*, August 1978, 3.

12. Ibid., 2.

13. Ibid.

14. *Ixim: Notas Indígenas*, October 1978, 2.

15. *Ixim: Notas Indígenas*, August 1978, 2.

16. *Ixim: Notas Indígenas*, September 1978, 5, reproducing columns published in *La Nación/Quetzaltenango*, September 1, 14, and 20, 1978. It is interesting and not accidental that Mayas such as Alvarez would use the word *mestizo*, with its connotation of racial mixing, rather than *Ladino*. The term is rarely used by Ladinos.

17. Ibid.

18. For its part, the EGP began to develop formal positions on the "indigenous problemática" when EGP commander Rolando Morán in late 1979

asked Mario Payeras to develop a position on ethnicity for internal debate. Personal communication with Arturo Arias, June 5, 2008.

19. Interview with Domingo Hernández Ixcoy, March 1, 2002, Chimaltenango.

20. Ibid., September 7, 2002, Chimaltenango.

21. Interview with Pablo Ceto, September 28, 2002, Guatemala City.

22. Interview with Emeterio Toj Medrano, August 24, 2002, Guatemala City.

23. The twenty-eight were listed in a manifesto by representatives of these communities, June 1978. Archivo Histórico, CIRMA.

24. CEH, *Memoria del silencio*, 6:163.

25. Telephone interview with Father Daniel Jensen, March 30, 2004.

26. For the former ambassador's own recounting of the episode, see Cajal, *¡Saber quién puso fuego ahí!*

27. See CEH, *Memoria del silencio*, 6:163–82.

28. Ibid., 6:176.

29. "Una monja habría muerto en la Embajada Española," *Diario Impacto*, May 28, 1980.

30. In Schirmer, *Guatemalan Military Project*, 303n2.

31. Interview with Emeterio Toj Medrano, August 24, 2002, Guatemala City. Soon afterward, in April and May of 1980, Toj, using the name José Us, traveled as a CUC representative with a group of four other political activists in the Democratic Front Against Repression (FDCR, which later joined the January 31 Popular Front, the FP-31), speaking out against the repressive Guatemalan government to audiences in Europe and several countries of Latin America. In apparent retaliation, his brother was assassinated in front of Radio Quiché that May. Emeterio then returned to Guatemala and lived and worked clandestinely in various places, including Antigua, Chimaltenango, and Quetzaltenango.

32. This is the same symbolic site employed for a different purpose two years earlier, when Iximché was chosen by leaders of the indigenous political party FIN and General Romeo Lucas García for the announcement of their political alliance, February 1978.

33. Interview with Ricardo Cajas Mejía, August 28, 2002, Quetzaltenango.

34. Ibid.

35. Interview with Miguel Alvarado, November 7, 2002, Cantel.

36. Interviews with Emeterio Toj Medrano, August 24 and September 29, 2002, Guatemala City, and with former activist who asked that her name not be mentioned. The text of the Declaration of Iximché was published in *Cuicuilco* 1 (July 1980): 2–5, as "Los pueblos indígenas de Guatemala ante el mundo."

37. Declaration of Iximché, February 14, 1980.

38. Interview with Ricardo Cajas Mejía, August 28, 2002, Quetzaltenango.

39. Fernández Fernández, *El Comité de Unidad Campesina*, 11.

40. Interview with Domingo Hernández Ixcoy, September 7, 2002, Chimaltenango.

41. Interview with Emeterio Toj Medrano, September 29, 2002, Guatemala City.

42. Mario Payeras, "Los indios guerrilleros," *Revista Compañero* 4:16–17.

43. Interview with Emeterio Toj Medrano, September 29, 2002, Guatemala City.

44. Interview with Ricardo Falla, November 12, 2002, Santa Maria Chiquimula.

45. The ORPA document known as "Racismo I" was entitled "Acerca del racismo," and "Racismo II" was entitled "Acerca de la verdadera magnitud del racismo." Bastos and Camus note the secrecy of ORPA, which results in confusion over authorship and publication dates. One scholar dates both documents 1978, another dates "Racismo I" as produced in 1976 and "Racismo II" in 1978 (Bastos and Camus, *Entre el mecapal y el cielo*, 61n9). In addition to the Lake Atitlán area and Sololá, ORPA recruited especially successfully around the department of Quetzaltenango.

46. Rother, *The Shepherd Cannot Run*, 10.

47. Ibid., 15 and 30.

48. Ibid., 30.

49. Ibid.

50. My deepest thanks to those at the Voz de Atitlán for their generous work in translating tapes of Gaspar Culán's programs from Tz'utujil to Spanish. The exact date of the program transcribed here is unknown; it was broadcast shortly before October 24, 1980.

51. Rother, *The Shepherd Cannot Run*, 31.

52. Interview with widow of Culán, June 28, 2002, Santiago Atitlán. For a long (and as always with such compilations, incomplete) listing of 265 dead and disappeared from Santiago Atitlán, 1980 through 1990, see the introduction to the Tz'utujil translation of the New Testament published by the Parroquia Santiago Apostol, Santiago Atitlán, 1991.

53. Interview with woman health worker who wishes not to be named, October 5, 2002, Santiago Atitlán.

54. Diócesis del Quiché, *El pueblo y su iglesia*, 147n141. For more on government repression of radio schools in indigenous communities, see "Investigarán las radios con programas en lengua," *Prensa Libre*, November 11, 1981.

55. The body found was that of the Voz de Atitlán board member Diego Sosof Alvarado, abducted in November 1980. See CEH, *Memoria del silencio*, 7:247–55; and Comisión de Derechos Humanos de Guatemala, "Santiago Atitlán," 56–65.

56. Rother reported hundreds of people sleeping in the church already on November 4, 1980, just a few weeks after the army set up its Santiago Atitlán camp (*The Shepherd Cannot Run*, 34).

57. See CEH, *Memoria del silencio*, 7:249.

58. Interviews with family of Felipe Vásquez Tuíz, Juan Atzip, and Pedro Esquina, July and October 2002, Santiago Atitlán.

59. *Prensa Libre*, November 10, 1981.

60. Ibid.

61. Ibid. The women were finally released and returned home in late 1982. Interviews with the women, who wish to remain unnamed, October 5, 2002, San Juan La Laguna. When I met them twenty years after their captivity, they were working as organizers of a weaving cooperative and women's group.

62. The letter, dated April 14, 1982, was addressed to Diego Coché, Juan Ajtzip [*sic*], and Diego Pop. It refers to a request from the group made to the Army Department of Culture and Public Relations for permission to resume broadcasting. Interviews with Juan Atzip and Diego Pop, June 27, 2002, Santiago Atitlán.

63. Details of Felipe's incarceration and abduction were provided by friends and family in Santiago Atitlán. See also CEH, *Memoria del silencio*, case #4245.

64. Interview with Miguel Sisay, July 2, 2002, Guatemala City. His brother Cruz was among those killed in the violence.

65. Interview with family member of Felipe Vásquez Tuíz, October 5, 2002, Santiago Atitlán.

66. Interview with activist who wished to remain anonymous, October 14, 2002, Quetzaltenango.

67. Interview with Alberto Mazariegos, September 3, 2002, Guatemala City.

68. Ibid.

Chapter 6

1. Interview with Domingo Hernández Ixcoy, September 7, 2002, Chimaltenango.

2. Interview with Miguel Alvarado, November 7, 2002, Cantel.

3. Ibid.

4. Ibid.

5. Interview with Emeterio Toj Medrano, September 29, 2002, Guatemala City.

6. Ibid. Toj felt that the resistance of the EGP leadership to Mayas in positions of authority extended to him. Even though he was well known after his European tour with the FDCR and thus terribly vulnerable, his requests in 1980 for a different kind of position were denied.

7. Interview with Ricardo Cajas Mejía, August 28, 2002, Quetzaltenango.

8. Ibid., August 29, 2002, Quetzaltenango.

9. Ibid.

10. Interview with Emeterio Toj Medrano, September 29, 2002, Guatemala City.

11. Ibid.

12. CEH, *Memoria del silencio*, 6:202.

13. Others have expressed the pain and torment that comes with collaboration under such circumstances. As one Argentine put it, "You had to walk a very fine line, making them believe you were useful, but without abetting them in a way that, morally, was going to do you in" (Feitlowitz, *A Lexicon of Terror*, 77).

14. Interview with Emeterio Toj Medrano, September 29, 2002, Guatemala City. Among the US delegation were Congresspersons Pat Schroeder and Thomas Petri.

15. "Sacerdote jesuita guerrillero se confesó ante la prensa," *Prensa Libre*, October 1, 1981. For a detailed account of the army's continuing use of this public relations tactic in 1992, with an alleged "self-kidnapping" of Maritza Urrutia followed by an army-orchestrated press conference, see Saxon, *To Save Her Life*.

16. Press Release, October 4, 1981, Jesuit Missions, "In Central America Concerning the Statements of Father Luis Pellecer," and "Further Information on Father Luis Eduardo Pellecer Faena," Amnesty International, AI Index: AMR 34/53/81.

17. Interview with Emeterio Toj Medrano, September 29, 2002, Guatemala City.

18. Ibid.

19. Ibid.

20. See "Otro dirigente campesino renunció al EGP; Gobierno presentó ayer a Emeterio Toc [sic] Medrano," *Diario La Hora*, October 23, 1981; "¡Fundador del CUC se entregó! Se trata de Emeterio Toc [sic] Medrano quien dio declaraciones ayer sobre su participación en el EGP," *El Gráfico*, October 23, 1981; "Co-fundador del CUC habla: Otro ex-militante de la guerrilla ofrece declaraciones a prensa nacional sobre EGP," *Diario Impacto*, October 23, 1981; "Se entrega guerrillero fundador del CUC," *Prensa Libre*, October 23, 1981. *Diario de Centro América* called the performance "one of the most eloquent calls that has been made to date for those who have fallen into subversive networks, especially the indígenas, to abandon those who have duped them, leaving only a fanatical minigroup, mostly foreigners, bringing on the aggression of which our country is a victim" ("Editorial: Hay que defender al indígena de los riesgos a que lo ha sometido la agresión soviética armada contra nuestro país," *Diario de Centro América*, October 23, 1981).

21. Interview with Emeterio Toj Medrano, September 29, 2002, Guatemala City. Maritza Urrutia in Saxon's *To Save Her Life* described virtually the same effort, to go along with her captors to a certain extent, but through body language, makeup, and voice, convey her own message that her words were false.

22. Interview with Emeterio Toj Medrano, September 29, 2002, Guatemala City.

23. Ibid.

24. "En una grabación, dice que no desertó del EGP," *Prensa Libre*, December 3, 1981.

25. Ejército Guerrillero de los Pobres, "Logramos la fuga del compañero Hemeterio [*sic*] Toj Medrano," no date. In interviews in 1982 with journalists and with Amnesty International, Toj refrained from giving details of the escape and did not contradict the EGP's assertion of a rescue. It was a time of war, he told them, and he did not want to provide information that would be useful to the enemy. See "Guatemala: Testimonio de Emeterio Toj Medrano," Amnesty International, AI Index: AMR 34/35/82/S, July 20, 1982.

26. "Supuesta fuga se explica," *El Imparcial*, December 3, 1981.

27. "Plan de reinfiltración en la guerrilla fue descubierto, asegura comunicado oficial en torno al ex-líder campesino," *El Gráfico*, December 4, 1981. Apparently there was a split within the EGP about what to do with Toj, with some leaders believing that he should be taught a lesson (maybe even killed, Toj believed) for his cooperation with the army. Meoño trusted him and protected him, most obviously by issuing the EGP statement about his rescue. As we'll see in the next chapter, Meoño was also instrumental in getting Toj's name mentioned in Rigoberta Menchú's memoir, sending another signal that he was a trusted part of the revolutionary Left. After his escape he finally went to the "mountains"—to a combat role—an assignment he had been requesting since 1980.

28. From testimony of army witness, in ODHAG, *Nunca más*, 3:207.

29. Interview with activist, November 13, 2002, Quetzaltenango.

30. Interview with Emeterio Toj Medrano, September 29, 2002, Guatemala City.

31. Interview with activist, November 13, 2002, Quetzaltenango.

32. Interview with Ricardo Cajas Mejía, August 28, 2002, Quetzaltenango.

33. Interview with Domingo Hernández Ixcoy, March 1, 2002, Chimaltenango.

34. The FP-31, announced on the one-year anniversary of the Spanish embassy massacre that its name commemorated, aimed to institutionalize the coalition of groups that had come together in 1980; it ended up being a short-lived umbrella organization of campesino, labor, and student groups supporting the revolutionary Left.

217

35. Arturo Arias observes that of the organizations grouped in FP-31, all except CUC were crushed by the state counterinsurgency offensive of 1981 to 1983. "By the end of 1983 there was no trace left of the January 31st Popular Front" (*The Rigoberta Menchú Controversy*, 5).

36. Interview with Domingo Hernández Ixcoy, September 7, 2002, Chimaltenango.

37. Ibid., August 20, 2002, Chimaltenango.

38. Interview with Ricardo Cajas Mejía, August 28, 2002, Quetzaltenango.

39. Interview with Miguel Alvarado, November 7, 2002, Cantel. Another group, Nuestro Movimiento, was an earlier and larger faction that separated from ORPA, with indígenas and Ladinos in its membership. It was very attuned to indigenous issues, organizers say, and maintained good relationships with the all-indigenous groups. Edgar Palma Lau was the founder and commander. The intent of the group was not to provoke the army into a guerrilla-style war, but to organize regionally, forming a corps of combatants that could secure a region and install regional governments, so the army couldn't enter and commit massacres. Palma and all of the group's leaders were killed in 1983 or 1984, and Nuestro Movimiento died with them.

40. Interview with Miguel Alvarado, November 7, 2002, Cantel.

41. Ibid.

42. Ibid.

43. Arias, "El movimiento indígena," 99. Miguel Alvarado is also mentioned in the version of the essay that was republished as "Changing Indian Identity: Guatemala's Violent Transition to Modernity," 253.

44. Arias explains that these were the "official" views of the EGP, not just his own, and that the phrase "indigenous bourgeoisie" came from Mario Payeras and was commonly used by activists on the Left, including Mayas such as Pablo Ceto and Domingo Hernández Ixcoy (personal communication, June 5, 2008). In later years Arias changed his views on these matters. See "Revisitando el genocidio guatemalteco a diez años de la firma de los acuerdos de paz," paper presented at the Central American Sociological Congress in Antigua, Guatemala in October 2006.

45. Interview with Miguel Alvarado, November 7, 2002, Cantel.

46. Interview with Ricardo Cajas Mejía, August 28, 2002, Quetzaltenango.

47. Ibid., August 30, 2002, Quetzaltenango.

48. Movimiento Indio Tojil, "Guatemala," in CIRMA Archivo Histórico, Colección Infostelle, binder 125, 27 pages. Exact dates of its publication are unclear; it seems to have been written and circulated in 1982 after Ríos Montt took power, since it mentions the "deceptive integrationist politics" related to the indio, programs including putting "indios in the Council of State," which took place in 1982 (see following). The revolutionary Left was clearly reacting to ideas expressed in the document by 1982, so if its publication date was later,

NOTES TO PAGES 146–49

the ideas in it, at least, were circulating by then. See chapter 7. Bastos and Camus suggest that its date of publication was likely 1984, since the document refers to 460 years of colonization; Alvarado arrived in Guatemala in 1524. See Bastos and Camus, *Entre el mecapal y el cielo*, 68n17. The Movimiento Indio Tojil, according to an account in Bastos and Camus, existed from 1980 to 1988 and may have included activists from Antonio Pop Caal's organization Cabracán. See Bastos and Camus, *Entre el mecapal y el cielo*, 65–66. Central demands of the Tojiles were rearticulated in the 1990s by the Mayanista movement. See next chapter.

49. Movimiento Indio Tojil, "Guatemala," 6.

50. Ibid., 1.

51. Ibid., 8.

52. Ibid., 6.

53. Ibid., 8. The document discusses preconquest Maya societies "constituted of various dynamic and interdependent nations" and colonial measures to break them down into controllable groups, while at the same time homogenizing them into indios. The *pueblos indios* now sought, they argued, not only to reclaim their individual ethnic identities, but to also claim a "national panethnic identity." See pages 7–8 and section 3.2, "La comunidad mayance: Una nacíon multiétnica?" 13–18.

54. Ibid., 23.

55. Ibid., 19.

56. Ibid., 23.

57. Ibid., 19.

58. Ibid., 20. A recent study by Wolfgang Gabbert suggests that "Mayas of the West" in Yucatán would have been very reluctant participants in any Maya nation. See Gabbert, *Becoming Maya*.

59. Movimiento Indio Tojil, "Guatemala," 5.

60. Ibid., 11.

61. Ibid., 24.

62. Ibid., 27.

63. Ibid. There are clear echoes here of Guzmán Böckler and Herbert.

64. Ibid., 8. References like this again point to the need for research on the sectors singled out by the Tojiles. Their critique was likely directed against those working (only) in the linguists and cultural fields and those involved in mainstream political parties.

65. We can see an example of this reaction from a Maya activist (margin notes identify him as "Fernando") from the Committee of Assistance and Solidarity with the Displaced, a group that publicized repression against Mayas. In correspondence sent to the German NGO Infostelle, "Fernando" comments on position papers by a "Coordinadora Kakchikel." The documents closely echo the Tojil manifesto, calling for a federated system in Guatemala and autonomy

for the pueblo maya. The papers set out a nationalist position with the same limitations as the Tojiles and like the Tojiles, argue not for a socialist revolution strictly following Marx or Lenin, but a "self-produced" socialism ("Nacionalismo indio y Marxismo," 1). "Fernando" told Infostelle that his organization saw some value in the documents: "The Committee uses them as training materials [material de formación], that is to say we are . . . in agreement with these proposals and a discussion is being established between the Coordinadora and the Committee regarding this line [of thought]." The typed letter is marked by several handwritten corrections, among them the crossing out of the word *completely* before "in agreement" (letter from "Fernando," July 1985, CIRMA Archivo Histórico, Colección Infostelle, del 11.01.09 al 11.02.02, Sig. 128). Striking similarities appear between the Tojil document, the documents attributed to the "Coordinadora Kakchikel," and "Mayanista" positions articulated by Demetrio Cojtí Cuxil beginning in the late 1980s. See chapter 7 for a discussion of Cojtí (a Kaqchikel from Tecpán, Chimaltenango) and the Mayanistas.

66. Interview with Pablo Ceto, September 28, 2002, Guatemala City.

67. Movimiento Indio Tojil, "Guatemala," 25.

68. Interview with Domingo Hernández Ixcoy, August 20, 2002, Chimaltenango.

69. CEH, *Memoria del silencio*, 1:183. The human rights record of the Guatemalan state has been extensively documented, most recently in the two lengthy Truth Commission reports, the twelve-volume work by the UN-sponsored CEH, *Memoria del silencio*, and the four-volume report by the Guatemalan Archbishop's Human Rights Office, ODHAG, *Nunca más*. See also several decades' worth of reporting by Amnesty International and Human Rights Watch/Americas.

70. Rother, *The Shepherd Cannot Run*, 86. The Diocese of El Quiché reports that at least 16 Catholic priests or nuns were kidnapped or assassinated during counterinsurgency violence, 155 were threatened or expelled from the country, and 30 Catholic Church–sponsored leadership training centers were closed (Diócesis del Quiché, *El pueblo y su iglesia*, 147n141).

71. Telephone interview with Father Daniel Jensen, March 30, 2004.

72. Azmitia and Salazar, *Rub'ix Qatinamit*, 20. Socorro, the more conservative of the two schools, attempted to resist politicization among its student body. The outspoken 1973 reina indígena of Quetzaltenango quoted previously, for example, was part of a class suspended from the school for girls' suspected political ideas and organizing. Interview with 1973 reina indígena, October 7, 2002, Quetzaltenango.

73. Affidavit of Father James P. Curtin, April 24, 1985, in James Curtin Media, Box 128, Maryknoll Mission Archives, Maryknoll, NY.

74. Ejército de Guatemala, *Historia del ejército*, cited in Schirmer, *Guatemalan Military Project*, 82. For a study of civil patrols in an area of Huehuetenango, see the PhD dissertation of Paul Kobrak, "Village Troubles."

75. See Schirmer, *Guatemalan Military Project*, 23–25, for discussion of the Ríos Montt plan of government.

76. *El Imparcial*, August 18, September 13, and October 12, 1982.

77. *New York Times*, December 5, 1982.

78. La Conferencia Episcopal de Guatemala, "Conferencia Episcopal de Guatemala condena masacre de campesinos," May 27, 1982, reproduced in Conferencia Episcopal de Guatemala, *Al servicio de la vida, la justicia, y la paz*, 297–300.

Chapter 7

1. Interview with community health worker and former Cabracán activist who wishes to remain anonymous, January 24, 2002, Cobán.

2. The URNG, founded in 1982, was made up of the four main guerrilla armies: the EGP and ORPA, along with the Rebel Armed Forces (FAR), and the Guatemalan Workers' Party (PGT), Guatemala's Communist Party.

3. See Jennifer Schirmer's examination of this process in *Guatemalan Military Project*.

4. A complicated package of constitutional reforms was rejected in a public referendum in May 1999, with most of the issues related to the indigenous rights accord grouped together in a proposal (Question 1) that was defeated 53 percent to 47 percent. Abstention rates were extremely high: nationwide 81 percent of the electorate did not vote on the measures. For analysis, see Warren, "Voting against Indigenous Rights in Guatemala"; Jonas, *Of Centaurs and Doves*; and Bastos and Camus, *Entre el mecapal y el cielo*.

5. See Bastos and Camus, *Entre el mecapal y el cielo*, 71–73. Arturo Taracena (formerly of the EGP) described the impact of revolutionary Mayas in European solidarity circles this way: "The indígenas conquered Europe before their own country" (quoted in Bastos and Camus, *Entre el mecapal y el cielo*, 71).

6. Of 669 massacres documented by the UN Truth Commission, 344 occurred in the department of El Quiché. See CEH, *Memoria del silencio*, "Conclusions and Recommendations."

7. Menchú and Hernández Ixcoy were *novios* (in a relationship) at the time.

8. For Stoll's accusations and the heated debates that have surrounded them, see Stoll, *Rigoberta Menchú*; Arias, ed., *Rigoberta Menchú Controversy*; and *Latin American Perspectives* 26, no. 6 (November 1999).

9. Burgos-Debray, ed., *I, Rigoberta Menchú*, chapter 32. The issue of Menchú's membership or nonmembership in the EGP has been the subject of much speculation in Guatemala. Menchú has publicly distanced herself from and criticized the URNG since winning the Nobel Peace Prize in 1992. Yet as Diane Nelson writes, she was "popularly understood to be, if not part of, then

quite sympathetic to the URNG." One of the many treasures of Nelson's *Finger in the Wound* is the jokes she compiled. At the time of Menchú's Nobel Prize, Nelson writes, a popular joke in Guatemala asked, "What is Rigoberta's blood type? URNG-positive" (*Finger in the Wound*, 362n3).

10. Greg Grandin, unpublished essay, written as the preface to a new edition of *I, Rigoberta Menchú*. Elisabeth Burgos-Debray, who holds author's rights to the book, refused its publication.

11. Beyond *I, Rigoberta Menchú*, Menchú spoke publicly throughout the 1980s about repression in Guatemala, to audiences in the US, and in international forums. In 1982 she helped found the United Representation of the Guatemalan Opposition (RUOG), which lobbied the UN and foreign governments to pressure the Guatemalan state to improve its human rights record. For her work in later years, see Menchú, *Crossing Borders*. She received the Nobel Peace Prize in 1992.

12. It was that guerrilla claim, and not so much the actual details of Menchú's narrative, that seems to have motivated Stoll's scrutiny of the text, though (using Menchú) he builds an illogical critique of the guerrilla forces and their responsibility for the war.

13. See Arturo Arias's introduction to the volume he edited, *Rigoberta Menchú Controversy*, 6, and in the same volume, "Arturo Taracena Breaks His Silence," interview by Luis Aceituno, 82–94.

14. See Arias, *Rigoberta Menchú Controversy*, 7.

15. Burgos-Debray, ed., *I, Rigoberta Menchú*, 153.

16. My thanks to Arturo Arias for helping to clear up the mystery of how Emeterio Toj's name made its way into Menchú's memoir. Arias was present in Taracena's house in Paris when Menchú was being interviewed and explained that afterward the group listened to a cassette tape (supplied by Meoño) of Emeterio announcing his rescue by the EGP (personal communication with Arturo Arias, June 5, 2008).

17. Quoted in Martí, "The Pitiful Lies of Rigoberta Menchú," 79.

18. Burgos-Debray, ed., *I, Rigoberta Menchú*, xiv.

19. Ibid., xiv–xv. Since the publication of her narrative, Rigoberta Menchú has been both praised and criticized for being a compelling speaker, something that non-Maya Guatemalans do not seem to expect of Mayas, nor, apparently, did Burgos-Debray. A *New York Times* opinion piece, "The Racial Politics of Speaking Well," takes on this issue, explaining how a frequently used characterization like "articulate" can be a "toxic adjective" when it implies that the speaker is "notably different" from his or her racial peers. The reference "often carries a subtext of amazement, even bewilderment," writes Lynette Clemetson. The occasion prompting the article was then senator Joseph Biden's unforgettable description of a future president of the United

States as "the first mainstream African-American who is articulate and bright and clean and a nice-looking guy" (*New York Times*, February 4, 2007).

20. Burgos-Debray, ed., *I, Rigoberta Menchú*, 1.

21. Ibid., xiii.

22. Ibid., xvii.

23. See the Infostelle collection, CIRMA Archivo Histórico. The collection also includes explicitly multiethnic writings, arguing for a collective indigenous-Ladino struggle. An unsigned document from November 1981, for example, asserts, "Today beside our *hermanos ladinos* [Ladino brothers] we will make the revolution." It quotes the *Popol Vuh*, "May all rise up," and ends with the slogans, "Indios y ladinos, a luchar para triunfar; Por la revolución guatemalteca, indios y ladinos a luchar." See "Siempre en pie de guerra," Infostelle collection, CIRMA Archivo Histórico. Bastos and Camus describe the document as written by someone linked to the EGP (*Entre el mecapal y el cielo*, 62).

24. CIRMA Infostelle collection, no title, dated by hand, 1982.

25. "Los pueblos maya-quiches de Guatemala a todos los pueblos del mundo consecuentes con los valores humanos," signed Las Naciones Maya-Quichés, July 7, 1982, in Infostelle Collection, CIRMA Archivo Histórico.

26. "Planteamientos del movimiento indio de Guatemala," signed Movimiento Indio de Guatemala, August 1983, in Infostelle Collection, CIRMA Archivo Histórico.

27. From the PGT, in Smith, "Conclusion: History and Revolution," 266.

28. EGP, "The Indian Problem and the Guatemalan Revolution," *Compañero* 5 (1982): 17–26, quoted in Smith, "Conclusion: History and Revolution," 269–70, emphasis in original.

29. Personal communication with Arturo Arias, June 5, 2008.

30. Ibid. Revolutionary October was led by Payeras, Gustavo Porras (formerly of Cráter), and Miguel Angel Albizúrez. See "Razones de una ruptura política," in the bulletin of Revolutionary October, *Opinión política: Por la comunicación, el intercambio y el debate entre los revolucionarios* 3 (March–April 1985), which includes excerpts from the group's "Carta de ruptura con la dirección nacional del EGP."

31. Two of the women were sisters from Santa Cruz del Quiché, and two were Mayas who had, with Hernández Ixcoy, occupied Guatemala's Brazilian embassy in 1982 to protest escalating rural violence. About twenty activists, including Hernández Ixcoy and the two Maya women, occupied the Brazilian embassy in May of that year, taking eight hostages including the ambassador. Speaking in the name of the January 31 Popular Front, CUC, and a student organization, the group condemned the "massacres, torture, rape and burning of crops and ranches" under Guatemalan head of state Ríos Montt and

claimed that three thousand mostly Maya peasants had been murdered since Ríos Montt's coup less than two months before. After negotiations with the Brazilian government, the occupiers released the hostages and were granted safe conduct to Mexico City (*Los Angeles Times*, May 13, 1982, and *New York Times*, May 14, 1982). Certainly the 1980 Spanish embassy massacre would have been on the minds of occupiers and Brazilians alike.

32. From personal communication with Arturo Arias, June 5, 2008. On the CPRs, see Falla, *The Story of a Great Love*.

33. See Revolutionary October, "Tésis sobre la cuestión étnico-nacional," *Opinión política* 11 (September 1987): 8.

34. Paper presented by Domingo Hernández Ixcoy of Ja C'Amabal I'b, "Algunos elementos de aproximación a la situación de la población india guatemalteca," in the United States, July 1986, 8.

35. Ibid., 9.

36. Ibid.

37. Ibid., 11.

38. Ja C'Amabal I'b, "Ponencia del taller Ja C'Amabal I'b (Casa de la Unidad del Pueblo) ante el Simposio Internacional 'Estado, Autonomia y Derechos Indígenas,'" July 1986, 1.

39. Ibid., 2.

40. See Schirmer, *Guatemalan Military Project*, 29–34.

41. Ibid., 30.

42. Manuel de Jesús Girón Tánchez, in 1988 interview with Jennifer Schirmer, ibid., 32.

43. General Héctor Alejandro Gramajo Morales, minister of defense, in early 1990s interview with Jennifer Schirmer, ibid., 1. There is ample evidence that military officials across the region shared such interpretations. Marguerite Feitlowitz notes the same explanation of "peace" as "war by other means" in Argentina's Dirty War (see Feitlowitz, *Lexicon of Terror*, 32–33 and 263–64n50). Karl von Clausewitz (1780–1831) had described the reverse, war as "the continuation of politics by other means."

44. In Schirmer, *Guatemalan Military Project*, 32. For an analysis of negotiations between the military and economic elites at this juncture, see McCleary, *Dictating Democracy*.

45. Doing justice to developments in the 1990s and 2000s would require another book, and in fact several excellent ones have been written! For detailed treatment of indigenous groups and coalitions since 1986, see especially the works by Bastos and Camus, *Quebrando el silencio*, *Abriendo caminos*, and *Entre el mecapal y el cielo*; and Jonas, *Of Centaurs and Doves*.

46. Interview with Rosalina Tuyuc, June 1995, Guatemala City. Tuyuc, along with human rights leaders Nineth Montenegro of GAM and Amílcar Méndez of CERJ, was elected to Congress in 1995.

47. Cojtí Cuxil, *El movimiento maya*, 102–3.

48. There is strong similarity between these Mayanista arguments and those of US anthropologist David Stoll. See Stoll, *Between Two Armies*.

49. Cojtí Cuxil, *El movimiento maya*, 103.

50. For a discussion of contemporary Guatemala's "sanctioned Maya," see Hale, "Rethinking Indigenous Politics," 16–21. Demetrio Cojtí Cuxil was named vice minister of education in the Portillo administration, 2000–2004. See also Hale, "Does Multiculturalism Menace?"

51. See CEDIM, *Foro del pueblo maya*.

52. Cojtí, ibid., 33.

53. Ibid., 33–36.

54. Jorge Serrano Elías, ibid., 73–74.

55. The Mayanistas grouped together in the Council of Maya Organizations of Guatemala, COMG, organized in the late 1980s and announced publicly in 1990.

56. Warren, "Voting against Indigenous Rights," 172.

57. Cojtí Cuxil, *El movimiento maya*, 113. Cojtí goes on to say that the *sector Maya-popular* in the late 1990s could consider itself part of the *movimiento Maya* since it had begun to demand indigenous rights, but earlier in the same work he expressed considerable skepticism about the authenticity of these positions. "Now it is a question of finding out," he wrote, "if the [popular movement's] adoption of indigenous ethnic demands is a tactical move or if it is real and authentic support" (*El movimiento maya*, 83).

58. Edward Fischer makes the argument that the Maya movement has been largely free of political repression because of their "moderate message" and "their use of savvy diplomacy when presenting it" (see Fischer, "Induced Culture Change as a Strategy for Socioeconomic Development," 69–70).

59. Kay Warren notes that in negotiations on the Accord on Identity and the Rights of Indigenous Peoples, "major issues such as the recognition of regional autonomy . . . and the officialization of Maya leadership norms were deemed irreconcilable and dropped" (*Indigenous Movements and Their Critics*, 56).

60. Santiago Bastos and Manuela Camus studied popular organizations' paid statements in two daily newspapers from 1985 to 1991, finding that specific references in those announcements to ethnicity increased considerably over time. They found few references to ethnicity in the 1985–1988 period; an increase between 1988 and 1990; and by 1991, ethnicity had become a common theme. From 1990 to 1991, in fact, popular organizations' references to ethnicity nearly doubled in the papers, from twenty-three instances in 1990 to forty-four in 1991 (see Bastos and Camus, *Quebrando el silencio*, 125).

61. Majawil Q'ij, ibid., 166. Majawil Q'ij was founded in 1990 and made up of organizations with ties to the revolutionary Left. They included CUC, CONAVIGUA, CERJ, campesino groups, and organizations of the displaced.

62. CUC, "Hunahpu: Personaje mítico de la religión maya," ibid., 161–162. In the case of CUC, such a rhetorical emphasis was temporary. In 1992 a group of Mayas led by Pedro Esquina and another Maya from Santiago Atitlán, Juan Tiney, broke from CUC to found the more ethnically focused CONIC, the National Indigenous and Campesino Coordination. In time CUC recentered its efforts and rhetoric on "lo campesino," again understood as multiethnic.

63. Ibid., 163.

64. Majawil Q'ij, "Life, Resistance, and the Future," in Nelson, *Finger in the Wound*, 24. The Indigenous Rights Accord made vague reference to communal land rights, but the topic was largely relegated to another agreement, the Accord on Social and Economic Aspects and the Agrarian Situation. The peace agreements as a whole, including both of these accords, have brought about little substantive change in Guatemala.

65. Warren, *Indigenous Movements*, 35. On the meeting, see also Hale, "Between Che Guevara and the Pachamama."

66. For various explanations of the defeat, see Warren, "Voting against Indigenous Rights."

67. Lieutenant colonel of the ministry of defense, in Schirmer, *Guatemalan Military Project*, 273, emphasis added.

68. Ibid.

69. Interview with Alberto Mazariegos, September 3, 2002, Guatemala City.

70. In Bastos and Camus, *Quebrando el silencio*, 182. Menchú resigned from a leadership role in CUC in 1993 and, as mentioned, has distanced herself from the URNG.

71. Ibid.

72. Quoted in McAllister, "Good People," 4.

73. Ibid. Victor Montejo, an indigenous teacher and anthropologist who has written on his experiences of violence, expressed a sentiment similar to Lux's as he commented on the Rigoberta Menchú/David Stoll controversy. "Don't we realize," he wrote, "that Maya now need to reconstruct their lives by trying to remove themselves from those who brought the guns and did the killing?" ("Truth, Human Rights, and Representation," 376–77).

74. Consider, for example, the statement by Juan Atzip when he and the other directors of the radio Voz de Atitlán were imprisoned by the army in Santiago Atitlán and that in the press conference by Emeterio Toj after his capture.

75. After serving on the Truth Commission, Otilia Lux became Guatemalan minister of culture (2000–2004) and was a member of the UN Permanent Forum on Indigenous Issues. She joined the executive board of the UN Educational, Scientific, and Cultural Organization (UNESCO) and was honored for her advocacy work by the governments of Spain and France.

Bibliography

Archives and Document Collections

Archivo de Gobernación, Quetzaltenango
Archivo General de Centro América (AGCA), Hemeroteca,
    Guatemala City
Archivo INAREMAC, San Cristóbal de las Casas, Chiapas
Biblioteca Nacional de Guatemala, Hemeroteca, Guatemala City
Centro de Investigaciones Regionales de Mesoamérica (CIRMA),
    Archivo Histórico, Antigua
Instituto Indígena Santiago, Guatemala City
Instituto Nuestra Señora del Socorro, Antigua
Maryknoll Mission Archives, Maryknoll, New York
Municipal Archive, San Cristóbal, Alta Verapaz
Parish Archive, Momostenango
Parish Archive, Santiago Atitlán
Sociedad El Adelanto, Quetzaltenango

Newspapers and Magazines

Acción Social Cristiana
Boletín del Instituto Indigenista Nacional
Boletín Indigenista, Instituto Indigenista Interamericano
Boletín Misionero Salesiano
Cha'b'l Tinamit
Cuicuilco
Día
Diario de Centro América
Diario Impacto
Diario La Hora
El Gráfico

El Impacto
El Imparcial
El Periódico
Guatemala Indígena
Inforpress
Ixim: Notas Indígenas
La Nación
La Nación/Quetzaltenango
La Nación/Sur
La Ruta
La Semana
La Tarde
Nuestro Diario
Opinión Política, Octubre Revolucionario
Prensa Libre
Revista Compañero
Revista Cultural del Ejército
Siglo Veintiuno
Xucaneb

Other Works

Adams, Abigail. "¿Diversidad cultural en la nacionalidad homogénea? Antonio Goubaud Carrera y la fundación del Instituto Indigenista Nacional de Guatemala." *Mesoamérica* 50 (Enero–Diciembre 2008): 66–95.

Adams, Richard. "Ethnic Images and Strategies in 1944." In *Guatemalan Indians and the State: 1540–1988*, edited by Carol Smith, 141–62. Austin: University of Texas Press, 1990.

———. "Las masacres de Patzicía de 1944: Una reflexión." *Winak Boletín Intercultural* 7, nos. 1–4 (June 1991–March 1992): 3–40.

———. "Some Premodernist Thoughts on the Mayan Population in Guatemala." Latin American Studies Association annual meeting, 1998. Electronic document, lasa.international.pitt.edu/LASA98/Adams.pdf., accessed November 16, 2009.

———, and Santiago Bastos. *Las relaciones étnicas en Guatemala, 1944–2000.* Antigua, Guatemala: CIRMA, 2003.

Alonzo, Marco Aurelio. "Los objetivos del Festival Folklórico." Unpublished manuscript, n.d.

Andrews, George Reid. *Afro-Latin America, 1800-2000.* New York: Oxford University Press, 2004.

Annis, Sheldon. *God and Production in a Guatemalan Town*. Austin: University of Texas Press, 1987.

Appelbaum, Nancy, Anne Macpherson, and Karin Rosemblatt. *Race and Nation in Modern Latin America*. Chapel Hill: University of North Carolina Press, 2003.

Arenas Bianchi, Clara, Charles R. Hale, and Gustavo Palma Murga, eds. *Racismo en Guatemala? Abriendo el debate sobre un tema tabú*. Guatemala: AVANCSO, 1999.

Arias, Arturo. "Changing Indian Identity: Guatemala's Violent Transition to Modernity." In *Guatemalan Indians and the State, 1540–1988*, edited by Carol Smith, 230–57. Austin: University of Texas Press, 1990.

———. "El movimiento indígena en Guatemala: 1970–1983." In *Movimientos populares en Centroamérica*, edited by R. Menjívar and D. Camacho, 62–119. Costa Rica: FLACSO, 1985.

———. "Revisitando el genocidio guatemalteco a diez años de la firma de los acuerdos de paz." Paper presented at the Central American Sociological Congress, Antigua, Guatemala, October 2006.

———, ed. *The Rigoberta Menchú Controversy*. Minneapolis: University of Minnesota Press, 2001.

Asociación Voz de Atitlán. "La verdad está en la historia." Unpublished manuscript, Santiago Atitlán, n.d.

Asturias, Miguel Angel. *Guatemalan Sociology: The Social Problem of the Indian*. Tempe: Arizona State University, 1977. First published 1923.

———. *Men of Maize*. Translated by Gerald Martin. Pittsburgh, PA: University of Pittsburgh Press, 1993.

AVANCSO. *Se cambió el tiempo: Conflicto y poder en territorio K'iche'*. Guatemala: AVANCSO, 2002.

Azmitia, Oscar, and Manuel Salazar, *Rub'ix Qatinamit: El canto del pueblo, Estudiantina del Instituto Indígena Santiago*. Guatemala: Instituto Indígena Santiago, n.d.

Barrios Escobar, Lina. *La alcaldía indígena en Guatemala: De 1821 a la Revolución de 1944*. Guatemala: Universidad Rafael Landívar Instituto de Investigaciones Económicas y Sociales, 1998.

Bastos, Santiago, and Manuela Camus. *Abriendo caminos: Las organizaciones mayas desde el Nobel hasta el acuerdo de Derechos Indígenas*. Guatemala: FLACSO, 1995.

———. *Entre el mecapal y el cielo: Desarrollo del movimiento maya en Guatemala*. Guatemala: FLACSO, 2003.

———. *Quebrando el silencio: Organizaciones del Pueblo Maya y sus demandas, 1986–1992*. Guatemala: FLACSO, 1993.

229

————, and Aura Cumes. *Mayanización y vida cotidiana: La ideología multicultural en la sociedad guatemalteca.* Vols. 1, 2, and 3, and Texto para el debate. Guatemala: FLACSO/CIRMA/Editorial Cholsamaj, 2007.

Behrens, Susan Fitzpatrick. "From Symbols of the Sacred to Symbols of Subversion to Simply Obscure: Maryknoll Women Religious in Guatemala, 1953-1967." *Americas* 61, no. 2 (October 2004): 189–216.

Bélisle, Jean-François. "Macy's vs. Ubico." Paper presented at the annual meeting of the American Society for Ethnohistory, New Orleans, October 3, 2009.

Berryman, Philip. *The Religious Roots of Rebellion: Christians in Central American Revolutions.* Maryknoll, NY: Orbis Books, 1984.

————. *Stubborn Hope: Religion, Politics and Revolution in Central America.* Maryknoll, NY: Orbis Books, 1994.

Bonfil Batalla, Guillerrmo. *Utopía y revolución: El pensamiento político contemporáneo de los indios en América Latina.* Mexico: Editorial Nueva Imágen, 1981.

Brintnall, Douglas. "The Birth of Indian Political Activism in Western Guatemala." *Katunob* 9, no. 1 (March 1976): 71–77.

————. *Revolt against the Dead: The Modernization of a Mayan Community in the Highlands of Guatemala.* New York: Gordon and Breach, 1979.

Burgos-Debray, Elisabeth, ed. *I, Rigoberta Menchú: An Indian Woman in Guatemala.* New York: Verso, 1984.

Cajal, Máximo. *¡Saber quién puso fuego ahí!: Masacre en la Embajada de España.* Madrid: Siddharth Mehta Ediciones, 2000.

Cajas Mejía, Ricardo. "Lógica local de participacón política maya: La experiencia de Xel-jú en Quetzaltenango, 1972–1998." Tésis de Maestría en Gerencia para el Desarrollo Sostenible, Instituto Chi Pixab', Quetzaltenango, 1998.

Calder, Bruce. *Crecimiento y cambio de la Iglesia Católica guatemalteca, 1944–1966.* Guatemala: Seminario de Integración Social Guatemalteca, 1970.

Cambranes, J. C., ed. *500 años de lucha por la tierra: Estudios sobre propiedad rural y reforma agraria en Guatemala.* Vol. 2. Guatemala: FLACSO, 1992.

Carlsen, Robert. *The War for the Heart and Soul of a Highland Maya Town.* Austin: University of Texas Press, 1997.

Carmack, Robert, ed. *Harvest of Violence: The Maya Indians and the Guatemalan Crisis.* Norman: University of Oklahoma Press, 1988.

————. *Rebels of Highland Guatemala: The Quiché-Mayas of Momostenango.* Norman: University of Oklahoma Press, 1995.

————. "The Story of Santa Cruz del Quiché." In *Harvest of Violence: The Maya Indians and the Guatemalan Crisis*, edited by Robert Carmack, 39–69. Norman: University of Oklahoma Press, 1988.

Casaus Arzú, Marta. *Genocidio: ¿La máxima expresión del racismo en Guatemala?* Guatemala: F&G Editores, 2008.

————. *Guatemala: Linaje y racismo.* San José, Costa Rica: FLACSO, 1992.

Castro Torres, Carlos Felipe. "Crecimiento de las luchas campesinas en Guatemala, February 1976–May 1978." *Estudios Centroamericanos* 33, nos. 356/357 (June/July 1978): 462–77.

CEDIM. *Foro del pueblo maya y los candidatos a la presidencia de Guatemala.* Guatemala: Editorial Cholsamaj, 1992.

CEH (Comisión para el Esclaracimiento Histórico). *Guatemala: Memoria del silencio.* 12 vols. Guatemala: UNOPS, 1999.

Chávez, Adrián Inés, trans. *Pop-Wuj: Poema mito-histórico Ki-ché.* Guatemala: Centro de Estudios Mayas, 1997.

Cohen, Colleen Ballerino, Richard Wilk, and Beverly Stoeltje, eds. *Beauty Queens on the Global Stage: Gender, Contests, and Power.* New York: Routledge, 1996.

Cojtí Cuxil, Demetrio. *Configuración del pensamiento político del pueblo maya.* Quetzaltenango: Asociación de Escritores Mayances de Guatemala, 1991.

———. *Políticas para la reivindicación de los Mayas de hoy.* Guatemala City: Editorial Cholsamaj, 1994.

———. *Ri maya' moloj pa iximulew, El movimiento maya (en Guatemala).* Guatemala: Editorial Cholsamaj, 1997.

———. *Ub'anik Ri Una'ooj Uchomab'aal Ri Maya' Tinamit, Configuración del pensamiento político del pueblo maya.* 2nd part. Guatemala: Editorial Cholsamaj, 1995.

Comisión de Derechos Humanos de Guatemala. "Santiago Atitlán, Preparación de una masacre." *Polémica* 1, no. 16 (January–March 1985): 56–65.

Conferencia Episcopal de Guatemala. *Al servicio de la vida, la justicia, y la paz: Documentos de la Conferencia Episcopal de Guatemala, 1956–1997.* Guatemala: Conferencia Episcopal de Guatemala, 1997.

Craig, Maxine Leeds. *Ain't I a Beauty Queen?: Black Women, Beauty, and the Politics of Race.* New York: Oxford University Press, 2002.

Dary, Claudia, ed. *La construcción de la nación y la representación ciudadana en México, Guatemala, Perú, Ecuador y Bolivia.* Guatemala: FLACSO, 1998.

de la Cadena, Marisol. *Indigenous Mestizos: The Politics of Race and Culture in Cuzco, Peru, 1919–1991.* Durham, NC: Duke University Press, 2000.

Depestre, René. "An Interview with Aimé Césaire." In *Discourse on Colonialism,* by Aimé Césaire, 88–94. New York: Monthly Review Press, 2000.

Diócesis del Quiché. *El Quiché: El pueblo y su iglesia, 1960–1980.* Santa Cruz del Quiché, Guatemala: Diócesis del Quiché, 1994.

———. *Y dieron la vida por el Quiché.* Santa Cruz del Quiché, Guatemala: Diócesis del Quiché, 2000.

Dirección General de Estadística. *VII Censo de Población, 1964.* Guatemala: Dirección General de Estadística, 1971.

———. *Quinto Censo de Población, levantado el 7 de abril de 1940.* Guatemala: Dirección General de Estadística, 1942.

231

———. *Sexto Censo de Población, 1950.* Guatemala: Dirección General de Estadística, 1950.

Ejército de Guatemala. *Historia del ejército, 1981–1984.* Guatemala: Departamento de Información y Divulgación, 1994.

England, Nora. *Autonomía de los idiomas mayas: Historia e identidad; Rukutamil, Ramaq'il, Rutzijob'al: Ri Mayab' Amaq'.* Guatemala City: Editorial Cholsamaj, 1992.

Euraque, Darío, Jeffrey Gould, and Charles Hale, eds. *Memorias del mestizaje: Cultura política en Centroamérica de 1920 al presente.* Antigua, Guatemala: CIRMA, 2004.

Falla, Ricardo."El movimiento indígena." *Estudios Centroamericanos* 23, nos. 356/357 (June/July 1978): 437–61.

———. *Quiché Rebelde: Religious Conversion, Politics, and Ethnic Identity in Guatemala.* Austin: University of Texas Press, 2001. First published 1978.

———. *The Story of a Great Love: Life with the Guatemalan "Communities of Population in Resistance": A Spiritual Journal.* Washington, DC: Ecumenical Program on Central America and the Caribbean, 1998.

Federación Guatemalteca de Escuelas Radiofónicas (FGER). *Pensemos juntos.* Guatemala: Centro de Investigación y Experimentación Pedagógica, 1976.

Feitlowitz, Marguerite. *A Lexicon of Terror: Argentina and the Legacies of Torture.* New York: Oxford University Press, 1998.

Fernández Fernández, José Manuel. *El Comité de Unidad Campesina: Origen y desarrollo.* Cuaderno 2. Guatemala/Madrid: Centro de Estudios Rurales Centroamericanos (CERCA), 1988.

Fischer, Edward. "Induced Culture Change as a Strategy for Socioeconomic Development: The Pan-Maya Movement in Guatemala." In *Maya Cultural Activism in Guatemala,* edited by Edward Fischer and R. McKenna Brown, 51–73. Austin: University of Texas Press, 1996.

———, and R. McKenna Brown, eds. *Maya Cultural Activism in Guatemala.* Austin: University of Texas Press, 1996.

500 Años de Resistencia Indígena, Negra, y Popular. *Nosotros conocemos nuestra historia.* Guatemala: 500 Años de Resistencia Indígena, Negra, y Popular, 1992.

Frank, Luisa, and Philip Wheaton. *Indian Guatemala: Path to Liberation.* Washington, DC: EPICA, 1984.

Gabbert, Wolfgang. *Becoming Maya: Ethnicity and Social Inequality in Yucatán since 1500.* Tucson: University of Arizona Press, 2004.

Gálvez Borrell, Víctor, Claudia Dary Fuentes, Edgar Esquit Choy, and Isabel Rodas. *Qué sociedad queremos? Una mirada desde el movimiento y las organizaciones mayas.* Guatemala: FLACSO, 1997.

Garzon, Susan, R. McKenna Brown, Julia Becker Richards, and Wuqu' Ajpub'. *Life of Our Language: Kaqchikel Maya Maintenance, Shift, and Revitalization.* Austin: University of Texas Press, 1998.

Gleijeses, Piero. *Shattered Hope: The Guatemalan Revolution and the United States, 1944–1954*. Princeton, NJ: Princeton University Press, 1991.

Goldman, Francisco. *The Art of Political Murder: Who Killed the Bishop?* New York: Grove Press, 2008. First published 2007.

González Ponciano, Ramón. "Diez años de indigenismo en Guatemala (1944–1954)." BA thesis, Escuela Nacional de Antropologia e Historia, Mexico, DF, 1988.

————. "'Esas sangres no están limpias': Modernidad y pensamiento civilizatorio en Guatemala (1954–1977)." In *¿Racismo en Guatemala? Abriendo el debate sobre un tema tabú*, edited by Arenas Bianchi et al., 15–46. Guatemala: AVANCSO, 1999.

Gotkowitz, Laura. *A Revolution for Our Rights: Indigenous Struggles for Land and Justice in Bolivia, 1880–1952*. Durham, NC: Duke University Press, 2007.

Gould, Jeffrey. *To Die in This Way: Nicaraguan Indians and the Myth of Mestizaje, 1880–1965*. Durham, NC: Duke University Press, 1998.

Graham, Richard, ed. *The Idea of Race in Latin America, 1870–1940*. Austin: University of Texas Press, 1990.

Grandin, Greg. *Blood of Guatemala: A History of Race and Nation*. Durham, NC: Duke University Press, 2000.

————. *The Last Colonial Massacre: Latin America in the Cold War*. Chicago: University of Chicago Press, 2004.

————. "To End with All These Evils: Ethnic Transformation and Community Mobilization in Guatemala's Western Highlands, 1954–1980." *Latin American Perspectives* 24, no. 2 (March 1997): 7–34.

Guzmán Böckler, Carlos. *Colonialismo y revolución*. Mexico: Siglo Veintiuno Editores, 1975.

————, and Jean-Loup Herbert. *Guatemala: Una interpretación histórico-social*. Mexico: XXI Editores, 1970.

————, and Julio E. Quan R. *Las clases sociales y la lucha de clases en Guatemala*. Asunción, Paraguay: Centro Paraguayo de Estudios Sociológicos, 1971.

Hale, Charles. "Between Che Guevara and the Pachamama: Mestizos, Indians and Identity Politics in the Anti-quincentenary Campaign." *Critique of Anthropology* 14, no. 1 (1994): 9–39.

————. "Consciousness, Violence, and the Politics of Memory in Guatemala." *Current Anthropology* 38, no. 5 (December 1997): 817–38.

————. "Does Multiculturalism Menace? Governance, Cultural Rights and the Politics of Identity in Guatemala." *Journal of Latin American Studies* 34, no. 3 (August 2002): 485–524.

————. *Más Que un Indio (More Than an Indian): Racial Ambivalence and Neoliberal Multiculturalism in Guatemala*. Santa Fe: School of American Research, 2006.

233

————. *Resistance and Contradiction: Miskitu Indians and the Nicaraguan State, 1894–1987*. Stanford, CA: Stanford University Press, 1994.

————. "Rethinking Indigenous Politics in the Era of the 'Indio Permitido.'" *NACLA Report on the Americas* 38, no. 2 (September/October 2004): 16–21.

Handy, Jim. *Revolution in the Countryside: Rural Conflict and Agrarian Reform in Guatemala, 1944–1954*. Chapel Hill: University of North Carolina Press, 1994.

————. "'A Sea of Indians': Ethnic Conflict and the Guatemalan Revolution, 1944–1952." *Americas* 46, no. 2 (October 1989): 189–204.

Harss, Luis, and Barbara Dohmann. "Miguel Angel Asturias, or the Land Where the Flowers Bloom." In *Men of Maize*, by Miguel Angel Asturias. Translated by Gerald Martin. Pittsburgh, PA: University of Pittsburgh Press, 1993.

Heckt, Meike, and Gustavo Palma Murga, eds. *Racismo en Guatemala: De lo políticamente correcto a la lucha antiracista*. Guatemala: AVANCSO, 2004.

Hendrickson, Carol. "Images of the Indian in Guatemala: The Role of Indigenous Dress in Indian and Ladino Constructions." In *Nation-States and Indians in Latin America*, edited by Greg Urban and Joel Sherzer, 286–306. Austin: University of Texas Press, 1991.

————. *Weaving Identities: Construction of Dress and Self in a Highland Guatemala Town*. Austin: University of Texas Press, 1995.

Instituto Indigenista Nacional. *Por qué es indispensable el indigenismo?* Guatemala: IIN, 1969.

————. *Santa Eulalia: Tierra de nuestros antepasados y esperanza para nuestros hijos (Escrito por un comité de vecinos)*. Guatemala: IIN, 1968.

Jonas, Susanne. *Of Centaurs and Doves: Guatemala's Peace Process*. Boulder, CO: Westview Press, 2000.

Kicza, John E., ed. *The Indian in Latin American History: Resistance, Resilience, and Acculturation*. Wilmington, DE: SR Books, 2000.

Kita, Bernice. *What Prize Awaits Us: Letters from Guatemala*. Maryknoll, NY: Orbis Books, 1988.

Kobrak, Paul. "Village Troubles: The Civil Patrols in Aguacatán, Guatemala." PhD diss., University of Michigan, 1997.

Konefal, Betsy. "Subverting Authenticity: Reinas Indígenas and the State, 1978." *Hispanic American Historical Review* 89, no. 1 (February 2009): 41–72.

Lavenda, Robert. "'It's Not a Beauty Pageant!': Hybrid Ideology in Minnesota Community Queen Pageants." In *Beauty Queens on the Global Stage: Gender, Contests, and Power*, edited by Colleen Ballerino Cohen, Richard Wilk, and Beverly Stoeltje, 31–46. New York: Routledge, 1996.

Le Bot, Yvon. *La Guerra en las tierras mayas: Comunidad, violencia y modernidad en Guatemala, 1970–1992*. Mexico: Fondo de Cultura Económica, 1995.

Levenson-Estrada, Deborah. *Trade Unionists against Terror: Guatemala City, 1954–1985*. Chapel Hill: University of North Carolina Press, 1994.

Little, Walter. "Outside of Social Movements: Dilemmas of Indigenous Handicrafts Vendors in Guatemala." *American Ethnologist* 31, no. 1 (2004): 43–59.

López, Rick. "The India Bonita Contest of 1921 and the Ethnicization of Mexican National Culture." *Hispanic American Historical Review* 82, no. 2 (May 2002): 291–328.

Lovell, W. George, and Christopher Lutz. "'A Dark Obverse': Maya Survival in Guatemala, 1520–1994." *Geographical Review* 86, no. 3 (July 1996): 398–407.

Lund, Joshua. "They Were Not a Barbarous Tribe." *Journal of Latin American Cultural Studies* 12, no. 2 (August 2003): 171–89.

Manz, Beatriz. *Paradise in Ashes: A Guatemalan Journey of Courage, Terror, and Hope*. Berkeley: University of California Press, 2004.

Mariñas Otero, Luis. *Las constituciones de Guatemala*. Madrid: Instituto de Estudios Políticos, 1958.

Martí, Octavio. "The Pitiful Lies of Rigoberta Menchú." In *The Rigoberta Menchú Controversy*, edited by Arturo Arias, 78–81. Minneapolis: University of Minnesota Press, 2001.

Martínez Peláez, Severo. *La patria del criollo: Ensayo de interpretación de la realidad colonial guatemalteca*. Guatemala: Editorial Universitaria, 1970.

Maryknoll Fathers. *5 Year Plan, Guatemala–El Salvador Region*. Guatemala City: Maryknoll Fathers, 1969.

Mattiace, Shannan. *To See with Two Eyes: Peasant Activism and Indian Autonomy in Chiapas, Mexico*. Albuquerque: University of New Mexico Press, 2003.

McAllister, Carlota. "Authenticity and Guatemala's Maya Queen." In *Beauty Queens on the Global Stage: Gender, Contests, and Power*, edited by Colleen Ballerino Cohen, Richard Wilks, and Beverly Stoeltje, 105–24. New York: Routledge, 1996.

———. "Good People: Revolution, Community, and *Conciencia* in a Maya-K'iche' Village in Guatemala." PhD diss., Johns Hopkins University, 2003.

———. *The Good Road: Conscience and Consciousness in a Postrevolutionary Guatemalan Village*. Durham, NC: Duke University Press, forthcoming.

———. "This Pageant Which Is Not Won: The Rabín Ahau, Maya Women, and the Guatemalan Nation." MA thesis, University of Arizona, 1994.

McCleary, Rachel. *Dictating Democracy: Guatemala and the End of Violent Revolution*. Gainsville: University Press of Florida, 1999.

McCreery, David. *Rural Guatemala, 1760–1940*. Stanford, CA: Stanford University Press, 1994.

Melville, Thomas. *Through a Glass Darkly: The US Holocaust in Central America.* Philadelphia: Xlibris, 2005.

———, and Marjorie Melville. *Whose Heaven, Whose Earth?* New York: Knopf, 1971.

———. *Guatemala: Another Vietnam?* Middlesex, England: Penguin Books, 1971.

Menchú, Rigoberta. *Crossing Borders.* Translated by Ann Wright. New York: Verso, 1998.

———, with Gianni Miná and Dante Liano. *La nieta de los mayas.* Madrid: El País-Aguilar, 1998.

Menchú Tum, Rigoberta, and the Comité de Unidad Campesina. *El clamor de la tierra: Luchas campesinas en la historia reciente de Guatemala.* Donostia, Gipúzkoa, Spain: Tercera Prensa, 1992.

Metz, Brent. "Without Nation, Without Community: The Growth of Maya Nationalism among Ch'orti's of Eastern Guatemala." *Journal of Anthropological Research* 54, no. 3 (Fall 1998): 325–49.

Montejo, Victor. *Testimony: Death of a Guatemalan Village.* Willimantic, CT: Curbstone Press, 1987.

———. "Truth, Human Rights, and Representation: The Case of Rigoberta Menchú." In *The Rigoberta Menchú Controversy,* edited by Arturo Arias, 376–77. Minneapolis: University of Minneapolis Press, 2001.

Movimiento Indio Tojil. "Guatemala: De la república burguesa centralista a la república popular federal." CIRMA Archivo Histórico, Colección Infostelle, binder 125, 27 pages.

Nelson, Diane. *A Finger in the Wound: Body Politics in Quincentennial Guatemala.* Berkeley: University of California Press, 1999.

ODHAG (Oficina de Derechos Humanos del Arzobispado de Guatemala). *Guatemala: Nunca más, Informe proyecto interdiocesano de recuperación de la memoria histórica.* 4 vols. Guatemala: ODHAG, 1998.

Oglesby, Elizabeth, and Amy Ross. "Guatemala's Genocide Determination and the Spatial Politics of Justice." *Space and Polity* 13, no. 1 (April 2009): 21–39.

Opazo Bernales, Andrés. "La iglesia y el pueblo como sujeto político." *Polémica* 2, no. 3 (September–December 1987): 2–25.

Otzoy, Irma. "Tekum Umam: From Nationalism to Maya Resistance." PhD diss., University of California–Davis, 1999.

Oxlajuuj Keej Maya' Ajtz'iib' (Maya Linguistic Research Group). *Maya' Chii': Los idiomas mayas de Guatemala.* Guatemala: Editorial Cholsamaj, 1993.

Parroquia Santiago Apostol. *Traducción del Nuevo Testamento en Tzutuhil.* Santiago Atitlán, Guatemala: Parroquia Santiago Apostol, 1991.

Partido Guatemalteco del Trabajo. *El camino de la revolución guatemalteca.* Mexico: Ediciones de Cultura Popular, 1972.

Payeras, Mario. *Days of the Jungle: The Testimony of a Guatemalan Guerrillero, 1972–1976.* New York: Monthly Review Press, 1983.

———. "Los indios guerrilleros." *Revista Compañero* 4 (1981): 13–17.

Pop Caal, Antonio. *Li Juliisil Kirisyaanil ut li Minok i'b, Judeo cristianismo y colonización*. Guatemala: Seminario Permanente de Estudios Mayas, 1992.

———. "Replica del indio a una disertación ladina." *La Semana*, December 12, 1972, 41–43.

Recinos, Adrián, trans. *Popol-Vuh: Las antiguas historias del Quiché*. Mexico: Fondo de Cultura Económica, 1953. First published 1947.

Rother, Stanley. *The Shepherd Cannot Run: Letters of Stanley Rother, Missionary and Martyr*. Edited by Rev. David Monahan. Oklahoma City: Archdiocese of Oklahoma City, 1984.

Rubin, Jeffrey. *Decentering the Regime: Ethnicity, Radicalism, and Democracy in Juchitán, Mexico*. Durham, NC: Duke University Press, 1997.

Rus, Jan, Aída Hernández Castillo, and Shannan Mattiace, eds. *Mayan Lives, Mayan Utopias: The Indigenous Peoples of Chiapas and the Zapatista Rebellion*. Lanham, MD: Rowman & Littlefield, 2003.

Salazar, Oswaldo. *Historia moderna de la etnicidad en Guatemala. La visión hegemónica: De 1944 al presente*. Guatemala: Universidad Rafael Landívar Instituto de Investigaciones Económicas y Sociales, 1996.

Sanford, Victoria. *Buried Secrets: Truth and Human Rights in Guatemala*. New York: Palgrave Macmillan, 2003.

Saxon, Daniel. *To Save Her Life: Disappearance, Deliverance, and the United States in Guatemala*. Berkeley: University of California Press, 2007.

Schirmer, Jennifer. *The Guatemalan Military Project: A Violence Called Democracy*. Philadelphia: University of Pennsylvania Press, 1998.

———. "'Those Who Die for Life Cannot Be Called Dead': Women and Human Rights Protest in Latin America." *Harvard Human Rights Yearbook* 1 (Spring 1988): 41–76.

Skinner Klée, Jorge. *Legislación indigenista de Guatemala*. Mexico: Instituto Indigenista Interamericano, 1995.

Smith, Carol. "Conclusion: History and Revolution in Guatemala." In *Guatemalan Indians and the State, 1540–1988*, edited by Carol Smith, 258–85. Austin: University of Texas Press, 1990.

———, ed. *Guatemalan Indians and the State, 1540–1988*. Austin: University of Texas Press, 1990.

———. "Interpretaciones norteamericanas sobre la raza y el racismo en Guatemala: Una genealogía crítica." In *¿Racismo en Guatemala?* edited by Clara Arenas Bianchi, Charles R. Hale, and Gustavo Palma Murga, 93–126. Guatemala: AVANCSO, 1999.

———. "Local History in Global Context: Social and Economic Transitions in Western Guatemala." In *Constructing Culture and Power in Latin America*, edited by Daniel H. Levine, 75–117. Ann Arbor: University of Michigan Press, 1993.

————. "The Militarization of Civil Society in Guatemala: Economic Reorganization as a Continuation of War." *Latin American Perspectives* 17, no. 4 (Fall 1990): 8–41.

————. "Race-Class-Gender Ideology in Guatemala: Modern and Anti-Modern Forms." *Comparative Studies in Society and History* 37, no. 4 (October 1995): 723–49.

Stabb, Martin. "Indigenism and Racism in Mexican Thought: 1857–1911." *Journal of Inter-American Studies* 1, no. 4 (October 1959): 405–23.

Steele, Diane. "Guatemala." In *Indigenous People and Poverty in Latin America: An Empirical Analysis*, edited by George Psacharopoulos and Harry Anthony Patrinos, 97–126. Washington, DC: World Bank, 1994.

Stoll, David. *Between Two Armies in the Ixil Towns of Guatemala*. New York: Columbia University Press, 1993.

————. *Rigoberta Menchú and the Story of All Poor Guatemalans*. Boulder, CO: Westview Press, 1999.

Taracena Arriola, Arturo. *Etnicidad, estado y nación en Guatemala, 1808–1944*. Vol. 1. Antigua, Guatemala: CIRMA, 2002.

————. *Etnicidad, estado y nación en Guatemala, 1944–1985*. Vol. 2. Antigua, Guatemala: CIRMA, 2004.

Tedlock, Dennis, trans. *Popol Vuh: The Definitive Edition of the Mayan Book of the Dawn of Life and the Glories of Gods and Kings*. New York: Simon and Schuster, 1985.

Tilley, Virginia. *Seeing Indians: A Study of Race, Nation, and Power in El Salvador*. Albuquerque: University of New Mexico Press, 2005.

Treacy, Mary Jane. "Killing the Queen: The Display and Disappearance of Rogelia Cruz." *Latin American Literary Review* 29, no. 57 (January–June 2001): 40–51.

Tzian, Leopoldo. *Mayas y ladinos en cifras: El caso de Guatemala*. Guatemala: Editorial Cholsamaj, 1994.

Tzunun M., Gloria Virginia, and Olegario Obispo Nimatuj I. *1934–1984: Historial del certamen de la belleza indígena de Quetzaltenango*. Quetzaltenango: Casa Publicitaria "GOF," 1985.

Urban, Greg, and Joel Sherzer. *Nation-States and Indians in Latin America*. Austin: University of Texas Press, 1991.

Van Cott, Donna Lee, ed. *Indigenous Peoples and Democracy in Latin America*. New York: St. Martin's Press, 1995.

Vela, David. "Tecun Uman en la historia y la leyenda." *Revista Cultural del Ejército* 6, nos. 16–17 (January–June 1979): 11–14. Guatemala: Ministerio de la Defensa Nacional, Relaciones Públicas del Ejército.

Wade, Peter. *Race and Ethnicity in Latin America*. Sterling, VA: Pluto Press, 1997.

Warren, Kay. *Indigenous Movements and Their Critics: Pan-Maya Activism in Guatemala*. Princeton, NJ: Princeton University Press, 1998.

———. *The Symbolism of Subordination: Indian Identity in a Guatemalan Town.* Austin: University of Texas Press, 1978.

———. "Voting against Indigenous Rights in Guatemala: Lessons from the 1999 Referendum." In *Indigenous Movements, Self-Representation, and the State in Latin America,* edited by Kay B. Warren and Jean E. Jackson, 149–80. Austin: University of Texas Press, 2002.

Wasserstrom, Robert. "Revolution in Guatemala: Peasants and Politics under the Arbenz Government." *Comparative Studies in Society and History* 17, no. 4 (October 1975): 443–78.

Watanabe, John. *Maya Saints and Souls in a Changing World.* Austin: University of Texas Press, 1992.

Wilk, Richard. "Connections and Contradictions: From the Crooked Tree Cashew Queen to Miss World Belize." In *Beauty Queens on the Global Stage: Gender, Contests, and Power,* edited by Colleen Ballerino Cohen, Richard Wilk, and Beverly Stoeltje, 217–32. New York: Routledge, 1996.

Wilson, Richard. *Maya Resurgence in Guatemala: Q'eqchi' Experiences.* Norman: University of Oklahoma Press, 1995.

Zur, Judith. *Violent Memories: Mayan War Widows in Guatemala.* Boulder, CO: Westview Press, 1998.

Index